Education and Information Technology Annual – 2014

A Selection of AACE Award Papers

Edited by

Theo J. Bastiaens, Ph.D.

Gary H. Marks, Ph.D.

Published by

AACE--Association for the Advancement of Computing in Education

Education and Information Technology Annual – 2014 A Selection of AACE Award Papers
(ISBN # 978-1-939797-09-4) is published by
AACE, PO Box 719, Waynesboro, NC 28786, USA
E-mail: info@aace.org

www.aace.org Available at http://www.aace.org/bookshelf.htm

Introduction

The Association for the Advancement of Computing in Education (AACE), http://AACE.org, founded in 1981, is an international, not-for-profit, educational organization with the mission of advancing Information Technology in Education and E-Learning research, development, learning, and its practical application.

AACE serves the profession with international conferences, high quality publications, leading-edge Digital Library (http://EdITLib.org), Career Center, and other opportunities for professional growth.

We are proud to present to you this selection of 22 award winning papers from AACE's conferences (http://AACE. org/conf). This year's selection includes papers from the annual conference of the Society for Information Technology & Teacher Education (SITE) in New Orleans, Louisiana, the World Conference on Educational Multimedia, Hypermedia and Telecommunications (Ed-Media) in Victoria, Canada and the World Conference on E-Learning in Corporate, Government, Healthcare, and Higher Education (E-Learn) in Las Vegas, NV. The decision to nominate a conference paper for an award was made by peer reviewers. All authors were honored during the conference and received a certificate that serves as testimony to their outstanding research and contribution to the conference.

This AACE finest of 2014 book groups the award winning papers in four parts. These four parts provide a timely overview and record of topics that are of primary interest in educational technology this year.

We hope that the reader enjoys this selection as much as we enjoyed working with these cutting-edge scholars. It is the third year that we publish this edition. We are grateful for all the feedback and all the nice comments we got on the 2012 and 2013 book. We look forward to many new future editions of AACE's award papers.

Thank you very much for your support and participation in AACE events and activities.

Theo J. Bastiaens, Gary H. Marks

Part 1

The learning Environment

In part 1 of this collection the focus is on the learning environment. Many practitioners and researchers in education experiment with new technologies as for example online video or mobile phones, and also implement new methods of instructions as for example flipped classrooms or MOOC's. All these experiments have their influence on education in general and have a huge impact on the innovation of the curriculum. In chapter 1, Casey discusses the multiplicity of communication channels offered through the integration of social and participatory media into the face-to-face classroom. It connects the multimodality of social environments with the need to redesign classroom programs.

In chapter 2, author Dove explores how community college students perceived a flipped classroom approach and their learning opportunities after completing a flipped Statistics I course. In a flipped classroom model, lectures are watched outside of the class and time in class is spent practicing and applying the material.

The next chapter investigates the effect of the design of instructional video based on the Cognitive Theory of Multimedia Learning on preservice teachers' learning outcome and the perceived difficulty in an online course. Authors Ibrahim, Callaway and Bell employed a three-group pretest-posttest design to assess whether there were significant differences in the students' test scores after watching an instructional video introducing the TPACK framework.

Chapter 4 is a short paper. Author Walsh & VanOverschelde provide preliminary data on a MOOC to accelerate student readiness.

The purpose of the study in chapter 5 is to investigate the determinants of the Korean college students' mobile learning (m-learning) acceptance based on the extended Unified Theory of Acceptance and Use of Technology (UTAUT) model. In this study from Liew, Kang et al. 173 college students from two universities in Seoul and Busan, Korea participated. Key determinants of behavioral intention to use m-learning were performance expectancy, effort expectancy, social influence, perceived playfulness and self-management of learning.

Chapter 6 focuses on online course quality and the students perception. Authors Robins, Simunich and Kelly investigate whether "findability", an aspect of usability, is an important component in student perceptions of/satisfaction with online courses and, as such, should be considered more heavily in online course design. Using standard usability testing measures, such as eye-tracking, time-on-task, and think-alouds, participants were asked to find essential course components in either a course with high findability or a modified version of the course with low findability, in order to determine the impact on student perceptions of course quality and experience.

In the last chapter of part 1 Zap and Montgomerie take a more traditional variable in consideration, the web accessibility.
Their recent follow-up study is based on two earlier studies in 2001 and 2002 that evaluate the web accessibility of all Canadian postsecondary institutions top-level front entry pages.

Part 2

Teacher and Students Impact on Learning

Part 2 stresses the individual impact of both teachers and students on learning. More specific it deals with teacher's abilities to put technology into practice and the possibilities within technology for student's self-directed learning.
In chapter 8, the aim of the study is to understand how teachers, across various career stages, reason with technology. Smart, Sim and Finger have given teachers access to their online SCDPL-Digital Pedagogical License. Accordingly these were reviewed using Shulman's Model of Pedagogical Reasoning and Action as a lens.
Authors Schwartz and Garofalo, in Chapter 9, try to document improvements in pre-service mathematics teachers' (PSMTs) use of technology in their standards-based teaching over a two-semester mathematics pedagogy course through the use of a multidimensional instructional observational tool, the Mathematics Scan (M-Scan). This tool is based on the NCTM's vision of quality mathematics instruction, and its' *Multiple Representations* and *Students' Use of Tools* dimensions.
According to Redmond and Lock, twenty-first century teacher educators need to design learning experiences integrating technology for transformative learning. In Chapter 10 they describe the TPACK findings of secondary pre-service teachers who have just completed their second professional experience placement in conjunction with a curriculum and pedagogy course.
Swan, Hynes, et al. report of a statewide study (Florida) that assesses the effectiveness of online teachers in two critically needed courses. In Chapter 11 they examine which teacher attributes are most likely to translate into successful course completion; and the relationship of course completion rates with students' satisfaction and frequency of teacher-student interactions.
In chapter 12, Self-Directed Learning (SDL) is identified as a critical skill for students. Little empirical research, however, is available regarding the SDL capabilities of younger students, particularly as they work and learn in technology rich classroom contexts. Authors Fahnoe and Mishra present their mixed-methods study that examines the development of self-directed learning skills by middle school students as they engage in an intentionally designed, technology rich learning environment. The Self-Directed Learning with Technology Scale (SDLTS), an assessment focusing on younger learners, was utilized for the study to collect data.
In the final chapter in part 2, Salter takes a more critical look on technology and reports on a technology-related theme examining a whole-school approach to self-regulated learning. An in-depth case study of an Australian secondary school was used to explore approaches taken to developing self-regulated learners and the perceptions of the school community

with respect to these approaches. As part of this study, students' and parents' perceptions of the impact of technology on self-regulated learning were examined.

Part 3

Gamification

Gamification is a relatively new concept in education and is becoming a buzzword. Author Glover tries to define the concept by providing an overview of the background of gamification, the relevant key game concepts and examples from outside education. He provides some suggestions for implementing gamification in education generally, and e-learning specifically. This chapter 14 is intended to give readers an overview of gamification, allowing an informed analysis of the technique in their own context to be made.

Chapter 15 goes into detail on motivational aspects of gaming. Authors Kang & Liu review research, both empirical and theoretical studies, on motivation and attributes of game-based learning from 2009 to the present. The purpose of the literature review is to identify game attributes and examine the relationship between the attributes as exhibited in educational games and learner motivation as discussed in the recent literature.

The purpose of Chapter 16 is to describe a ludic simulation designed for middle school space science and examines students' experiences with it. It is an attempt of authors Liu, Horton et al. to explore the value of ludic simulations in education and better understand how such environments can be designed to support learning.

Code and Zap state that the key to education reform lies in exploring alternative forms of assessment. Alternative performance measures provide a more valid measure than multiple-choice tests of students' conceptual understanding and higher-level skills such as problem solving. Advances in immersive virtual environment technologies are creating new possibilities for learning and assessment. Rigorous, empirically based research studies are underway that aim to explore this potential. One such possibility is through the use of immersive 3D technologies that aim to situate students in an environment that promotes inquiry and sets the context for assessment. In chapter 17 they describes three on-going research projects that are using immersive 3D virtual environments as a platform in which to enable the summative, self-, and formative assessments of student learning.

Part 4

Digital change, reading, writing and libraries

In part 4 of this educational and information technology annual the focus is on libraries, librarians, reading and writing. In chapter 18 author Gregersen explains that for many years libraries have adapted to digital change as this has been expressed on the immediate and tangible levels - books, journals, search & retrieval etc. But they have done so within established institutional and conceptual borders. A wider set of technological, economic and socio-cultural changes are now impacting universities at the framework level. This has consequences for all agents and subunits within the mother institution. In this new situation the academic librarians need to reassess not only their functions and modus operandi, but also their ethos and professional identity. Gregersen's chapter traces such core challenges facing a library at an institution of higher learning in transition and suggest practical solutions.

Chapter 19 continues in the same context of the previous chapter. Author Nilsen reports on a project in where they have managed to maintain and integrate a development project for student guidance as a permanent feature of the Library and Learning Center in an institution of higher learning. The chapter describes the characteristics of the project as such and the mechanisms with which the process grew deeper and permanent roots within the existing organization.

In Chapter 20 the author Hoivik discusses the reasons that libraries need to move towards the html5 solution from Flash in the future. Using the national library of Norway as an example, the paper describes a developing mobile web application with HTML5/jQuery Mobile to deploy across multiple browser and OS platforms with several accesses to library resources, including free text search, location maps, sound books and video display. Interactive solution for books and journals, for example, zooming function, page turning function, online order form have been presented.

Yang and Li explore in chapter 21 the use of an assessment model adapted for College English teaching at a Chinese University. The target goal of the assessment is English-based digital literacy skills, which consist of search skills, evaluation skills, organization skills and presentation skills. The major assessment task was built around a web-based research project combined with a textbook.

In the last chapter Slykhuis and Cline introduce a Trans-Media book written in conjunction with NASA about the upcoming Magnetospheric Mulitscale Mission. The book called 'iMAGiNETICspace, was implemented with almost 300 8th grade students and STEM aptitudes and science content knowledge was pre- and post tested. Statistical Results are presented in the chapter.

TABLE OF CONTENTS

PART 1 THE LEARNING ENVIRONMENT

Chapter 1 'From Telling the World to Showing the World in an Era of Social Media'
G. Casey, School of Education, Deakin University, Australia 21

Chapter 2 Students' Perceptions of Learning in a Flipped Statistics Class
A. Dove, Radford University, United States 35

Chapter 3 The effect of the design of instructional video on students' learning outcome and perceived difficulty in online learning environment
M. Ibrahim, R. Callaway & D. Bell, College of Education, Arkansas Tech University, United States 43

Chapter 4 Leveraging a MOOC Platform to Accelerate College Readiness
L. Walsh & K. VanOverschelde, Walden University, United States 53

Chapter 5 Investigating the determinants of mobile learning acceptance in Korea
B.T. Liew, M. Kang, E. Yoo & J. You, Educational Technology Department, Ewha Womans University, South Korea 57

Chapter 6 The Impact of Findability on Student Perceptions of Online Course Quality and Experience
D. B. Robins, B. Simunich & V. Kelly, School of Library and Information Science & Office of Continuing and Distance Education, Kent State University, United States 67

Chapter 7 The Status of Web Accessibility of Canadian Universities and Colleges: A Follow-up Study 10 Years Later
N. Zap, Simon Fraser University & C. Montgomerie University of Alberta, Canada 77

PART 2 TEACHER AND STUDENTS IMPACT ON LEARNING

Chapter 8 A view into teachers' digital pedagogical portfolios showing evidence of their Technological Pedagogical Reasoning
V. Smart, C. Sim & G. Finger, Griffith University, Australia 89

Chapter 9 Pre-Service Mathematics Teachers' Growth in Incorporating Technology into their Teaching Practices
B.A. Swartz & J. Garofalo, University of Virginia, United States 101

Chapter 10 TPACK: Exploring a Secondary Pre-service Teachers' Context
P. Redmond, University of Southern Queensland, Australia & J. Lock, University of Calgary, Canada 113

Chapter 11 How Online Teacher Educational Backgrounds, Student Satisfaction, and Frequency of Teacher-Student Interactions Relate to Completion Rates for Two Critically Needed Courses Statewide
B. Swan, University of Central Florida, M. Hynes, University of Central Florida, B. Miller, Florida Virtual School, J. Godek, Florida Virtual School, K. Childs, University of Central

Florida, X.Coulombe-Quach, University of Central Florida, Y. Zhou, University of Central Florida, United States 125

Chapter 12 Do 21st Century Learning Environments Support Self-Directed Learning?
C. Fahnoe & P. Mishra, Michigan State University, United States 139

Chapter 13 Helping or Hindering? Technology's Impact on Secondary Students' Self-Regulated Learning
P. Salter, University of Technology Sydney, Australia 151

PART 3 GAMIFICATION

Chapter 14 Play As You Learn: Gamification as a Technique for Motivating Learners
I. Glover, Sheffield Hallam University, United Kingdom 165

Chapter 15 Attributes and Motivation in Game-Based Learning: A Review of the Literature.
J. Kang & M. Liu, The University of Texas at Austin, United States 179

Chapter 16 Making Learning Fun Through a Ludic Simulation
M. Liu, L. Horton, J. Kang, R. Kimmons & J. Lee, The University of Texas at Austin, United States 193

Chapter 17 Assessments for Learning, of Learning, and as Learning in 3D Immersive Virtual Environments
J. Code, University of Victoria & N. Zap, Simon Fraser University, Canada 209

PART 4 DIGITAL CHANGE, READING, WRITING AND LIBRARIES

Chapter 18 The Academic Librarians: New Roles and Challenges: a Comparison to Kurt De Belder's "Partners in Knowledge"
A. Gregersen, Learning Center & Library Oslo and Akershus University College of Applied Sciences, Norway 221

Chapter 19 New Library Tasks: A Dialog-based Approach to Guidance on Academic Writing.
I. Nilsen, The Culture, Language and Learning Unit, Learning Center & Library Oslo and Akershus University College of Applied Sciences, Norway 229

Chapter 20 From Flash to HTML5: making a mobile web application for library with jQuery Mobile
J. Hoivik, The National Library of Norway, Norway 237

Chapter 21 Applying the Model of Digital Literacy Assessment in English Reading and Writing
F. Yang & L. Li, Beijing University of Technology, China 243

Chapter 22 Results from implementation of the Trans-Media book iMAGiNETICspace
D. Slykhuis, James Madison University & T. Cline, NASA, United States 255

AUTHORS AND EDITORS CONTACT INFORMATION

Chapter 1. 'From Telling the World to Showing the World in an Era of Social Media'
Gail Casey, School of Education, Deakin University, Australia
E-mail: gcas@deakin.edu.au

Chapter 2. Students' Perceptions of Learning in a Flipped Statistics Class
Anthony Dove, Radford University, United States of America
E-mail: adove3@radford.edu

Chapter 3. The effect of the design of instructional video on students' learning outcome and perceived difficulty in online learning environment
Mohamed Ibrahim, Rebecca Callaway & David Bell, College of Education, Arkansas Tech University, United States of America
E-mail: mibrahim1@atu.edu

Chapter 4. Leveraging a MOOC Platform to Accelerate College Readiness
Laurel Walsh & Keri VanOverschelde, Walden University, United States of America
E-mail: laurel.walsh@waldenu.edu

Chapter 5. Investigating the determinants of mobile learning acceptance in Korea
BaoYng Teresa Liew, Myunghee Kang, Eunjin Yoo , Jiwon You, Educational Technology Department, Ewha Womans University, South Korea
E-mail: teresalby@ewhain.net

Chapter 6. The Impact of Findability on Student Perceptions of Online Course Quality and Experience
David B. Robins, Bethany Simunich & Valerie Kelly, Kent State University, United States
E-mail: drobins@kent.edu

Chapter 7. The Status of Web Accessibility of Canadian Universities and Colleges: A Follow-up Study 10 Years Later
Nick Zap, Simon Fraser University & Craig Montgomerie, University of Alberta, Canada
E-mail: nick_zap@sfu.ca

Chapter 8. A view into teachers' digital pedagogical portfolios showing evidence of their Technological Pedagogical Reasoning
Vicky Smart, Cheryl Sim & Glenn Finger, Griffith University, Australia
E-mail: vicky.smart@bigpond.com

Chapter 9. Pre-Service Mathematics Teachers' Growth in Incorporating Technology into their Teaching Practices
Barbara Ann Swartz & Joe Garofalo, University of Virginia, United States
E-mail: bswartz@virginia.edu

Chapter 10. TPACK: Exploring a Secondary Pre-service Teachers' Context

Petrea Redmond, University of Southern Queensland, Australia & Jennifer Lock, University of Calgary, Canada,
E-mail: redmond@usq.edu.au

Chapter 11. How Online Teacher Educational Backgrounds, Student Satisfaction, and Frequency of Teacher-Student Interactions Relate to Completion Rates for Two Critically Needed Courses Statewide
Bonnie Swan, University of Central Florida, Michael Hynes, University of Central Florida, Beth Miller, Florida Virtual School, Jaime Godek, Florida Virtual School, Kristopher Childs, University of Central Florida, Xuan-Lise Coulombe-Quach, University of Central Florida, Yan Zhou, University of Central Florida, United States
E-mail: bonnie.swan@ucf.edu

Chapter 12. Do 21st Century Learning Environments Support Self-Directed Learning? Middle School Students' Response to an Intentionally Designed Learning Environment
Christopher Fahnoe & Punya Mishra, Michigan State University, United States
E-mail: fahnoech@msu.edu

Chapter 13. Helping or Hindering? Technology's Impact on Secondary Students' Self-Regulated Learning
Prue Salter, University of Technology Sydney, Australia
E-mail: Prue.E.Salter@student.uts.edu.au

Chapter 14. Play As You Learn: Gamification as a Technique for Motivating Learners
Ian. Glover, Sheffield Hallam University, United Kingdom.
E-mail: i.glover@shu.ac.uk

Chapter 15. Attributes and Motivation in Game-Based Learning: A Review of the Literature.
Jina. Kang & Min. Liu, The University of Texas at Austin, United States
E-mail: jina.kang@austin.utexas.edu

Chapter 16. Making Learning Fun Through a Ludic Simulation
Min Liu, Lucas Horton, Jina Kang, Royce Kimmons & Jaejin Lee, The University of Texas at Austin, United States
E-mail: mliu@austin.utexas.edu

Chapter 17. Assessments for Learning, of Learning, and as Learning in 3D Immersive Virtual Environments
Jillianne Code, University of Victoria & Nick Zap, Simon Fraser University, Canada
E-mail: jcode@uvic.ca

Chapter 18. The Academic Librarians: New Roles and Challenges: a Comparison to Kurt De Belder's "Partners in Knowledge"
Anne-Berit Gregersen, Learning Center & Library Oslo and Akershus University College of Applied Sciences, Norway
E-mail: anne-berit.gregersen@hioa.no

Chapter 19. New Library Tasks: A Dialog-based Approach to Guidance on Academic Writing.
Ingunn Nilsen, The Culture, Language and Learning Unit, Learning Center & Library Oslo and Akershus University College of Applied Sciences, Norway
E-mail: Ingunn.Nilsen@hioa.no

Chapter 20. From Flash to HTML5: making a mobile web application for library with jQuery Mobile
Jingru Hoivik, The National Library of Norway, Norway
E-mail: jingru.hoivik@nb.no

Chapter 21. Applying the Model of Digital Literacy Assessment in English Reading and Writing
Feng Yang & Lihua Li, Beijing University of Technology, China
E-mail: yy88ff99@163.com

Chapter 22. Results from implementation of the Trans-Media book iMAGiNETICspace
David Slykhuis, James Madison University & Troy Cline, NASA, United States
E-mail: slykhuda@jmu.edu

Editors

Theo Bastiaens is professor of Educational Technology at the Fernuniversität in Hagen, Germany and part time professor at the Open University, The Netherlands. He is a member of the AACE board of directors. •E-mail: Theo.Bastiaens@fernuni-hagen.de

Gary Marks is CEO and founder of AACE. E-mail: info@aace.org

 Abstracts for all journal issues are available at www.EdITLib.org

Education & Information Technology Digital Library – Electronic

The EdITLib is your source for peer-reviewed, published articles (100,000+) and papers on the latest research, developments, and applications related to all aspects of Educational Technology and E-Learning. Included are 1,000s of articles from AACE journals and international proceedings.

International Journal on E-Learning

(Corporate, Government, Healthcare, & Higher Education)

(IJEL) ISSN# 1537-245 Quarterly

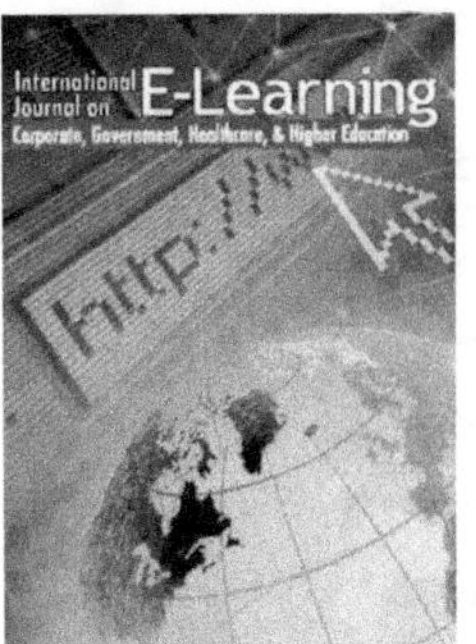

IJEL serves as a forum to facilitate the international exchange of information on the current theory, research, development, and practice of E-Learning in education and training. This journal is designed for researchers, developers and practitioners in schools, colleges, and universities, administrators, policy decision-makers, professional trainers, adult educators, and other specialists in education, industry, and government.

Journal of Educational Multimedia & Hypermedia

(JEMH) ISSN# 1055-8896 Quarterly

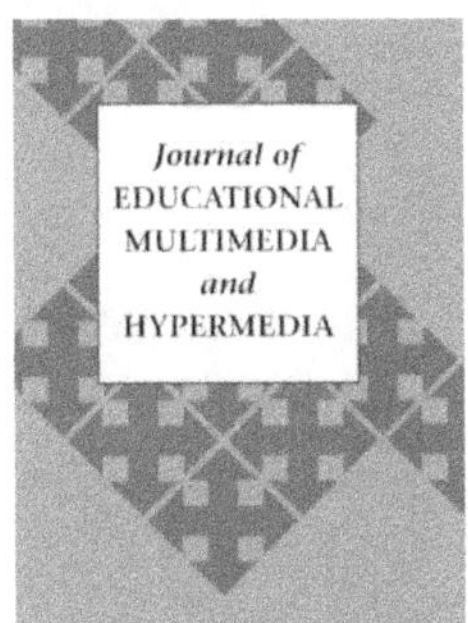

Designed to provide a multidisciplinary forum to present and discuss research, development and applications of multimedia and hypermedia in education. The main goal of the Journal is to contribute to the advancement of the theory and practice of learning and teaching using these powerful and promising technological tools that allow the integration of images, sound, text, and data.

Journal of Interactive Learning Research

(JILR) ISSN# 1093-023X Quarterly

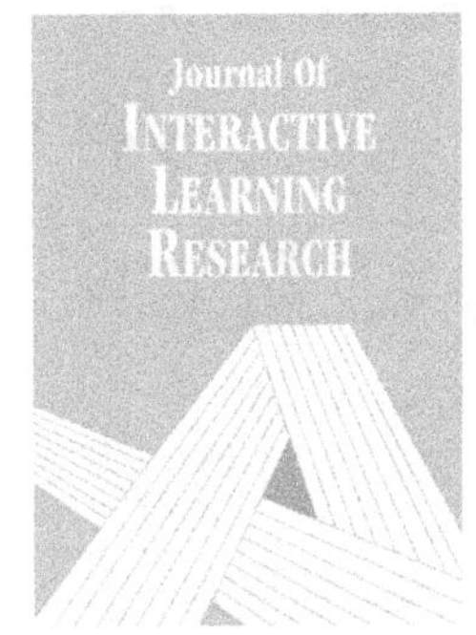

The Journal's published papers relate to the underlying theory, design, implementation, effectiveness, and impact on education and training of the following interactive learning environments: authoring systems, CALL, assessment systems, CBT, computer-mediated communications, collaborative learning, distributed learning environments, performance support systems, multimedia systems, simulations and games, intelligent agents on the Internet, intelligent tutoring systems, micro-worlds, and virtual reality-based learning systems.

Journal of Technology and Teacher Education

(JTATE) ISSN# 1059-7069 Quarterly

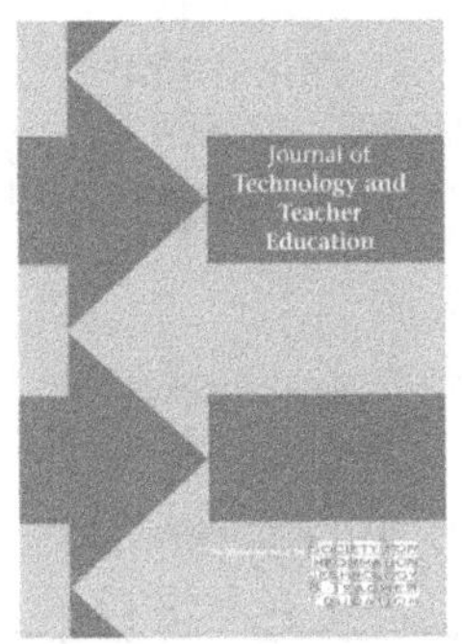

A forum for the exchange of knowledge about the use of information technology in teacher education. Journal content covers preservice and inservice teacher education, graduate programs in areas such as curriculum and instruction, educational administration, staff development, instructional technology, and educational computing.

Journal of Computers in Mathematics & Science Teaching

(JCMST) ISSN# 0731-9258 Quarterly

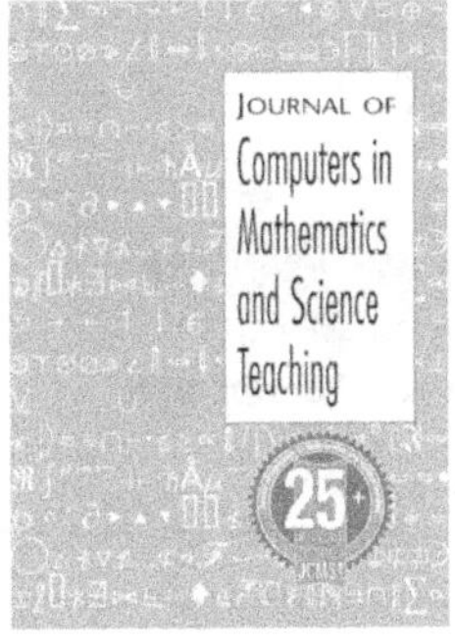

JCMST is the only periodical devoted specifically to using information technology in the teaching of mathematics and science. The Journal offers an in-depth forum for the exchange of information in the fields of science, mathematics, and computer science.

CITE – Electronic Journal

CITE

CONTEMPORARY ISSUES IN TECHNOLOGY & TEACHER EDUCATION

An electronic publication of the Society for Information Technology and Teacher Education (SITE), established as a multimedia, interactive electronic counterpart of the Journal of Technology and Teacher Education.

aace.org/pubs • pubs@aace.org

AACE MEMBERSHIP

Membership Application **You can also apply online at aace.org/my/membership/**

Membership Options

- Subscription to 1 AACE print Journal (see below)
- Full online access to back issues of that journal
- Online subscription to the AACE Journal
- Discounted conference registrations and proceedings
- Discount subscriptions to additional journals
- Access to the AACE Career Center and Job Board
- All the benefits of AACE Membership.

US $125 Non-US $145

- All the same benefits of a Professional Membership
- Offered at a discount for students
- MUST be enrolled as a full-time student in an accredited educational institution and provide school information below

US $45 Non-US $65

The *Only* Digital Library Dedicated to Education & Information Technology

- All the same benefits of a Professional Membership
- PLUS 1-year subscription to the EdITLib with thousands of peer-reviewed journal articles, conference papers and presentations, videos, webinars and much more

$175

The *Only* Digital Library Dedicated to Education & Information Technology

- All the same benefits of a Professional Membership
- PLUS 1-year subscription to the EdITLib
- Offered at a discount for students
- MUST be enrolled as a full-time student in an accredited educational institution and provide school information below

$75

New Option!

- **Registration as a virtual participant for the following events:**
  EdMedia – World Conference on EdMedia & Technology (Value $225)
  E-Learn – World Conference on E-Learning in Corp. Govt., Health, & Higher Ed. (Value $225)
- **Conference proceedings** for AACE events, accessible in EdITLib – Education and Information Technology Digital Library
- **Full access** to EdITLib - The Only Digital Library Dedicated to Education & Information Technology (Value $150)
- **AACE F2F Conference Registration discounts**

$395
(Value $600)

- Libraries may purchase subscription to AACE print Journal(s) and/or the EdITLib

❑ International Journal on E-Learning (IJEL) **$195**
❑ Journal of Educational Multimedia and Hypermedia (JEMH) **$195**
❑ Journal of Computers in Math and Science Teaching (JCMST) **$195**
❑ Journal of Interactive Learning Research (JILR) **$195**
❑ Journal of Technology and Teacher Education (JTATE) **$195**
❑ EdITLib – Education & Information Tech. Library (electronic) **$1895**

Additional shipping charge of $15 per journal per year for non-U.S. addresses

- **Professional & Student Memberships include a subscription to 1 AACE print Journal** *(not included in virtual membership)*
- **Additional journals can be added to your membership**

- **Please choose ONE option:**

❑ Add 1 Journal $115 prof / $35 student
❑ Add 2 Journals $150 prof / $60 student
❑ Add 3 Journals $205 prof / $85 student
❑ Add 4 Journals $260 prof / $110 student
❑ Add 5 Journals $315 prof / $135 student

Additional shipping charge of $15 per journal per year for non-U.S. addresses

Applicant Information

Name: ______________________ E-mail: ______________________

Address: ______________________ City: ____________ State: ______

Postal Code: __________ Country: ______________ ☐ New Member ☐ Renewal Membership # __________

If applying as a student please provide School/Institution Name: ______________ Expected Graduation Date: __________

Select Journal(s) to receive: (*Membership includes 1 journal. See above for adding addit.*) ☐ IJEL ☐ JEMH ☐ JCMST ☐ JILR ☐ JTATE

Method of Payment (US Dollars)

TOTAL:
$

Enclosed: ❑ Check (U.S. funds & bank, payable to AACE) ❑ Purchase Order *(PO must be included plus $10 service charge)*
❑ Bank Wire *(Wire info must be included plus $25 service charge)*

Credit Card: ❑ MasterCard ❑ VISA ❑ AMEX ❑ Discover

Card # ______________________ Card Exp. Date ___/___ Signature: ______________________

Return to: AACE P.O. Box 719, Waynesville, NC 28786 USA • E-mail: info@aace.org • www.aace.org

PART 1 THE LEARNING ENVIRONMENT

1.'From Telling the World to Showing the World in an Era of Social Media'

Gail Casey, School of Education, Deakin University, Australia

Introduction

This article reports on the interdisciplinary learning and literacy aspects of my PhD action research study that took place started in 2010 and continued throughout 2011 and 2012. During this time, I taught thirteen Middle Years classes over an eighteen month period, in an Australian public high school. Students were aged 13 to 16 years and were generally from the mid socio-economic range. I had been a teacher at the school for some years and during the data collection period I taught two Year 8 and one Year 9 Mathematics classes, four Information Technology (IT) classes, including Programming and Multimedia, as well as six classes of Year 7 IT as part of a Year 7 integrated curriculum program where Year 7 is the first year of high school. My interest in interdisciplinary learning and literacy has influenced my classroom teaching for many years and this interest continued to grow as I experienced teaching English as a second language in South Korea in 2007 and completed a Masters in Language and Literacy Education in 2009. I was further supported, in recent years, through the literacy policies and implementation programs of my state department of education (DEECD) which focused on literacy education as the foundation for success in all areas of the curriculum (see, http://www.education.vic.gov.au/studentlearning/litnum/).

As part of my school's literacy policy I, along with other teachers, was expected to identify the literacy practices within my curriculum and discuss these at both specific learning area meetings and in larger mixed learning area meetings. These meetings allowed teachers to share and build on their knowledge and understanding of literacy as well as their literacy practices. Options were provided for teachers to observe the classroom literacy practices of others and also to obtain constructive peer feedback on these practices. The administration at the research site fully supported the literacy policies from DEECD. Of particular note, for this research, was the drive the school had for the literacy practices across different discipline areas which can be framed in the following quote published on the DEECD website.
Literacy is not a practice in isolated classroom activities. Teachers need to support literacy practices across different discipline areas and link the children's literacy practices for home and outside school activities with school learning (DEECD, 2007).

Multimodality and Social Practice

They read because they are part of social groups or because they are in search of role models or information. They write for self-expression, to get through periods of crisis, to document their beliefs, or to communicate with other youth. Thus, we see the world of adolescent literacy as complex, not only because both "adolescent" and "literacy" are ill-defined constructs, but also because young people are so different from one another (Moje et al, 2008, p. 108).

One reason for this study was my frustration, in the classroom, with student disengagement with my traditional teaching and learning practices. The above words of Moje et al challenge some of the prevailing myths about adolescents and their choices related to reading. Their research, on adolescent literacy (p. 146), found that youth do read and write outside of school, but they may not read and write the kinds of texts that adults value. In looking at the reading practices of youth, they found that reading and writing frequently occur in a range of literacy contexts outside school. They explain that adolescents read texts that are embedded in social networks, allowing them to build social capital. Their findings present a number of important possible implications for education practice, which this study investigates, but also pose questions regarding how to build on what motivates adolescents' literacy practices in order to both promote the building of their social selves and improve their academic outcomes. Moje et al (2008) take a sociocultural perspective on literacy, as does this study, and add a critical stance, arguing that power, identities, and agency also play important roles in whose social and cultural practices are valued. Their critical stance has strong implications for this study as I attempt to tease out the changes in my pedagogical approach to interdisciplinary literacy brought about by combining social media, Web 2.0 and face-to-face teaching in my Middle Years classroom. I allowed my students to create their own online identity using pseudonyms, profiles and avatars of their choice. Students also had the freedom to create their own interest groups for interaction, publication and enjoyment while working on teacher directed projects. I used the action research cycle to help redesign my teaching practice where I encouraged the active participation of my students beyond their face-to-face classroom friendship groups. I used social media to allow all of my classes to interact both formally and informally. Adolescent reading and writing practices, as described by Moje et al, were encouraged between classes as well as within classes.

In education, as argued by Kress (2009, p. 212), the question of what theories are needed to deal with learning and assessment in a multimodally constituted world of meaning is becoming newly and insistently urgent. Siegel (2012, p. 671) notes that it is increasingly rare to open a professional journal or attend a conference without encountering the argument that multimodality is central to literate practice everywhere except in schools. Like Siegel, I assert that there are three main arguments for including multimodality in school literacy curricula.

- Literacies are changing and so must school literacy curricula.
- Youth bring multimodal practices to school.
- Multimodal practice can reframe at-risk students as learners of promise.

I do not subscribe to merely entertaining students by integrating their out-of-school online activities into the curriculum. There is considerable research, now, that does indicate that such media can enhance literacy practices in the face-to-face classroom (Bertram, 2002; Dillon, 2006; Jewitt, Clark, & Hadjithoma-Garstka, 2011; Kelly, 2012; A. Luke, 2010; C. Luke, 2002; Walsh, Asha, & Sprainger, 2007). In the redesign of my curriculum through the action research cycle, I looked for teachable moments to build on my student's conversations and I promoted these in our online social network. Cervetti and Pearson (2012, p. 585) argue that we need to know more about how to support teachers in capitalizing on (and occasionally engineering) teachable moments as they bring the tools of literacy to disciplinary learning. All too often, especially in high fidelity implementations of basal programs, as discussed by Cervetti and Person, reading and writing strategies are taught as content-free routines that can be applied to any text. They should be taught in exactly the opposite way – as tools that help readers unlock the meanings of particular texts in the interest of particular knowledge and inquiry pursuits (Cervetti & Pearson, 2012, p. 582).

The concept of literacy is in a profound state of transition and the current landscapes of communication can be characterised, as described by Kress (2003, p. 139), through the metaphor of the move from "telling the world" to "showing the world". In understanding that the world of communication is not standing still and all of us now inhabit this new world, I accept Kress' call for a new way of thinking about literacy resources, their use and the users (2003, p. 32). This study lends itself for Kress' call for a new theory of meaning and meaning-making and a new theory of semiosis.

Research Context and Methods

This study takes a qualitative approach where I categorised and tagged data into 'Teacher', 'Student' and 'Learning' themes and created data collection templates to provide some consistency with documentation. I used a Tablet PC to scribe notes of actions, feelings, reflections and points of interest; when time permitted, I wrote these in the classroom and they were completed after class, if that was needed. I also documented my classroom planning notes and after-class reflections. I analysed action plans and reflections at the end of each week and at the end of each five week period. I also collected and documented student work and critical friend discussions and feedback. Fig. 1 provides a visual summary of the direction of the research and the underlying concepts used for the data tags.

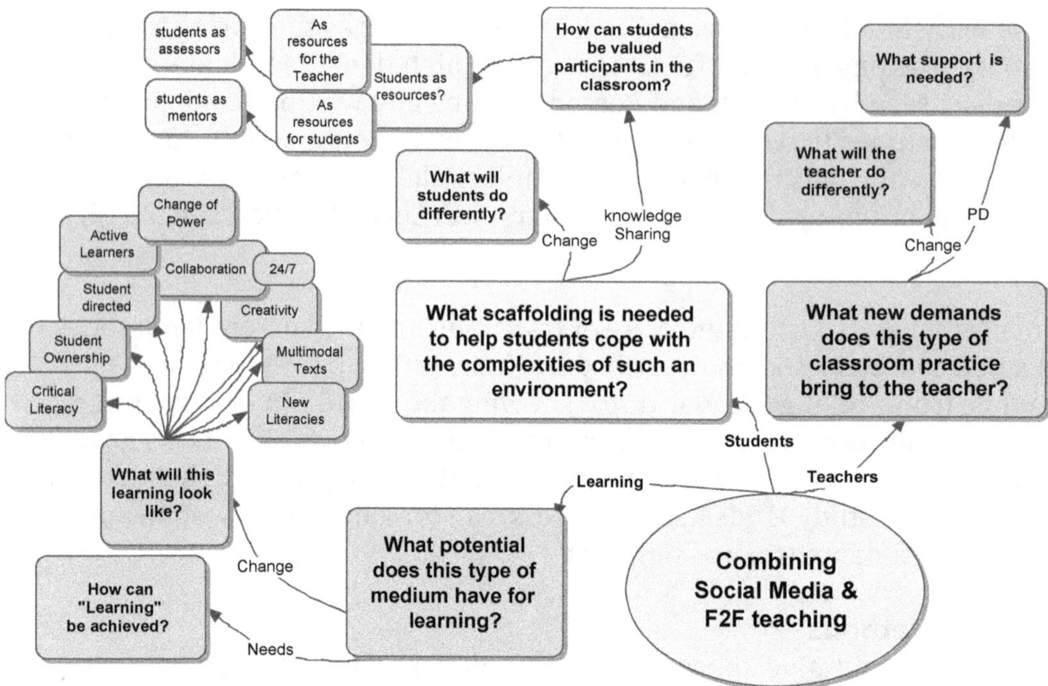

Figure 1: Research focus for which the data was categories and tagged.

The research took place in all of my classes over three semesters, eighteen months, and each class was one semester in length. This included thirteen classes and each class had approximately twenty-five students. Most students from the study were part of the initial stages (first or second year) of the school's one-to-one laptop program. I developed one social media site, called a Ning, to share between my classes during each semester. Students were asked to use pseudonyms when online and were also encouraged not to disclose their online identity, even in the face-to-face classroom. I moderated all membership and activity for the site and I created three social media, Ning, sites over the eighteen month data collection period; one of these can be seen in Fig. 2.

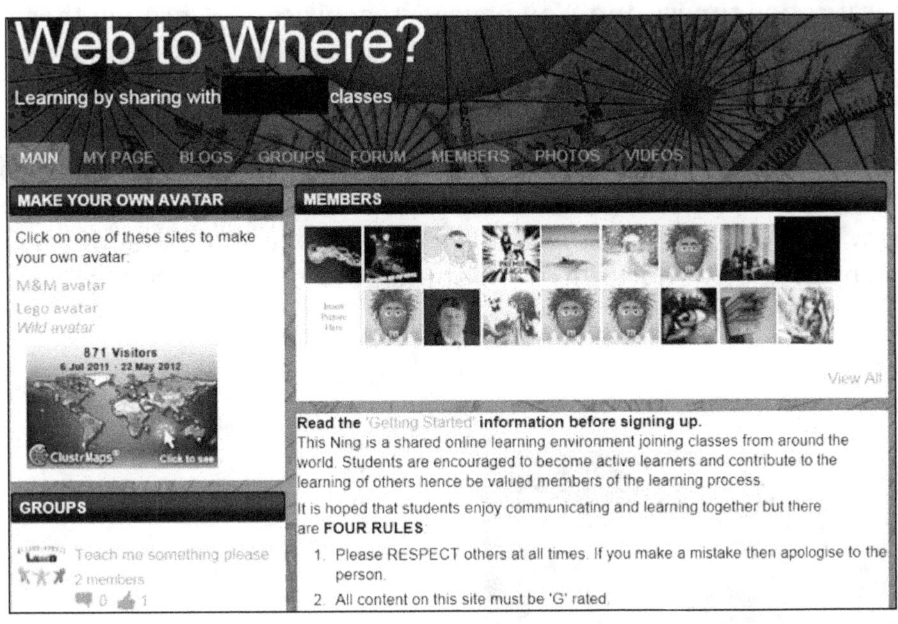

Figure 2: One of the three social media site used during the eighteen month data collection period.

Although many of the classroom projects posted online were specific to a particular class or classes, I did not specify a subject or year level in their online description; encouraging students of any age or subject to view and interact within the project. I used the Ning 'Groups' to post project work and within a particular Group I created 'Discussion Forums' which housed further instructions or spaces where students could post ideas and media. Students were encouraged to use blogs to post their project work which enabled them to receive one-to-one feedback and interaction from their peers. For many projects students had three online peer mentors who were responsible for providing constructive and critical feedback and, at times, peer assessment. Students were able to add their own tags and descriptions to photos and video before posting them to the site and they were encouraged to create their own interest groups for interaction and collaboration outside of their project work. I designed activities that encouraged students to interact within their own class and also with students from my other classes. Activities of this type usually involved students creating multimedia resources to support the learning of others. This I describe as knowledge-building activities (Casey, 2011). It was common for students from Year 7 to Year 10 to interact and become online friends. The following discussion provides examples of the literacy practices from my Middle Years classes. Within these classes I incorporated a wide range of Web 2.0 applications to help transform the way in which students not only presented their work, but also the way they thought, and how they valued their own work and the work of their peers. This type of approach encouraged students to become designers, creators and publishers.

From Telling the World to Showing the World

Throughout the study, a number of curricula activities included global classroom projects where my students interacted with students from outside Australia. Such projects drew on the students' day-to-day knowledge. These included 'What's in your closet?',

'What's for dinner?', 'A typical day at school', 'What's so interesting?', 'I bet you didn't know...', 'Celebrate good times!' and 'You have virtual visitors'. Through these types of projects, students were able to personally connect classroom literacy practices to their own daily activities inside and outside school. For example, students took photos of the clothes they were wearing. Fig. 3 shows how a student used his mobile phone to take a picture of his school uniform and pasted a picture of a pumpkin over the head, to ensure his identity was protected, before posting it online using his phone. These types of activities enabled students to draw personal comparisons and supported their understandings as 'Global Citizens'. It also opened up opportunities for students to think creatively and to critically evaluate the ideas of their peers.

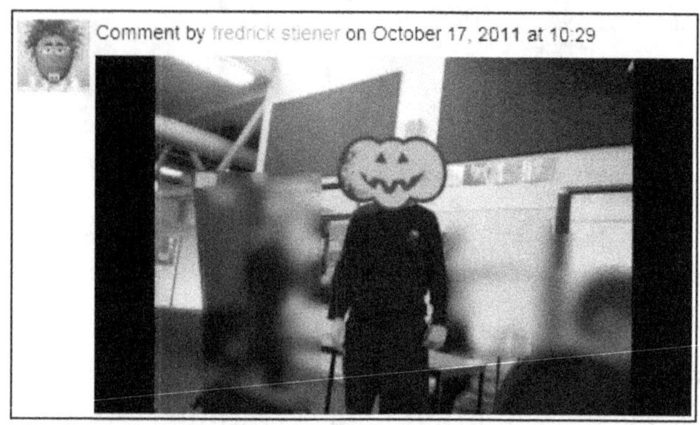

Figure 3: A student used his mobile phone to upload a picture of his school uniform to share. He also used his phone to cover his face for privacy purposes.

Discussion forums were created by students to provide a collaborative space to discuss the clothes they wore. It was encouraging to see that students with perceived lower levels of literacy felt comfortable posting pictures and typing comments. Students, at times, used shorthand forms of text when communicating in discussions; hence, they did not have the burden of traditional spelling and grammar. Fig. 4 shows five student discussion groups and the number of replies for each group.

StudentGroups Discussions (5)

Sort by: Latest Activity

Discussions	Replies	Latest Activity
CoolKidsClothes Ebony Sea, Paige Maslow and Tilah Unicorn. Started by Madeline Guetta	6	Nov 24, 2011 Reply by Madeline Guetta
Ghanda Gang group members: LOLing panther Hermione Granger Miss Beckham Gumball Started by Hermione Granger :)	1	Nov 7, 2011 Reply by Gail Casey
The Walk in Wardrobes The Initial Members of "The Walk in Wardrobes" are Dobby, Can't Tell you and 3 others that don't have a web to where account Yet. Started by Anonymous	11	Nov 7, 2011 Reply by Gail Casey
Evil monkeys The members of our group are- Barney Stinson, Ted Mosby, Telehasse, Hay Guys and enak Ic arke :) Started by Barney Stinson Started by Barney Stinson	7	Oct 20, 2011 Reply by Barney Stinson
Whats in your closet? Our group is called HighTops Started by Roxy Quicksilver	5	Oct 20, 2011 Reply by Anna Ann

Figure 4: Student discussion groups listing the replies to each discussion.

Other examples included the use of 'VoiceThread' <http://voicethread.com/>. Students uploaded photos of the food they liked and used the VoiceThread Web 2.0 application, shown in Fig. 5, to create a multimedia slideshow with options for text and verbal commentary. Students could also leave text or verbal comments for their peers on a VoiceThread.

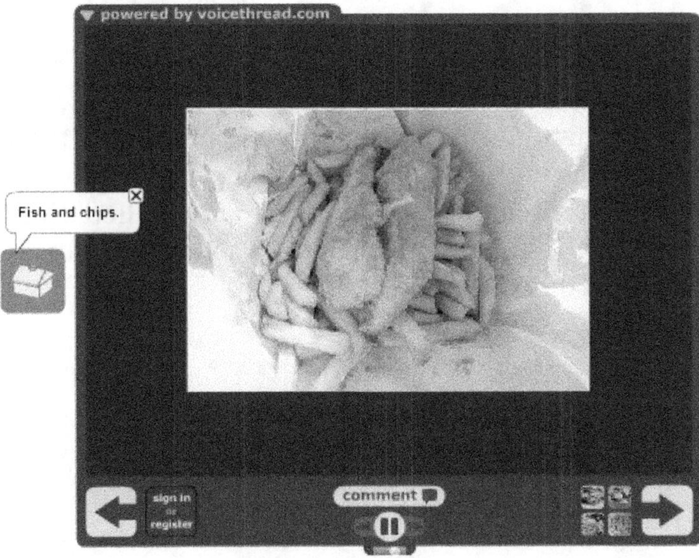

Figure 5: Vociethread combined text, voice and pictures as well as allowing peers to post text and verbal comments.

Students used online video creation software including Animoto <http://animoto.com/> in projects such as 'Digital Footprints' and 'Internet Safety'. These multimedia products were shared across subjects and year levels to warn students of the possible dangers associated with using the Internet. Examples can be seen at <http://ghs2010.ning.com/group/digitalfootprints>. I used a host of other Web 2.0 applications, some are listed below and some are further discussed in Casey (2012), to help students present visual representations of their thinking, to express themselves in many different ways and to provide them with a mechanism to create content, to publish their knowledge and contribute further to the learning of their peers.

- http://click7.org/image-mosaic-generator/?create – creates mosaics from uploaded pictures
- http://www.toondoo.com/ and http://www.makebeliefscomix.com/ - generates cartoons
- http://www.tagxedo.com/ - word cloud generator
- http://www.voki.com/ - creates animated podcasts
- http://blabberize.com/ - creates animated podcasts
- https://bubbl.us/ - online mind mapping
- http://www.xtranormal.com/ - creates animated stories
- http://polldaddy.com/ - survey generator
- http://wallwisher.com/ - online notice board
- http://taggalaxy.de/ - generates a revolving globe of pictures
- http://www.befunky.com/ - fun editing with pictures

The multimodal social semiotics within these activities supports Kress' theory of meaning-making beyond language. Students developed a range of skills which included the social protocols, formal and informal language as well as reading and interpreting both the text and graphics of their peers. Students were able to participate in 'Real world' projects and produce their own representations of 'new texts', as described by Walsh (2011, p. 18).

All members of the social networking site could develop their own 'My Page' which provided them with quick links to their own content such as 'friends', blogs, groups, photos and latest activities. Each student's 'My page' also provided peers with a space to leave direct comments for the owner of that page. At times, students used their 'My Page' to post some of their feelings and emotions. Fig. 6 provides an example of one student who used his 'My Page' to express the loss of his dog. This student used the pseudonym 'metalhead 1997' and he held personal connections and experiences with this name. Students also created groups to express their disapproval and frustrations. Examples include groups called 'Not enough chairs' and 'Why'. Another group called 'RIP Dan Wheldod' was also used to express feelings about the loss of a racing car driver who died in a high speed race.

Figure 6: Each member had their own 'My Page' where they could express themselves.

Many students displayed ownership qualities when editing their 'My Page' by designing their own backgrounds and themes. Some students also changed the privacy settings of their page so that only those allocated with online 'friend' status could view or post comments. As supported by Moje etal (2008, p. 112), the complexity of literacy in which youth engage demonstrates that many young people are able to read across a variety of symbol systems, including print, Internet messaging, video and computer games and other digital environments. The students in this study created their own identity by designing their own avatar, profile and pseudonym, which they were able to change at any time. They published their own fictitious personal details which allowed them to take on a new identity, whenever they desired, while remaining anonymous.

The social media I used in this study, provided students with mechanisms not only to showcase their strengths and expertise but also to use these to support their peers. As the study progressed, the action research cycle enabled the design of the social media site and the projects within the site to improve and develop in flexibility and complexity. Some of these complexities contributed to aspects which could be described as chaotic (Casey & Evans, 2011) as students created informal discussion forums and changed their profiles whenever they desired. These student-directed discussion forums provided students with opportunities to interact and publish content as well as having fun and being entertained: but students were also learning. Some could argue that student interest groups such as 'Formula One', 'Gaming', 'Funny Pictures', 'Football' and 'gifs', to name just a few, were distractions to the learning process. I would argue that they actually helped students manage and understand online relationships and to gain personal confidence. This in turn helped with their participation in teacher-directed activities. These student-directed groups and forums also provided a means for other students to learn more about the activities and the interests of their peers. They also, at times, allowed me to learn more about my student's interests and out-of-school activities which then helped me to find 'teachable moments'.

In Math, students used 'Google Earth' < http://www.google.com/earth/index.html> to find the area of part of the school and then created help-video tutorials to teach other students aspects of the Google Earth online software. This type of activity, as described by Walsh (2011, p. 19), involved the students in a process of reading and writing (as well as calculations) which could be described as new literacy practices; in the way that the activities with print and digital texts converge. Students were expected to read the screen to understand how Google Earth could be manipulated. Recording of new information was taken and then this learning was transferred into the digital form for others to use. Students were not only documenting their own learning but designing ways for others to access information and to learn. Walsh (p. 19) describes such activities as authentic learning and literacy processes, requiring detailed metacognitive strategies. The affordances of digital technology, combined with the way in which I designed the tasks, provided an environment where students were motivated to work together, not only to use the technology, but also to create products that were evidence of their learning. Walsh (2011, p. 23) explains that while a reader's interaction with a text has long been established as an important aspect of comprehension, interaction occurs in further ways. Both in the face-to-face classroom and the social media site, reading activities were usually linked to other speaking, listening, writing or creative activities involving both peers and the teacher.

Implications for Teaching

Students in this study could create interest groups unrelated to their class work and, through these interest groups, they built friendships and relationships which in turn supported their class work. This type of learning is supported by Gee and Hayes (2011, p. 130) who explain that throughout the Internet (not just in virtual worlds) more and more people are joining groups with shared interests and passions. These groups often agree to behave in certain ways that ensure yet more uniformity. Gee and Hayes go on to explain that the interests and passions that people pursue on the Internet are not uncorrelated with social classes, genders, and lifestyles in the real world. This can be seen throughout this study, but in particular during the first semester of data collection when I taught seven classes who shared the one site; seventy-seven online 'Groups' were formed with more than forty of these groups being created by students and not related to class projects.

In his discussion of a 'decline in standards' and the context from which such a statement is drawn, Kress (2003) asserts that "The young are teaching themselves because the old cannot or will not" (p.175). He gives 'texting' as an example. From data taken from my reflections after school meetings and informal teacher discussions, I would argue that most teachers were not interested in using forms of social media or mobile devices in their teaching practices. Often teachers saw these as student leisure activities and they felt that they should be left outside the classroom. I would assert that for teachers and teachers-to-be, it is important to venture beyond the walls of the classroom and build, with students, a shared framework for learning. Without doubt, it is important to be willing and accountable to school and state-driven testing, but in doing so we need to also support the students' strengths and abilities which are often linked to students' lives. This author believes that González, Moll and Amanti provide an appropriate metaphor in support of this type of thinking: "Our perspective is that learning does not take place just 'between the ears,' but is eminently a social process" (González et al, 2005, p. ix).
Their book 'Funds of knowledge' (González, et al., 2005) is based on a simple premise: People are competent, they have knowledge and their life experiences have given them that knowledge. Fuller and Hood (2005, p. 63) also argue that placing the cultural and intellectual resources children have acquired outside the classroom at the centre of

curriculum design can turn around participation of children in classroom discourse and can enhance their learning.

This study suggests, like Gee and Hayes (2011), that multimodality is more pervasive, diverse and important today than ever before. Digital media can "power up" or enhance the powers of language, oral and written, just as written language "powered up" or enhanced the powers of oral language (Gee & Hayes, 2011, p. 1). Language itself, as explained by Gee and Hayes, has always been a mixture of sound, words, images created in the mind, and gestures used in contexts full of objects, sounds, actions and interactions; language has always been "multimodal". Textbooks and newspapers are available today on the Internet where they are usually accompanied by images and video.

Despite years of research and governments from all political persuasions trying just about everything to intervene, old patterns of literacy disaffection and disconnection prevail for certain groups of students (Comber & Kamler, 2005, p. 2). By positioning teachers as researchers and collaborators, Comber and Kamler have documented numerous ways teachers can turn around student literacy achievement and engagement by the redesigning of literacy practices. These ways support Kucer's (2009, p. 5) argument that literacy should be conceived as dynamic and multidimensional in nature, if literacy in education is to be effective.

Throughout the data collection period, I was able to construct a solid triangulation of assessment data for school reporting which included peer feedback followed by peer assessment, self assessment and teacher assessment. I found, as supported by Feng and Beaumont (2010, p. 428), that my initial concern over students copying the work of their peers and plagiarism and vandalism was not an issue. The research findings show that opportunities for collaborative learning and interaction were well supported by the integration of social media into the face-to-face classroom. The research also suggests that by providing students with opportunities to interact informally and create fluid identities online helped them to more fully engage with my teacher directed projects.

Creating an online site that could be used for informal social interaction, as well as for teacher directed class and project work required a solid understanding of social software tools, this is discussed further in Casey (2013). I hope that by designing such interactive projects into my Middle Years Mathematics and Information Technology classes, as well as my Year 7 integrated program class, that this research can contribute to a knowledge base which will support teachers from across disciplines to recognise and implement literacy practices, not as an isolated classroom activity, but across different discipline areas that link to adolescent out-of-school literacy practices.

Conclusion

In this research, it was not the technology itself, but it was my design of the class projects and the links they made to the learning environments that offered the potential for dynamic literacy learning. In an attempt to stay current, educators are beginning to incorporate social media tools more frequently in their classes; blogs along with social networks are being used more regularly to encourage curriculum based discourse outside of classroom walls (Moayeri, 2010, p. 41). But, many challenges exist within a changing classroom environment, as explained by Walsh (2011, p. 101). While teachers take on these challenges, I call for more teachers to document their changes in teaching and learning approaches and to become researchers of their own practice. I found that by using action research I could move my thinking when searching for success from "that did not work, what else can I try?" to a mode of analysis and empowerment such as "how can I do that better?". This encouraged me to position myself as a fellow learner, modelling for students. And, as found in the boys literacy study of Fisher and Frey (2012, p. 595), one's truths continue to be shaped by close readings; hence, my expertise was not an endpoint, but rather it continued to grow with my students.

I encouraged students to become publishers. They were given opportunities to use their 'voice' as part of their meaning-making. At times, students were empowered as authors, producing sophisticated pieces of multimodal work that would not have been possible to produce using conventional literacies. Their digital texts were able to be non-linear and students could draw on their cultural capital to support their in-school literacies. Integrating the social media site provided students with tools such as blogs, groups and discussion forums and also provided a space where students could create their own identity. These supported many reluctant classroom participants and provided models of learning for students of all abilities. Peer feedback, encouragement, support and assessment were easily built into the learning process. I allowed the site to be used for social purposes as well as teacher directed project work which raised pedagogical challenges for me both in implementing classroom practices and designing activities. I found, as did Hansford and Adlington (2009, p. 60) when examining wikis and blogs, that online learning with social media do not just provide neat online facilities capable of creating digital versions of conventional texts; they are new texts in themselves with their own potential and purpose" (p. 60). I found that the affordances and demands of these new texts, at times, challenged my traditional methods of teaching.

The view that literacy is a social practice is posited on the importance of context and, within this context, students help to shape their own learning environment, both with and without the consent of the teacher (Kelly, 2012). The literacy events co-constructed by my students promoted motivation and empowerment. In many ways, it personalised the students learning experiences. This research supports the research of Moje et al (2008); students do read and write outside of school and, although many adults, often, do not value the kinds of texts that adolescents read, the communication, relationships and self-expression which they foster, as seen in this study, offers them essential day-to-day literacy skills and can play an important role in the classroom.

We are reminded by Kress (2009, p. 212) that the world of meaning has always been multimodal and language alone cannot give us access to the meaning of the multimodally constituted message. His metaphor (p. 139) 'from telling the world to showing the world', points to a profound change in the act of reading and he asserts that this metaphor allows us to explore the questions that reading poses. This, he explains, could be as narrow as 'getting meaning from a written text', and as wide as 'making sense of the world around me' – through a new lens and new forms of reading, where texts showing the world rather than telling the world have consequences for the relations between makers and re-makers of meaning (writers and readers, image-makers and viewers). I share this metaphor with Kress in the title of this article because, in many ways, it provides a picture, for me, of the impact the action research cycle had on my own understanding of what it means to teach and learn.

Acknowledgements

I would like to acknowledge Dr Muriel Wells and Professor Terry Evans, Deakin University, for guiding me to supportive resources, for their professional interaction and for editorial advice.

References

Bertram, B. C. (2002). Diversity and critical social engagement : How changing technologies enable new modes of literacy in changing circumstances. In D. E. Alvermann (Ed.), *Adolescents and literacies in a digital world* (pp. 1-18). New York: P. Lang.

Casey, G. (2013). Social Media in the Classroom: a Simple Yet Complex Hybrid Environment for Students. Journal of Educational Multimedia and Hypermedia, 22(1), 5-24.

Casey, G. (2012). Social Media in the Math Classroom. Learning & Leading with Technology, 40(36-37).

Casey, G. (2011). Knowledge-building: Designing for learning using social and participatory media. *eLearning Papers*, (27), 1-7. Retrieved from http://elearningeuropa.info/en/node/111104?paper=111465

Casey, G., & Evans, T. (2011). Designing for learning: Online social networks as a classroom environment. *The International Review of Research in Open and Distance Learning*, 12(7), 1-26. Retrieved from http://www.irrodl.org/index.php/irrodl/article/view/1011

Cervetti, G., & Pearson, P. D. (2012). Reading, Writing, and Thinking Like a Scientist. *Journal of Adolescent & Adult Literacy, 55*(7), 580-586.

Comber, B., & Kamler, B. (2005). Designing turn-around dedagogies and contesting deficit assumptions. In B. Comber & B. Kamler (Eds.), *Turn-around Pedagogies: Literacy Interventions for At-risk Students*. Newtown, Australia: PETA.

DEECD. (2007). Overview of Literacy Learning. Retrieved 6th June, 2012, from http://www.education.vic.gov.au/studentlearning/teachingresources/english/literacy/litoview.htm

Dillon, N. (2006). skills FOR A NEW CENTURY. *American School Board Journal, 193*(3), 22-26.

Feng, S., & Beaumont, C. (2010). Evaluating the use of a wiki for collaborative learning. *Innovations in Education and Teaching International, 47*(4), 417-431.

Fisher, D., & Frey, N. (2012). Motivating Boys to Read: Inquiry, Modeling, and Choice Matter. *Journal of Adolescent & Adult Literacy, 55*(7), 587-596.

Fuller, R., & Hood, D. (2005). Utilising community funds of knowlege as resources for school learning. In B. Comber & B. Kamler (Eds.), *Turn-around Pedagogies: Literacy Interventions for At-risk Students*. Newtown, Australia: PETA.

Gee, J. P., & Hayes, E. R. (2011). *Language and Learning in the Digital Age.* Abingdon: Routledge.

González, N., Moll, L. C., & Amanti, C. (2005). *Funds of knowledge : theorizing practices in households, communities, and classrooms.* Mahwah, N.J.: L. Erlbaum Associates.

Hansford, D., & Adlington, R. (2009). Digital spaces and young people's online authoring: challenges for teachers. *Australian Journal of Language and Literacy, 32*(1), 55-68.

Jewitt, C., Clark, W., & Hadjithoma-Garstka, C. (2011). The use of learning platforms to organise learning in English primary and secondary schools. *Learning Media and Technology, 36*(4), 335-348.

Kelly, C. R. (2012). Recognizing the "Social" in Literacy as a Social Practice: Building on the Resources of Nonmainstream Students. *Journal of Adolescent & Adult Literacy, 55*(7), 608-618.

Kress, G. R. (2003). *Literacy in the new media age.* London Routledge.

Kress, G. R. (2009). *Multimodality : A social semiotic approach to contemporary communication.* London: Routledge.

Kucer, S. B. (2009). *Dimensions of Literacy : A Conceptual Base for Teaching Reading and Writing in School Settings* (3rd ed.). New York: Routledge.

Luke, A. (2010). Australia: The Challenges of Poverty, Pedagogy, and Pathways. In I. Rotberg (Ed.), *Balancing Change and Tradition in Global Education Reform* (pp. 339-347). Plymouth, United Kingdom: Rowman & Littlefield Education.

Luke, C. (2002). Re-Crafting Media and ICT Literacies. In D. E. Alvermann (Ed.), *Adolescents and literacies in a digital world* (pp. 132-146). New York: P. Lang.

Moayeri, M. (2010). Classroom Uses of Social Network Sites: Traditional Practices or New Literacies. *Digital Culture & Education, 2*(1), 25-43.

Moje, E., Overby, M., Tysvaer, N., & Morris, K. (2008). The Complex World of Adolescent Literacy: Myths, Motivations, and Mysteries. *Harvard Educational Review, 78*(1), 107-280.

Siegel, M. (2012). New Times for Multimodality? Confronting the Accountability Culture. *Journal of Adolescent & Adult Literacy, 55*(8), 671-680.

Walsh, M. (2011). *Multimodal Literacy.* Newtown, NSW: PETA.

Walsh, M., Asha, J., & Sprainger, N. (2007). Reading digital texts.(reading instruction). *Australian Journal of Language and Literacy, 30*(1), 40.

2 Students' Perceptions of Learning in a Flipped Statistics Class

Anthony Dove, Radford University, United States

Introduction

While teachers often wish to use collaborative discovery-based experiences during class, they are often concerned about the time needed for these activities when there is pressure to cover the breadth of material required in an era of high stakes testing (Hannafin et al., 2001; Ruthven et al., 2008). However, unique opportunities through the use of technological methods can assist in allowing such experiences to occur in the classroom. One such method that has received national publicity is the flipped classroom approach. In a flipped classroom, students are assigned video lectures to watch at home and then return to class to apply the learning through practice problems, projects, and discovery-based activities. While this method has received recognition in various settings, little research has explored student perception of the use of this approach in the mathematics classroom. For this reason, this study explored the question: How do students perceive learning Introduction to Statistics in a flipped classroom?

Background

While programs like the Kahn Academy have brought publicity to the concept of flipping the classroom, very little research has been done on the effectiveness of flipped classrooms. However, available research suggests that the flipped classroom can have a positive influence in the classroom. At the K-12 level, Clintondale High School in Detroit, Michigan significantly decreased their failure rate in mathematics and overall discipline referrals after teachers shifted their classroom instruction to the flipped method (Roscorla, 2011). At the collegiate level, Yoon and Sneedon (2011) found that availability of video lectures in mathematics courses provided significant increases in final grades.

Although there is limited research specifically on flipping the classroom, the method utilizes well-researched notions on how students learn. For example, findings have indicated that students who sit in the front row often perform significantly better in class (Rosengrant et al., 2011). Since lecture videos are watched outside the class and individually in a flipped classroom, students have a virtual front-row view of the material. In addition, research has suggested that building trusting relationships between students, teachers, and parents can have a positive influence on student achievement (Goddard, Tschannen-Moran, & Hoy, 2001). Since lecture videos are readily accessible, content and instruction become transparent, which can help build trust between parents, students, and teachers. Also, many of the classroom distractors that occur during lectures are no longer an issue since the student watches the videos individually (Rosengrant et al., 2011). Finally, lecture videos offer a unique learning opportunity since students can access the videos when they are most needed (Yoon & Sneedon, 2011). Students can rewind, rewatch, and skip to sections of the video that they need to specifically review. When students miss class for any reason, they have an opportunity to not fall behind on the content as the videos can be watched anytime, anywhere.

Methods

This study incorporated an action research design. The primary researcher served as the instructor of a Statistics I course at a large community college in the Mid-Atlantic region with the intent of changing his instruction via the flipped classroom method. This course provided four credits. The class met twice a week for 2.5 hours each meeting in a computer lab.

There were 21 students that completed the course. Students ranged in age from 18 – 55. The class was comprised of 15 females and 6 males. There were five minority students and three with special needs. The students had a diverse background upon entering the class as well, such as nursing majors at the community college for which the course was required, students just beginning their degrees at the community college, and students taking the course for transfer credit to one of the four-year universities near the community college.

The course utilized *Elementary Statistics 5th Edition* (Larson & Farber, 2011) and the classroom management system, *MyMathLab* (http://www.mymathlab.com/). To flip the classroom, the instructor created lecture videos using *Microsoft PowerPoint* and *Screencast-O-Matic* (http://screencast-o-matic.com/). A lecture video was created for each required section from the Statistics I course pacing guide. Videos were uploaded to a YouTube channel prior to each class and were linked to the corresponding section in *MyMathLab*. In addition, section materials required for all activities were uploaded in *MyMathLab* (Figure 1).

Ch 9.2: Linear Regression

- *Activity 1: Watch Lecture and Take Notes*
  - Click here to watch the Video Lecture
  - Click here to download the PowerPoint

- *Activity 2: CSI Forensics*
  - As you can see, we have a murder on our hands and we have limited data. With your help, hopefully we can solve this murder. To do so, we will have to use data about our class.

    Data Collection

    a) Measure your shoe (in centimeters). If necessary, 1 inch = 2.54 centimeters

    b) Measure your height in inches.

    c) Measure your stride from back of heel to back of heel (in centimeters)

    d) Enter your data: Click Here

    Now it is time to determine the murderer!

    1) Download the following Word document: Forensics Case File

    2) To answer the questions, use the following Excel file: Click here!

    3) Place your answers in the following form: Ch 9 Form

    4) Let's work to solve this case!

- *Activity 3*
  - Ch 9.2 Practice

Figure 1: Example of a Section in *MyMathLab*

During the first class of the semester, the instructor explained to the students the flipped classroom approach. As this was a new experience for all students involved, the class watched the lecture videos for the first two textbook sections together. During this time, the teacher focused both on the content and how to watch the video with the intent of taking notes. This time included instructions on how to use YouTube features such as viewing the video in full screen, pausing, and rewinding.

For the duration of the semester, students were assigned one to two lecture videos which they were to watch prior to the upcoming class. Students were required to show their lecture notes for the first two weeks of the semester to verify they were watching the videos and understanding how to take appropriate notes. During class, students completed practice problems, discovery-based activities, and projects. All activities were accessed via *MyMathLab* (Figure 1).

Throughout the semester, students were encouraged to collaborate with one another for all activities except quizzes and tests. During each activity, the instructor circulated throughout the class and assisted students individually or in pairs. Students were also required to complete online homework sets and quizzes that were assigned to all students taking Statistics I at the community college.

At the completion of the semester, students were asked to complete a 12 question *Google Forms* survey about their experiences in a flipped classroom (Figure 2). Questions included two questions on how often students watched the video lectures and took notes as well as eight Likert questions and two open-ended questions about the overall flipped classroom experience. For calculation of each question's mean and standard deviation, the Likert Scale was given values of 1 (Strong Disagree) to 4 (Strongly Agree). The open-ended questions were examined for common themes among the students. Completion of the survey was fully anonymous as no identifying questions were asked within the survey. In addition, the survey was not required and was presented as a tool for the professor to use to improve his flipped classroom method for future courses. Of the 21 students who completed the course, 20 completed the survey.

Statistics Survey

I am working to improve my class, and I am trying to figure out what worked well and what didn't with the "flipped lecture video" method (watching lecture videos at home instead of lecturing during class). Please take a moment to complete this very brief survey. This is completely anonymous. I would greatly appreciate your input.

How many of the lecture videos did you watch?

- Never
- I watched no more than 1/4 of the videos
- I watched more than 1/4 but no more than 1/2 of the videos
- I watched more than 1/2 but no more than 3/4 of the videos
- I watched between 3/4 and all of the videos

Of the videos you watched, did you take notes?

- I never watched the videos
- I never took notes
- I took notes for less than 1/4 of the videos
- I took notes for more than 1/4 but no more than 1/2 of the videos
- I took notes for more than 1/2 but no more than 3/4 of the videos
- I took notes for between 3/4 and all of the videos

Answer the following statements using a rating from "Strongly Disagree" to "Strongly Agree"

	Strongly Disagree	**Disagree**	**Agree**	**Strongly Agree**
I would have preferred having the lecture during class time	○	○	○	○
I appreciated having the lecture videos readily available	○	○	○	○

I appreciated having the lecture notes readily available	○	○	○	○
I found the practice problems completed in class helpful in learning concepts	○	○	○	○
I found the class assignments/activities to be helpful in learning concepts	○	○	○	○
I found the opportunity to work with other students during class to be helpful	○	○	○	○
If I were to take another math class, I would prefer it to use the "flipped lecture video" method	○	○	○	○
I would recommend other students to take a class using the "flipped lecture video" method	○	○	○	○

What did you like most about this class?

What did you like least about this class?

Figure 2: End of Semester Survey

Findings

Results suggested that students found the lecture videos helpful, the in-class activities relevant, and the opportunity to work with others a positive opportunity to enhance their learning. Of the respondents, 65% watched 75%-100% of the videos, while 70% took notes for 75%-100% of the sections. Student responses suggested that they perceived two values in the lecture videos: opportunity to build conceptual understanding; and opportunity to access and learn at their own pace. For example, one student commented, "Honestly, I didn't watch all the videos. The ones I did watch, however, greatly improved my understanding of the concepts." Another student stated that due to the access of the lectures, "I could learn at my own pace at home." Another student suggested, "The videos were nice because I could always go back to review before a test."

For the eight Likert questions, students were overwhelmingly in favor of the overall opportunities presented in the flipped classroom (Table 1). For example, only three students agreed or strongly agreed that they would prefer having lectures in class. In contrast, all but two agreed or strongly agreed that they would prefer taking another class using the flipped classroom approach. In addition, all students agreed or strongly agreed that they would recommend other students to take a class using the flipped classroom method. Student responses suggested that they preferred this method because it kept them actively engaged through various activities instead of passively listening to a lecture in class. One student suggested, "Lectures make me sleepy and I tend to zone out. It is much harder to zone out when I'm actively participating versus 'listening' to someone talk."

With no direct instruction occurring in class, students were asked their perception of the in-class activities. All students agreed or strongly agreed that the given practice sets and assignments were beneficial to their learning, and all but one student agreed or strongly agreed that student collaboration was helpful. Student responses suggested that the in-class time spent applying the concepts had a significantly positive influence on their understanding of the content. One student stated, "I liked that we used our class time to apply the materials learned on the lecture. The hands on experience in the classroom gave me a better understanding of the material." Another student suggested that the classroom assignments helped personalize the learning. "I really enjoyed the more interactive problems and exercises through the online surveys because it brought a more personal touch to the problems, and thus increased [my] interest in the problem itself." This method also helped students with different learning styles, as one student suggested, "I am a hands-on learner so working in class with other people and being able to do work during class was very helpful."

On the two open-ended responses, students were asked what was liked most and least about the flipped class. Responses were limited about the least favorite aspect of the flipped classroom. The majority of students suggested the class length and the time of day were their least favorite aspects. However, one student stated displeasure in working with partners and another wanted the lectures to occur in class. A third student specifically critiqued the videos, stating, "I would have liked it if the lecture videos were longer, going over more details a little deeper through more problems."

In contrast, there was a significant amount of responses for what was liked most about the flipped classroom. These responses suggested that the flipped classroom improved the students' perception of their mathematical abilities. One student stated, "This has been the easiest class for me, and I attribute it to your video method and practice time in class." Another student commented, "I always struggled with math prior to this class. I think the flipped class method should be used as much as possible, especially within the math and sciences." Responses also suggested the flipped classroom increased students' interest in math. "I am so excited and pleased to say that I have renewed confidence in my math skill set and overall interest in math."

Question	Mean	Standard Deviation
I would have preferred having the lecture during class time	1.7	0.86
I appreciated having the lecture videos readily available	3.5	0.83
I appreciated having the lecture notes readily available	3.9	0.31
I found the practice problems completed in class helpful in learning concepts	3.8	0.41
I found the class assignments/activities to be helpful in learning concepts	3.7	0.49
I found the opportunity to work with other students during class to be helpful	3.6	0.60
If I were to take another math class, I would prefer it to use the "flipped lecture video" method	3.6	0.69
I would recommend other students to take a class using the "flipped lecture video" method	3.6	0.50

Table 1: Student Perception Survey Results for the Flipped Statistics I Classroom

Discussion

This study focused on how students perceived the opportunity to learn in an Introduction to Statistics flipped classroom environment. Student results, both on Likert scaled questions and open-ended responses, suggested that they enjoyed and preferred the flipped classroom method of instruction. Student responses suggested that having lecture videos readily available in and out of class allowed them the time needed to process content so that it could be applied in a student-centered activity-based in-class setting.

One could argue that the overall positive assessment by the students reflected more on the opportunities and activities created in the classroom. However, that is the very essence of the flipped classroom method. Had in-class lectures been necessary, the amount of practice and hands-on activities completed by the students would have been significantly less. Removing lectures provided the only viable means for such activities to occur that students enjoyed. In addition, it provide students the time to practice, explore, and ask questions of the instructor, something that cannot be done as effectively when the majority of practice is completed outside the classroom as homework.

This study does have its limitations. For example, this was an evening class at a community college. Many of the students were working full time jobs during the day while completing classes at night. It is not known how this unique population influenced the results of this study and whether similar results would be found with any section of Introduction to Statistics. Also, this class was taught in a computer lab so that technology-based statistical programs such as *Microsoft Excel* could be used with the students. While all sections of Introduction to Statistics were taught in labs at the community college, it is unknown what influence this had on students' perception of the course. How would it change the activities that were completed in the class if limited or no technology was available, and how would it change students' perceptions of a flipped introductory statistics course?

The flipped classroom provides a unique opportunity that may not have been fully available prior to the increased use of technology and the internet. While there is little research on the flipped classroom, this study suggests that students are receptive to taking such classes at the collegiate level and that it can help them feel more positive about the overall learning experience. As one student summarized:

> At first I was really hesitant to take a class where the lectures were videos that we had to watch outside of class but I actually found it to be more helpful because we were able to practice the concepts during class. The layout of the class provided me plenty of time to ask questions and get help on all concepts that we were learning while in class and I was able to grasp the material really well.

References

Goddard, R. D., Tschannen-Moran, M., & Hoy, W. K. (2001). A multilevel examination of the distribution and effects of teacher trust in students and parents in urban elementary schools. *The Elementary School Journal, 102(1),* 3-17.

Hannafin, R. D., Burruss, J. D., & Little, C. (2001). Learning with dynamic geometry programs: Perspectives of teachers and learners. *The Journal of Educational Research, 94*(3), 132-144.

Roscorla, T. (2011). Clintondale high cuts freshman failure rates with flipped classes. *Converge*. Retrieved from http://www.convergemag.com/classtech/Clintondale-High-Flipped-Classes.html.

Rosengrant, D., Hearrington, D., Kerriann, A., & Keeble, D. (2012). Following student gaze patterns in physical science lectures. Proceedings of American Institute of Physics Conference 2011, 323 – 326.

Ruthven, K., Hennessy, S., & Deaney, R. (2008). Constructions of dynamic geometry: A study of the interpretative flexibility of educational software in classroom practice. *Computers & Education, 51*(1), 297-317.

Yoon, C. & Sneddon, J. (2011). Student perceptions of effective use of tablet PC recorded lectures in undergraduate mathematics courses. *International Journal of Mathematical Education in Science and Technology, 42(4),* 425-445.

3 The effect of the design of instructional video on students' learning outcome and perceived difficulty in online learning environment

Mohamed Ibrahim, Rebecca Callaway & David Bell College of Education, Arkansas Tech University, United States

Introduction

One of the frequently used medium across learning environments is instructional video. The use of instructional video has increased over the past decade and become an essential teaching medium. For example, in 2009, video becomes the third most popular genre for learning and reached 38% of adult Internet users (Purcell & American Life, 2010). Empirical research on the use of dynamic audiovisual learning materials demonstrates that learners not only prefer instructional video over text, but are also more likely to gain deeper conceptual understanding of the content from video than from words alone (Baggett, 1984; Mayer, 2002, 2003; Mayer & Moreno, 2002). In many learning contexts, knowledge acquisition better achieved through presenting materials in formats to use both the visual and auditory sensory channels at the same time (Mayer, 2001). Studies also found that content presented in video is more memorable than text-based instruction (Jonassen, Peck, & Wilson, 1999). A major assumption underlying this empirical work is that humans can construct a mental representation of the semantic meaning from either auditory or visual information alone, but when instruction presented in both formats, each source provides complementary information that is relevant to learning (Baggett, 1984).

Although video is increasingly becoming a key component in face-to-face, hybrid and online learning environments, there are few drawbacks such as presenting long videos or videos that contain complex topics. Some videos offer students no control over its pace and students can only view video in a sequential, linear and passive fashion. Furthermore, cognitive researchers argue that video requires high levels of cognitive processing to synthesize the visual and auditory streams of information and extract the semantics of the message (Homer, Plass, & Blake, 2008). This increased processing upturns the learner's cognitive load, especially when students are novices in the knowledge domain and lack appropriate prior knowledge to guide their attention (Moreno, 2004; Sweller, 1999). Therefore, a central problem in using video as an instructional device is how to direct learners' attention to relevant information and decrease cognitive load (perceived difficulty) by creating conditions for the learners' cognitive system to meet the processing demands needed to organize and integrate knowledge from a stream of visual and auditory information. More specifically, cognitive researchers have suggest that focusing students' attention on essential information in fast stream of visual and verbal information helps students' limited cognitive resources (e.g., Ayres, 2007; Lowe, 1999, 2003).

In an attempt to overcome the challenges associated with learning from multimedia materials, such as video, cognitive researchers suggested a number of research-based design principles to improve students' knowledge acquisition. These design principles based on Cognitive Theory of Multimedia Learning (CTML) (Mayer, 2001) and Cognitive Load Theory (CLT) (Sweller, Merrienboer, & Paas, 1998). Both theories based on several assumptions regarding the relationship between cognition and learning from dual representation information formats.

Four of these assumptions are particularly relevant to learning from video. First, the cognitive architecture assumption postulates that the human mind consists of an unlimited, long-term memory (LTM) in which all prior knowledge is stored and a limited working memory (WM) in which new information is processed. Second, the dual-channel assumption proposes that WM has two channels for visual/pictorial and auditory/verbal processing and that the two channels are structurally and functionally distinct (Clark & Paivio, 1991). Third, the limited capacity assumption states that each cognitive channel has limited capacity for information that can be processed at one time (Baddeley, 1986; Baddeley & Logie, 1999). Fourth, the active processing assumption explains that humans actively engage in the cognitive processes to select relevant verbal and non-verbal information from the learning materials, organize the selected information into cognitive structures, and integrate these cognitive structures with the existing knowledge to construct a new (or update an old) mental representation (Mayer, 1996).

According to cognitive research, the human cognitive system can process only small portions of the multimedia large amounts of visual and auditory stimuli received at a time. Unlike processing printed text, learners in face-to-face contexts typically do not have the opportunity to stop the video presentation and reflect on what learned and identify potential gaps in their knowledge. Thus, information processing in this situation frequently requires longer and more intense periods of cognitive and metacognitive activity. Regardless of the amount of information presented in each sensory channel, the learner's WM will accept, process, and send to LTM only a limited number of information units (Attneave, 1954; Jacobson, 1950, 1951). Thus, working memory requires direct prompting to accept, process, and send to the long-term storage only the most crucial information (Clark, Nguyen, & Sweller, 2006).

Empirical research informed by CTML and CLT suggested a number of prescriptive principles to help multimedia designers create learning materials better aligned with human cognitive architecture. These design principles categorized into two groups. The first group comprises strategies aimed at reducing extraneous cognitive load (i.e., processing that is not related to the instructional goal) and increasing germane load (i.e., processing that results in deeper learning). These strategies include adding cues to signal the main ideas such as signaling. In signaling, the presentation's main ideas summarized and highlighted to aid learners in selecting relevant information and organizing it into coherent mental representations. The second group of design principles aimed at managing intrinsic cognitive load (i.e., essential processing related to the learning goal), such as dividing the presentation into small units such as segmentation. With segmentation, learning material is broken up into several segments of information to help students to process one cluster of related information elements before moving to the next one.

Based on the prior research, the following questions guided this study:

The first question: How instructional video designed based on CTML effects preservice teachers' learning outcome in the context of in online environment? This primary research question was at the heart of the study, as the answer to this question will inform educational technology instructors and course developers the appropriate video design to introduce concepts such as TPACK framework to preservice teachers in online learning environment.

The second question: How video designed based on CTML effects students' perceived difficulty of the learning materials in online learning environment? Bases for this research question reported in a study by Moreno (2007), where participants who studied a segmented version of classroom video and animation reported lower mental effort. Students also perceived the learning materials as less difficult than participants who studied using non-segmented versions of the material.

The Study

This study employed a quasi-experimental, between-subjects design to assess the effect of learning from video introducing the TPACK framework on preservice teachers' learning outcome. The video explains the TPACK framework, its components and examples of how teachers successfully integrate technology in a lesson. The investigators created three different videos to introduce the TPACK framework: the first video designed by applying segmentation (divide the video into three short segments) and signaling (highlight and summarize the main ideas before and after each segment). The second video created by segmenting the video but without signaling. The third video was created continuance, without segmentation or signaling. The three videos used in this study presented in online module, where students control the time and duration to watch (self-paced). Participants were one hundred fifty six preservice teachers who enrolled in a technology integration course and divided randomly in three groups. The study has one independent variable: video design and two dependent variables: (1) learning outcome (2) the video perceived difficulty. Students' prior knowledge was included in the analysis as covariate. Students were divided into three-group based on the type of video they were watching

Participants were graduate and undergraduate, non-science majors. There were 50 students in the first group, 51 students in the second group and 55 students in the third group (35 male, 121 female). Students were from four different majors: Bachelor of professional studies, early childhood education, middle-level education and secondary education. All participations were fluent in English and consisted of 4 freshmen, 28 sophomores, 42 juniors, and 81 seniors in education major (Art 1, Early Childhood Education 85, English and Language Arts 9, Foreign Language 2, Health 7, History 14, Mathematics 5, Music, Science-Basic 10, Social Studies 4, Speech/Theater 2 and other major 16). Participant age was between 18 –above 41.

Instrumentation

All videos, pre-test, post-tests and surveys were online as part of the Blackboard course content and released to students based on the completion of the assigned learning materials using the Blackboard Adaptive Release function (AR). Blackboard AR is a function that controls the release of content to students based on a set of rules created by the instructor. The rules related to availability and the number of attempts for each student individually. The content and assessments instrumentations released individually to every student in sequence. The instrumentations consisted of the following items: demographic survey, a 15-question multiple-choice prior knowledge test (10-question retention and 5-question transfer), one-question instrument 9-level Likert scale to assess students' perceived difficulty of the module as an indirect subjective measure of cognitive load (Kalyuga, Chandler, & Sweller, 1999) and a 15-question multiple-choice post-test (10-question retention and 5-question transfer). All learning measures were selected or developed by the course instructors and were used regularly with students attending the technology integration course.

Pre-test

Demographic survey: This questionnaire was to collect information about the participants with regard to their makeup. The survey consists of five questions about students' gender, years in college, learning style, area of specialization and their age. Prior knowledge test: This measure consisted of 15 questions multiple-choice and true or false to assess participants' prior knowledge regarding the TPACK framework (ten retention questions and five transfer questions). Each correct answer yielded one point for a total of 15 points. Scores ranged from zero (no correct responses) to 15 (all correct responses).

Post-test

The Retention test: This measure consisted of 10 questions multiple-choice and true or false to assess participants' retention of the TPACK core components. An example of multiple-choice questions was "Pedagogical Knowledge is:" Participants could choose from the following responses: Knowledge about teachers' content area or discipline, Knowledge about how to teach a content area or discipline, Knowledge about how to teach, Knowledge about how to use technology in classroom. Each correct answer yields 1 point, for a total of 10 points. The score ranged from zero (no correct responses) to 10 (all correct responses).

The knowledge transfer test: This measure consisted of 5 multiple questions to elicit transfer of knowledge by asking participants to logically equivalent information presented in the video that required them to transfer knowledge from one context to another (Barnett Sm, 2002). The questions based on understanding the TPACK framework covered in the video and related to its components. For example, the participants had the following question: "An Instructor is developing an online module to encourage students to use collaboration tools to facilitate social learning for geographically separated learners. This is an example of". Students then asked the select the correct answer from the following choices: Technological Pedagogical and Content Knowledge, Technological Pedagogical Knowledge, Pedagogical Content Knowledge or Technology Knowledge. Students' responses based on their ability to infer and use the information included in the video. Every correct answer was worth one points and the sum score ranged from zero (no correct responses) to five (all correct responses). All learning measurements developed, selected and reviewed by the course instructors to construct validity. The ratings indicated that the tests adequately reflected and assessed the main concepts included in the video.

Materials

The video used in the present study was part of the instructors' materials for introducing TPACK framework to preservice teachers. Videos were identical in all three conditions, except adding segmentation and signaling to the one video and segmentation only to another. The first video designed by applying segmentation and signaling. These two design principles were adapted from Cognitive Theory of Multimedia Learning (CTML) (Mayer, 2001). Segmentation added to the first video through dividing the video content into three conceptual segments (i.e., segmentation) with highlighted 12 topics throughout the video. Blackboard released each segment upon the completion of the previous segment (Blackboard Adaptive Release) and students had control over the pace and the number of times of watching the video. The order of the topics discussed in video was the same in the three videos; however, there was no signaling of in the second video and segmentations or signaling in the third video.

In the first video, there were three segments, each segment began with an introduction showing the segment title and followed by a list of the core concepts presented as bulleted list. The signaling method was in a form of introducing the name of each segment followed by a list of the core concepts covered in that segment. At the end of each segment, a brief summary of the main concepts presented in the video (i.e., signaling). For example, the first concept was about explaining meaning of TPACK acronym followed by the meaning of teacher knowledge, content knowledge and the pedagogical knowledge. At the end of segment one, a summary presented in audio and concise bulleted lists of the concepts discussed in segment one. Example of summary of the Pedagogical Knowledge: "Pedagogical Knowledge or "PK," is about how to teach. This includes planning lessons and implementation strategies, such as establishing class rules, grouping students to provoke learning from each other, setting up class routines, using discipline techniques and teaching strategies to enhance the learning environment". The second video segmented but not signaled and in the third video, there was no segmentation or signaling of information. To maintain a fair design between all video design, the investigators retained the same sequence and information presented in all video conditions.

Procedure

First, all students randomly assigned to one of the following video conditions: (1) segmented and signaled, (2) segmented without signaling and (3) no segmentation or signaling. The random distribution of participants to each of the video condition was via Blackboard Random Selection tool. Course instructors then emailed the instruction of experiment to their students to explain the purpose and procedure of the module. The e-mail included a brief introduction about the module, the scope of the study and students' option to participate in the study for extra credit or to opt out. Second, students who agreed to participate in the experiment completed all tasks through the Blackboard adaptive release function (release a task after completing the previous task). Participants completed the module content on their own pace until a "Thank you" message appeared saying "Thank you for participating in this study".

Findings

Prior to the main analyses, the data was screened for out-of-range responses and systematic patterns of missing values and found small number of cases and no apparent patterns or clusters emerging.

First question: To answer the first question "How video effects preservice teachers' learning outcome in the context of the TPACK framework in online environment?" the investigators conducted one-way analysis of covariance (ANCOVA). First, homogeneity-of-regression (slope) was conducted to test the assumption of the interaction between the prior knowledge and the video design in the prediction of students' posttest scores. The results indicate that the interaction is not significant, F (2, 136) = .316, p = .730, p (.730) > α (.01). After confirming that the data meets the ANCOVA assumption, investigators proceed with our ANCOVA analysis. The ANCOVA analysis indicates that there was a significant effect of the TPACK video design on students' learning outcome after controlling for the effect of students' prior knowledge, F (2, 138) = 3.811, p = 024. The results produced an eta square of .052, indicating that segmentation and signaling accounted for a 5.2% improvement in students' learning outcome in the first group. Table 1 summarizes the ANCOVA results.

Table 1: The results of the one-way analysis of covariance (ANCOVA)

Dependent Variable: Post Test

Source	Type III SS	df	M S	F	Sig.	Partial Eta S.
Corrected Model	236.727[a]	3	78.909	16.582	.000	.265
Intercept	174.276	1	174.276	36.622	.000	.210
PRETEST	195.289	1	195.289	41.037	.000	.229
GROUP	36.271	2	18.136	3.811	.024	.052
Error	656.716	138	4.759			
Total	16049.000	142				
Corrected Total	893.444	141				

Note: Significant at $p < 0.05$ level

Second question: How video designed based on CTML about TPACK effects students' perceived difficulty of the learning materials in online learning environment?

To answer the second question, the investigators conducted a one-way between subjects ANOVA to assess the effect of video design on students' perceived difficulty of the learning materials. The ANOVA analysis indicated that there was difference in students' perceive difficulty of the instructional video, however these differences wasn't statistically significant as (F (2,147) = .505, p = .605). Table 2 summarizes the ANOVA results.

Table 2: The result of one-way between subjects (ANOVA)					
Difficulty	Sum of Squares	df	Mean Square	F	Sig.
Between Groups	2.748	2	1.374	.505	.605
Within Groups	400.292	147	2.723		
Total	403.040	149			
Note: Significant at $p < 0.05$ level					

Results and Discussion:

The main finding of this study is that educational video presented online has the potential to effectively help preservice teachers in online learning environment, but require design manipulations. The results of the present study support previous findings produced in the context of learning from educational animations and hypermedia and provide empirical evidence that validates Cognitive Theory of Multimedia Learning design manipulations of multimedia in several ways. The segmentation and signaling of the online video helped to introduce the TPACK concept to the preservice teachers and improved their learning outcome. Specifically, the preservice teachers' test scores improved when the online TPACK video presented in self-paced, segmented and signaled rather than continuous and non-signaled (Mautone & Mayer, 2001; Mayer & Chandler, 2001). According to cognitive research, segmentation and signaling are appropriate design strategies to help students to process long and complex multimedia learning materials. In this study, results showed that students' learning outcomes indeed benefited from cognitively appropriate design of the TPACK video. This benefit demonstrated by the statistically significant differences in learning outcomes between students in the three video groups, with the highest scores achieved by students in the segmented and signaled video condition and the least was in the no segmentation and no signaling condition. A possible interpretation of this result is that during processing long instructional video, novice learners may have to relate and reconcile too many new concepts presented in visual and auditory format included in the TPACK video. However, students in segmented and signaled condition were easily able to manage sequential segments with time breaks between them and highlighted the main concepts presented in the video. These design manipulations not only improve learning for novice learners for whom the learning concepts are new and lack adequate prior knowledge, but also eliminate a cognitive overload represented in students' perceived difficulty of the TPACK video. These results imply that segmenting and signaling the TPACK video provided cognitive guidance to help novice teachers learning about the TPACK concept.

Further, although the results indicated that there was improvement in students' perceived difficulty, with the lowest level of perceived difficulty reported by students in the segmented and signaled group, these differences were not statistically significant. This result is consistent with the evidence that segmentation and signaling principles reduce students' perceived difficulty by focusing their attention on important aspects of the learning material, providing concise cues about relevant information, and guiding them to engage in organizing and integrating only the essential information. These cognitive activities contributed to the optimization of learners' cognitive processes during learning and helped reduce students' perception of the learning task's difficulty. However, the self-paced learning environment found equally in all three groups, assists students further to control the video pace for their needs which minimized to certain extend students' perceived difficulty associated with extraneous cognitive load in all groups. Therefore, the perceived difficulty between the three group design was minimized.

References:

Attneave, F. (1954). Some informational aspects of visual perception. *Psychological review, 61*(3), 183-193.

Ayres, P. P. F. (2007). Making instructional animations more effective: a cognitive load approach. *Applied cognitive psychology., 21*(6), 695-700.

Baddeley. (1986). *Working memory*. Oxford; New York: Clarendon Press ; Oxford University Press.

Baddeley, & Logie. (1999). Working memory: The multiple-component model. In A. Miyake & P. Shah (Eds.), *Models of working memory: mechanisms of active maintenance and executive control*. New York: Cambridge University Press.

Baggett, P. (1984). Role of temporal overlap of visual and auditory material in forming dual media associations. *Journal of Educational Psychology, 76*(3), 408-417.

Barnett Sm, C. S. J. (2002). When and where do we apply what we learn? A taxonomy for far transfer. *Psychological bulletin, 128*(4), 612-637.

Clark, Nguyen, & Sweller. (2006). *Efficiency in learning: Evidence-based guidelines to manage cognitive load*: Pfeiffer.

Clark, & Paivio. (1991). Dual coding theory and education. *Educational Psychology Review, 3*(3), 60.

Homer, B. D., Plass, J. L., & Blake, L. (2008). The effects of video on cognitive load and social presence in multimedia-learning. *Computers in Human Behavior, 24*(3), 786-797.

Jacobson, H. (1950). The informational capacity of the human ear. *Science (New York, N.Y.), 112*(2901), 143-144.

Jacobson, H. (1951). The informational capacity of the human eye. *Science (New York, N.Y.), 113*(2933), 292-293.

Jonassen, Peck, & Wilson. (1999). *Learning with technology : a constructivist perspective*. Upper Saddle River, N.J.: Merrill.

Kalyuga, S., Chandler, P., & Sweller, J. (1999). Managing split-attention and redundancy in multimedia instruction. *Applied cognitive psychology., 13*(4), 351.

Lowe, R. K. (1999). Extracting information from an animation during complex visual learning. *European Journal of Psychology of Education, 14*(2), 225-244.

Lowe, R. K. (2003). Animation and learning: selective processing of information in dynamic graphics. *Learning and Instruction Learning and Instruction, 13*(2), 157-176.

Mautone, & Mayer. (2001). Signaling as a cognitive guide in multimedia learning. *Journal of Educational Psychology., 93*(2), 377.

Mayer. (1996). Learning Strategies for Making Sense out of Expository Text: The SOI Model for Guiding Three Cognitive Processes in Knowledge Construction. *Educational psychology review., 8*(4), 357.

Mayer. (2001). *Multimedia learning*. Cambridge; New York: Cambridge University Press.

Mayer. (2002). *The promise of educational psychology : Learning in the content areas.* Upper Saddle River, N.J.: Merrill.

Mayer. (2003). The promise of multimedia learning: Using the same instructional design methods across different media. *Learning and Instruction, 13*(2), 125.

Mayer, & Chandler. (2001). When learning is just a click away: Does simple user interaction foster deeper understanding of multimedia messages? *Journal of Educational Psychology., 93*(2), 390.

Mayer, & Moreno. (2002). Aids to computer-based multimedia learning. *Learning and Instruction, 12*(1), 107-119.

Moreno. (2004). Decreasing cognitive load for novice students: Effects of explanatory versus corrective feedback in discovery-based multimedia. *Instructional Science, 32*(1/2), 99-113.

Moreno, R. (2007). Optimising learning from animations by minimising cognitive load: cognitive and affective consequences of signalling and segmentation methods. *Applied cognitive psychology., 21*(6), 765-781.

Purcell, K. P. I., & American Life, P. (2010). The state of online video. from http://pewinternet.com/~/media//Files/Reports/2010/PIP-The-State-of-Online-Video.pdf

Sweller. (1999). *Instructional design in technical areas.* Camberwell, Vic.: ACER Press.

Sweller, Merrienboer, V., & Paas. (1998). Cognitive Architecture and Instructional Design. *Educational Psychology Review, 10*(3), 251-296.

4 Leveraging a MOOC Platform to Accelerate College Readiness

Laurel Walsh & Keri VanOverschelde, Walden University, United States

To accelerate student readiness, the university created a micro-course available to selected students who unsuccessfully participated in their foundational course. By leveraging a MOOC platform, students who were unable to successfully complete the first two weeks of course work were taught by a first term faculty member paired with a peer mentor. This 3-week skill refresher provides students with (a) feedback on writing, (b) an introduction to university support services, and (c) a preview of first term assignments with strategies for success in coursework. Students are given an opportunity to explicitly articulate a plan for academic success in an online classroom. Students complete an Academic Success Narrative that enumerates and details the supports that they will use to stay on track. This optional micro-course is not credit bearing, although students can earn a certificate of completion. Because it is built in a MOOC, it is offered completely free for students.

As research continues to show the negative impact of long periods of remediation for adult students, MOOC delivery of skill activation content becomes an essential consideration. Universities and community colleges can leverage free online learning platforms to enhance the onboarding experience of nervous new students. Online environments are ideal for remediation as they can be leveraged before a term start or concurrently with curriculum delivery. Viewed by many in higher education as a disruptive force, MOOCs represent an amazing opportunity to provide adults with skill activating activities that will enhance persistence in post-secondary settings. Preliminary data has shown that students who successfully complete the 3-week intervention are able to successfully complete first term courses (n = 15).

Educators across the nation are grappling with issues associated with remediation for college readiness. Unfortunately for teachers, student skill gaps in non-cognitive factors have as much to do with attrition as academic gaps. Attempting to remediate across all domains for students from a mix of academic backgrounds presents a number of difficulties. One size fits all skill activation of short duration can positively impact student readiness for college re-enrollment. Longer term effects of this type of competency accelerating activity must be studied longitudinally. This micro-course includes explicit instruction in critical reading, thinking, and writing skills. Interpersonal communication skills are introduced through academic networking, lessons in cyber civility, and modeling and promoting e-communication best practices.

Professional and Academic Skill Refresher

Walden University allows students to try the first two weeks of courses for free. At day 14, if students have successfully completed all assignments in their first term course, they are considered to have made Adequate Academic Progress (AAP). Students who have not made AAP are dropped from Walden entirely. This population is targeted for direct outreach, and the students are encouraged to enroll in a skill activating classroom. On the day that the AAP drop occurs, the Professional and Academic Skills Refresher (PASR) invitation is sent from the free blackboard platform (www.coursesites.com). Students who decide to participate in PASR are provided a free three week course that runs until the next term start. It is assumed that students will re-enroll in the following term.

Predicting the Needs of Adult Learners

PASR curriculum is designed to activate dormant skills for adults. The primary assignment is to craft an academic success narrative that delineates the exact personal and professional skills and auxiliary resources that the student will employ to be successful in their next attempt at Walden. PASR discussion boards help students articulate the ways that they will work on (a) time management, (b) technology competencies, and (c) academic writing skills in order to thrive in an asynchronous setting.

Leveraging a MOOC Platform

Walden University uses Blackboard as a platform. Coursesites houses the free unbranded Blackboard platform to provide students with a similar educational experience. By leveraging this platform, Walden doesn't incur any cost for course delivery. This allows us to offer the course free of charge to students. The course puts students into contact with (a) Walden faculty and staff, (b) fellow students who have experienced an academic misstep, (c) Walden's Writing Center material, and (d) synchronous webinars.

By incorporating webinars, students have the chance to speak to faculty, staff, and advisors regarding any issues that might arise in the classroom. Each week, students are invited to participate in a presentation with the PASR instructor and support staff. This weekly touch base meeting provides students with an opportunity to get clarification about assignments and answer questions about the first term courses. Advisors are on hand to help offer help and suggestions regarding a student's program of study.

Virtual High Touch

Online students are drawn to asynchronous settings because of the convenience for time poor adults. Students are able to balance work, school, and family because school comes into their living rooms via the computer. The problem is that when school enters your living room, your living room cannot help but enter your classroom. When a child becomes ill, a spouse is laid off, or a death occurs in the family, online access is an additional stressor. Classroom assignments loom, and students can feel forced to choose between school and life.

PASR was designed to provide students with more synchronous opportunities to connect with faculty via webinar and phone than occurs in a standard online classroom. These high touch experiences allow students to feel that they have a coach/advocate in the classroom. By employing the Academic Success Narrative, students are provided with strong goal statements to elevate self-efficacy around issues of academic expression. Walden uses the same prompt for students who have to apply for admissions via the admissions committee. Internal research reveals that students who write on to Walden are retained at a higher rate than students who were admitted through the traditional process.

Asynchronous options for synchronous instruction play a vital role in the PASR classroom. The weekly webinars that students are invited to attend allow for a synchronous interaction with faculty and staff that online classrooms frequently omit. This is beyond a Jing video classroom tour; it is a chance for students to connect directly with first term faculty and Walden staff. Some scholarship suggests that podcasts (in this case a webinar) must allow for knowledge to be applied. It is not enough to merely place the lecture in a form that is available for listening to at the student's leisure. "Simply reproducing a lecture with the sole purpose of providing the student with the possibility of re-viewing and with no other correlation to what is going on in the course are not the best way to enhance the student's knowledge acquisition and learning" (Blok & Godst, 2009, p. 123). The weekly webinars are available to students in real time, relate to the lessons covered in the course curriculum that week, and are then archived and readily available to students to view in the classroom following the presentation.

Celebrating Success

The student population for PASR is far from uniform. Students who have high transfer of credit as well as students who have never attended college can experience an academic hiccup in the first 14 days of class. In this one size fits all skill activation classroom, it can be difficult for the very least prepared student to feel fully supported. Also, some high performing students are alienated by the remediation content that they are asked to review. Mixed level online classrooms are typical of first term courses at Walden, and some of the students really need more support than others. Research shows that asynchronous instruction puts more responsibility on the adult learner and that "students in e-learning courses must be self-motivated and willing to spend an ample amount of time of self-directed study" (Shivetts, 2011, p. 336). Supporting students who enter the classroom with varying levels of readiness is a difficult task.

Each PASR student who has successfully completed the course is sent a certificate of completion to his or her home address. These students are encouraged to contact the instructor to ensure that the name of the certificate is correct. Because the course is not credit bearing and not financial aid eligible, a certification of completion was seen as a positive reinforcement for completion of course content. The certification is only provided if students complete all germane classroom activities.

Moving Forward

College readiness means different things to different students. For some students, navigating the online learning platform is the primary difficulty. For other students, academic writing skill deficits are the primary issue impeding retention. Still for other adults, intense academic remediation is required. Walden currently lacks learning assistance centers or specialized skills labs where students can be provided individualized remediation. These support options "are an important means of increasing students' academic preparedness for postsecondary study" (Campbell, Cook, Kusch, & Moulton, 2009, p. 1). Although Walden has a robust and fully professional Writing Center, it doesn't have explicit individualized support for associated academic skills. Until Walden builds a more robust support infrastructure, a MOOC platform for accelerating academic readiness can help some students become more comfortable and confident learners.

Moving forward, explicitly directing students to the PASR curriculum at the time of the AAP drop might help empower student learners to view this material as an academic enhancement. Using student testimony regarding the experience, Walden could promote positive social change at the individual level to enhance student persistence and accelerate dormant skills. The use of PASR to promote Walden's Writing Center, library, and advisor services helps students fully understand the level of academic support available at the university. This offering aligns with Walden's mission of positive social change by providing underprepared adults with a second shot at entering into a fully accredited institution, even after an academic misstep in the first 14 days of the student lifecycle.

References

Blok, R. & Godsk, M. (2009). Podcasts in Higher Education: What Students Want, What They Really Need, and How This Might be Supported. In T. Bastiaens et al. (Eds.), Proceedings of World Conference on E-Learning in Corporate, Government, Healthcare, and Higher Education 2009 (pp. 117-128). Chesapeake, VA: AACE. Retrieved October 7, 2013 from http://www.editlib.org/p/32442.

Chen, L.H. (2011). Enhancement of Student Learning Performance Using Personalized Diagnosis and Remedial Learning System. Computers & Education, 56(1), 289-299. Retrieved September 7, 2013 from http://www.editlib.org/p/66779.

Campbell, D., Cook, K.J., Kusch, B. & Moulton, S. (2009). Inspiring Learning and Teaching: Using e-tools to Facilitate Change. In T. Bastiaens et al. (Eds.), Proceedings of World Conference on E-Learning in Corporate, Government, Healthcare, and Higher Education 2009 (pp. 172-181). Chesapeake, VA: AACE. Retrieved October 7, 2013 from http://www.editlib.org/p/32454.

Perin, D. (2004). Remediation Beyond Developmental Education: The Use of Learning Assistance Centers to Increase Academic Preparedness in Community Colleges. Community College Journal of Research and Practice, 28(7), 559-582. Retrieved October 7, 2013 from http://www.editlib.org/p/98150.

Shivetts, C. (2011). E-Learning and Blended Learning: The Importance of the Learner A Research Literature Review. International Journal on E-Learning, 10(3), 331-337. Chesapeake, VA: AACE. Retrieved October 7, 2013 from http://www.editlib.org/p/33111.

5 Investigating the determinants of mobile learning acceptance in Korea

BaoYng Teresa Liew, Myunghee Kang, Eunjin Yoo , Jiwon You, Educational Technology Department, Ewha Womans University, South Korea

Introduction

For decades, the Korean government has provided primary and secondary school teachers with teacher training that integrates Information and Communications Technologies (ICTs) into their teaching (Hwang, Yang, & Kim, 2010 ; Severin & Capota, 2011). Since mobile devices have become more affordable and easier to use, the number of students in higher education with mobile devices is growing in Korea. Corresponding to this phenomena, education trends in Korea are now moving from e-learning to mobile learning (m-learning) in both formal and informal education (Jung, 2009; Park, Nam, & Cha, 2012). Some Korean universities even provide their students with mobile devices for free so that they can use them for their studies (Park, Nam, & Cha, 2012).

M-learning happens when learners are not at a fixed and predetermined location or when learners take advantage of learning opportunities offered by mobile technologies (Kukulska-Hulme, 2005). According to Liew, You and Kang (2012), m-learning is any educational activity offered by mobile technologies regardless of devices. M-learning provides students and institutions various benefits including cost savings, ubiquitous communication, study aids, and accessibility, among others (Cheon, Lee, Crooks, & Song, 2012). Researchers and practitioners, however, found several challenges facing m-learning, such as unstable connectivity, small screen sizes, limited processing power and restricted input capabilities which might affect the acceptance of m-learning by potential users (Wang, Wu, & Wang, 2009). Furthermore, although the majority of adult learners have their own mobile devices, they do not use the devices for learning purposes (Keller, 2011). The success of m-learning highly depends on whether users are willing to adopt this new technology in education (Wang, Wu, & Wang, 2009). In Korea, many studies on m-learning had been conducted to investigate the educational effectiveness of using mobile devices (Jung, 2009; Um & Kim, 2007), but only few studies have been conducted on m-learning acceptance (Joo, Kim, & Lim, 2012; Park, Nam, & Cha, 2012). Moreover, these studies were limited to students who had experience in e-learning environments or distance learning experience.

Based on previous researches, the used of Information System (IS) models in m-learning research had been clearly identified and the scales used to measure had been developed and validated (Joo, Kim, & Lim, 2012; Park, Nam, & Cha, 2012; Wang, Wu, & Wang, 2009). Among several IS models which explained technology acceptance, the extended Unified Theory of Acceptance and Use of Technology (UTAUT) model (Wang, Wu, & Wang, 2009) was chosen in this study based on the literature review. The purpose of this study is to investigate the determinants of m-learning acceptance among college students. The main research question is do the predictors in the extended UTAUT model (performance expectancy, effort expectancy, social influence, perceived playfulness and self-management of learning) predict behavioral intention to use m-learning in Korea?

Technology Acceptance in m-learning

Dillon and Morris (1996) defined user acceptance as "the demonstrable willingness within a user group to employ information technology for the tasks it is designed to support" (p. 4). In this paper, user acceptance is the willingness of students in higher education to use mobile devices and m-learning applications (Liew, You, & Kang, 2012). For decades, there have been numerous IS theories and models which explain how and why people accept technology and intend to use it. For m-learning, users utilize m-learning systems for learning which may be explained by IS theories or models.

UTAUT and the Extended UTAUT model in m-learning

The UTAUT developed by Venkatesh, Morris, Davis and Davis (2003), accounted for 70% of the variance in behavioral intention to use technology in a longitudinal field study of employee technology acceptance (Venkatesh et al., 2003). The UTAUT was developed by integrating eight prominent models in the field of IS user acceptance research. The UTAUT holds that performance expectancy, effort expectancy, social influence, and facilitating conditions are key determinants of information system usage intention and usage behavior. Also, it suggests that gender, age, experience, and voluntariness of use moderate the impact of the four key constructs on usage intention and behavior. In m-learning context, Wang, Wu and Wang (2009) adopted and extended the UTAUT to investigate the determinants of m-learning acceptance among working adults in Taiwan. Their results showed that the determinants of UTAUT and the extended determinants (perceived playfulness and self-management of learning) predicted behavior intention of m-learning. Their study explained 58% of variance of behavioral intention in m-learning acceptance. The extended UTAUT model holds that performance expectancy, effort expectancy, social influence, perceived playfulness and self-management of learning are key determinants of m-learning acceptance. Also, it suggests that gender and age moderate the impact of the constructs on behavioral intention to use m-learning.

In this study, we adopted their extended UTAUT model in the Korean higher educational context. Similar to their study, since m-learning is still in its infancy, this study only used behavioral intention as a dependent variable. Also, since our participants were year one and year two students, therefore we excluded the age and gender as moderating variables on the determinants. Many recent studies also found that m-learning perception did not differ significantly according to gender differences (Oğuz Serin, 2012; Uzunboylu & Ozdaml, 2011).

Performance Expectancy

According to Venkatesh et al. (2003), performance expectancy is defined as "The degree to which an individual believes that using the system will help him or her to attain gains in job performance." (p. 448). In the context of m-learning, performance expectancy suggests that individuals will find m-learning useful because it enables them to access information quickly, at a time and place of their convenience, and on the device of their choice (Donaldson, 2011). Wang, Wu and Wang (2009) and Lowenthal (2010) found that performance expectancy predicted behavioral intention to use m-learning in their study in Taiwan.

Effort Expectancy

Effort expectancy is defined as "The degree of ease associated with the use of the system." (Venkatesh et al., 2003, p. 448). Previous studies also showed that effort expectancy had a significant influence on individual intention to use m-learning (Lowenthal, 2010; Wang, Wu, & Wang, 2009).

Social Influence

As defined by Venkatesh et al. (2003), social influence is defined as "The degree to which an individual perceives that others believe it is important that he or she uses the new system." (p. 448). In the context of m-learning, social influence (e.g. teachers, parents, peers, etc.) will strongly affect younger students' intention to accept and use mobile devices for learning purposes. Wang, Wu and Wang (2009) also found that social influence had a significant effect on usage intention of m-learning.

Perceived Playfulness

Moon and Kim (2001) added perceived playfulness to TAM as an intrinsic motivation factor. An intrinsic motivator refers to an individual's performance or engagement in an activity due to his or her interest in the activity (Deci, 1975). Perceived playfulness has been found to be a significant positive predictor in mobile research. Cheong and Park (2005) found perceived playfulness was a positive predictor of behavioral intention to use the Internet on mobile devices. Wang, Wu and Wang (2009) found perceived playfulness to be a significant determinant of the behavioral intention to use m-learning. Therefore, this study assumed that intrinsic motivation in the form of perceived playfulness would have a significant impact on college students' intention to use mobile devices for their learning.

Self-management of Learning

Self-management of learning refers to the degree to which an individual perceives self-discipline and is able to engage in autonomous learning (Sharples, 2003). In the context of m-learning, students must manage their own learning because they are separated from faculty, peers, and institutional support. This autonomy entails an increased need to develop critical thinking skills, identify learning needs, and locate and evaluate resources (Liu, Han, & Li, 2010; McVay, 2001; Wang, Wu, & Wang, 2009). In a study using the UTAUT as its theoretical basis, Wang, Wu and Wang (2009) and Lowenthal (2010) found that self-management of learning is a significant determinant of m-learning acceptance.

Research Hypotheses

The above literature reviews suggest that performance expectancy, effort expectancy, social influence, perceived playfulness and self-management of learning play substantial role in predicting the behavioral intention to use m-learning. Therefore, these variables were used in our study which was formulated as five research hypotheses. The hypothesized research model tested in this study is illustrated in Figure 2.

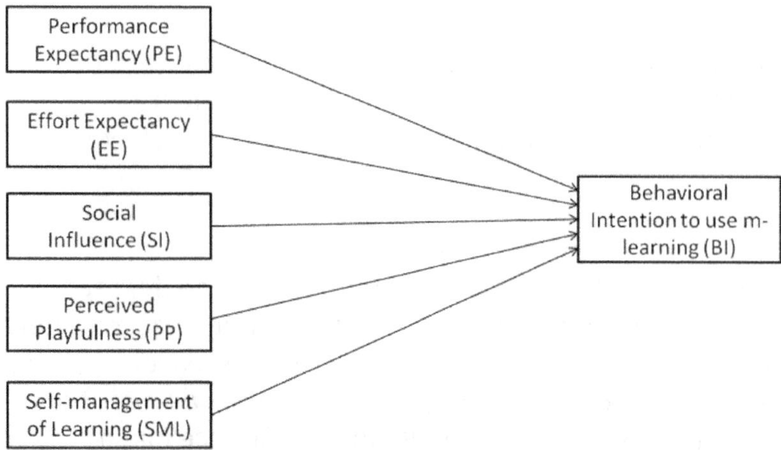

Figure 1: Hypothesized research Model

Hypothesis 1: Performance expectancy has a significant effect on behavioral intention to use m-learning.
Hypothesis 2: Effort Expectancy has a significant effect on behavioral intention to use m-learning.
Hypothesis 3: Social influence has a significant effect on behavioral intention to use m-learning.
Hypothesis 4: Perceived playfulness has a significant effect on behavioral intention to use m-learning.
Hypothesis5: Self-management of learning has a significant effect on behavioral intention to use m-learning.

Method

Participants

In this study, we used a convenient sampling technique. A total of 185 college students from two universities in Seoul and Busan, Korea participated in this study. Surveys were distributed during the spring semester in 2012. After excluding cases that had unreliable or missing responses among all collected data, 173 cases were obtained and analyzed for the study. The participants in this study were first and second year students. The sample included 114 (66%) men and 59 (34%) women. The mean age of participants was 20.82 years (SD = 3.06, range 18 ~ 42). 150 (86.7%) students were between the ages of 18 and 23, and 22 (12.7%) students were between the age of 24 and 28, and only 1 student was at the age of 42. In order to have better understanding of the sample, we also asked if participants had a smart phone, and what mobile devices and mobile applications they were using. Among all the students, only 6 (4%) of them did not have a smart phone. Moreover, besides the basic calling and texting features, most of students who had smart phones reported that they used Social Networking Services (SNS) such as Facebook for getting connected with their friends.

Measurements

A survey instrument which consisted of two main parts was developed. The first part focused on gathering the data for key constructs as represented in the conceptual research model. As a second part, the open-ended questions were developed to gather information about demographics of participants and the type of mobile devices and mobile applications they were using. Items measuring performance expectancy, effort expectancy, social influence, perceived playfulness and self-management of learning were adapted from Wang, Wu and Wang (2009). The survey items were translated from English to Korean, and a professor in the Educational Technology reviewed the items to check the content validity, and the survey was refined based on the feedback. Since there were subtle differences between two languages, the survey was administered and refined three times with a total of 90 college students to see if they had clear understanding of each item. Lastly, the final version of survey was determined. All the items in the first section used 5-point Likert scales ranging from 1 – "Strongly disagree" to 5 – "Strongly agree". Reliability was examined using Cronbach's alpha for each variable. The reliability of all variables was ranged from .62 to .83 as presented in Table 1. Since all the Cronbach's alpha values of constructs were exceed .60, the instruments were considered as reliable (Thompson, Barclay, & Higgins, 1995).

Variables	# of items	Cronbach's alpha
Performance Expectancy	4	.83
Effort Expectancy	4	.62
Social Influence	4	.70
Perceive Playfulness	5	.74
Self-management of learning	4	.81
Behavioral Intention	2	.85
Total	23	

Table 1. Variables and reliabilities

Procedure

All the data were collected via offline surveys in June, 2012 in Seoul and Busan, South Korea. The data were analyzed using SPSS 18.0 for descriptive analysis, Pearson correlations analysis and multiple regression analysis. The significance level for hypotheses testing was set at .05.

Results

The means and standard deviations of each variables and correlations among constructs were presented in Table 4. Almost all the constructs were significantly correlated with each other except the correlation between (1) self-management of learning and social influence and (2) self-management of learning and perceived playfulness. All the independent variables (performance expectancy, effort expectancy, social influence and self-management of learning) correlated with the dependent variable (behavior intention), and independent variables, the social influence ($r = .42$, $p < .01$) showed the highest correlation with the dependent variable.

	(n = 173)				
	1	2	3	4	5
1. Performance Expectancy	1				
2. Effort Expectancy	.66**	1			
3. Social Influence	.559**	.46**	1		
4. Perceive Playfulness	.25**	.38**	.38**	1	
5. Self-management of learning	.18*	.30**	.11	.064	1
6. Behavioral Intention	.39**	.39**	.42**	.38**	.23**
Mean	3.53	3.95	2.94	3.23	3.12
Standard deviation	.86	.65	.84	.76	.77

$*p < .05$, $**p < .01$

Table 2: Descriptive statistics and correlations among the variables

Hypotheses testing

A stepwise multiple regression analysis was conducted to test the hypotheses. Five variables including performance expectancy, effort expectancy, social influence, perceived playfulness and self-management of earning were set as predictors, and behavioral intention to use m-learning was set as a dependent variable. As a result, performance expectancy, social influence, perceived playfulness and self-management of learning emerged as significant factors of behavioral intention. Performance expectancy (β= .18, $p < .05$), social influence (β= .21, $p < .05$), perceived playfulness (β= .25, $p < .01$) and self-management of learning (β= .19, $p < .05$) had a positively significant influence on behavioral intention to use m-learning. Therefore, we concluded that Hypothesis 1, Hypothesis 3, Hypothesis 4 and Hypothesis 5 were supported. In the results, effort expectancy was not significant to predict behavioral intention. Therefore, Hypothesis 2 was not supported. The results of multiple regression analysis were presented in Table 3. These results suggest that 29% ($F = 18.31$, $p < .05$) variance of behavioral intention to use m-learning can be explained by four critical variables in this study.

(*n*=173)

Criterion	*Predictor*	B	SE	β	*t*	*p*	*F*	R^2 (*adj.* R^2)
Behavioral Intention to use m-learning	Performance Expectancy	.21	.09	.18	2.34*	.02	18.31**	.31(.29)
	Social Influence	.25	.09	.21	2.62*	.01		
	Perceive Playfulness	.33	.09	.25	2.66**	.00		
	Self-management of Learning	.24	.84	.19	2.85*	.01		

$^*p < .05$, $^{**}p < .01$

Table 3. Results of stepwise regression analysis on behavioral intention.

Discussion

The purpose of this study was to examine the determinants of the Korean college students' m-learning acceptance by using the extended UTAUT model from Wang, Wu and Wang (2009). Since there has been little research on user acceptance of m-learning especially using the extended UTAUT in Korea, the findings of this study provide several important implications for m-learning research and practice in Korea. The results showed that only performance expectancy, social influence, perceived playfulness and self-management of learning were significant determinants of behavioral intention to use m-learning which were consistent with previous researches (Lowenthal, 2010; Moon & Kim, 2001; Wang, Wu, & Wang, 2009). In contrast to the previous findings, the results indicated that effort expectancy had no significant effects on behavioral intention (Lin, Wu & Tsai, 2005; Venkatesh et al., 2003; Wang, Wu, & Wang, 2009). This may due to that fact that Korea is one of the most advanced countries in ICTs' development. Park, Nam and Cha (2012) described that university students in Korea, whom we call the M-generation, were very flexible in adapting and using mobile devices and applications in their daily life. As seen in this study, 96% of the participants owned smart phones (i.e. iPhone, Samsung Galaxy, etc.) and had been using various mobile applications in their daily life; therefore, effort expectancy seem to be no longer critical for predicting behavioral intention to m-learning acceptance in Korea.

Our results revealed that performance expectancy, social influence, perceived playfulness and self-management of learning were found as critical factors to predict the intention of m-learning acceptance for Korean college students. Perceived playfulness is the strongest predictor of m-learning acceptance in this study. Therefore, besides meeting users' needs and highlighting the benefits of m-learning, developers and practitioners need to develop strategies for fostering students' perception of perceived playfulness in m-learning. Therefore, m-learning practitioners need to focus on not only developing high quality of m-learning contents but also developing strategies which promote m-learning implementation in formal and informal education.

Finally, this study is limited to generalize findings in that the sample size was not huge enough and limited to only first and second year college students in Korea. Therefore, testing the model with a bigger sample sizes and a wide range of university students (e.g. undergraduate and graduate, online and offline students) and instructors is suggested. Also, with our model only explained 29% variance of behavioral intention to use m-learning, further research should be conducted to explore other significant determinants of accepting m-learning as well as other competitive models for Korean users. Especially, this study was implemented in Korea where culture factors maybe influence findings of the study. In addition, it is recommended to employ mixed research method (combining quantitative and qualitative research) for future research, so more insights and better understandings on user acceptance of m-learning will be available. With the limited amount of empirical research in this area especially by using UTAUT, the findings of the present study are significant in that it clearly illustrates the need for and directions of future research. This study not only provides implications for future studies on m-learning acceptance especially in the Korean context, but also guides m-learning designers and practitioners to develop strategies for successful implementation of m-learning in Korea.

Reference

Bandura, A. (1986). Social foundations of thought and action: a social cognitive theory. Prentice Hall, Englewood Cliffs, NJ.

Baron, S., Patterson, A., & Harris, K. (2006): Beyond technology acceptance: understanding consumer practice. International Journal of Service Industry Management, 17(2), 111-135.

Cheong, J., & Park, M. (2005) Mobile internet acceptance in Korea. Internet Research: Electronic Networking Applications and Policy, 15, 125- 140.

Deci, E. L. (1975). Intrinsic motivation. New York: Plenum.

Dillon, A., & Morris, M. G. (1996). User acceptance of information technology: Theories and models. Annual Review of Information Science and Technology, 31, 3-32.

Donaldson, R. L. (2011). Student acceptance of mobile learning. Unpublished doctoral dissertation, The Florida State University, Florida.

Hwang, D. J., Yang, H., & Kim, H. (2010). E-learning in the Republic of Korea. UNESCO Institute for Information Technologies in Education, Russian Federation: UNESCO

Joo, Y. J., Kim, N. H., & Lim, E. (2012). Analysis of factors affecting adoption of mobile learning in cyber university. Korean Journal of Educational Technology and Society, 28(1), 79-102.

Jung, H. J. (2009). Determinants influencing mobile-learning for English learning. Korean Journal of English21, 22(2), 234-255.

Keller, J. (2011). The slow-motion mobile campus. The Chronicle of Higher Education, B4-B6.

Kukulska-Hulme, A. (2005). Mobile usability and user experience. In A. Kukulska-Hulme & J. Traxler (Eds.), Mobile learning: A handbook for educators and trainers (pp. 45–56). London: Routledge.

Liew, B. T., You, J., & Kang, M. (2012). User acceptance for mobile learning: A review and future directions. Proceedings of 10th Anniversary International Conference of Hanyang Cyber University. Seoul, Korea.

Lin, C. S., Wu, S., & Tsai, R. J. (2005). Integrating perceived playfulness into expectation-confirmation model for web portal context. Information & Management, 42, 683-693.
Liu, Y., Han, S., & Li, H. (2010) Understanding the factors driving m-learning adoption: a literature review. Campus-Wide Information System, 27(4), 210-226.
Lowenthal, J. N. (2010). Using mobile learning: Determinates impacting behavioral intention. The American Journal of Distance Education, 24, 195-206
McVay, M. (2001). How to be a successful distance learning student: Learning on the Internet. New York: Prentice Hall.
Moon, J., & Kim, Y. (2001). Extending the TAM for a World Wide Web context. Information & Management, 38, 217–230.
Oğuz, S. (2012). Mobile learning perceptions of the prospective teachers (Turkish Replybic of Northern Cyprus Sampling). The Turkish Online Journal of Educational Technology, 11(3), 222-233.
Park, S. Y. (2009). An analysis of the technology acceptance model in understanding university student's behavioral intention to use e-learning. Educational Technology & Society, 12(3), 150-162.
Park, Y. S., Nam, M., & Cha, S. (2012). University students' behavioral intention to use mobile learning: Evaluating the technology acceptance model. British Journal of Educational Technology, 43(4), 592-605.
Pedersen, P. E., & Ling, R. (2003). Modifying adoption research for mobile internet service adoption: Cross-disciplinary interactions. Proceedings of the 36th Hawaii International Conference on System Sciences (HICSS-36), Big Island, HI. Los Alamitos, CA: IEEE Computer Society Press.
Rogers, E. M. (2003). Diffusion of innovations (5th ed.). New York: Free Press.
Severin, E., & Capota, C. (2011). The use of technology in education: Lessons from South Korea. Washington: Inter-American Development Bank.
Shapka, J. D. & Ferrari, M. (2003). Computer-related attitudes and actions of teacher candidates. Computers in Human Behavior, 19(3), 319-334.
Straub, E. T. (2009). Understanding technology adoption: Theory and future directions for informal learning. Review of Educational Research, 79(2), 625-649.
Thompson, R. L. , Barclay, D. , & Higgins, C. (1995). The partial least squares approach to casual modeling: Personal computer adoption and use as an illustration. Technology Studies: Special Issue on Research Methodology, 2(2), 285-324.
Um, M. Y., & Kim, M. R. (2007). A study on factors affecting users' satisfaction level in using PMP for learning purpose. The Journal of Korean Association of Computer Science, 10(1), 77-88.
Uzunboylu, H., & Özdamlı, F. (2011). Teacher perception for m-learning: scale development and teachers' perceptions. Journal of Computer Assisted Learning, 27(6), 544-556.
Venkatesh, V., Morris, M. G., Davis, G. B., & Davis, F. D. (2003). User acceptance of information technology: Toward a unified view. MIS Quarterly, 27(3), 425-478.
Volman, M., van Eck, E., Heemskerk, I., & Kuiper, E. (2005). New technologies, new differences: Gender and ethnic differences in pupils' use of ICT in primary and secondary education. Computers & Education, 45, 35-55.
Wang, Y., Wu, M., & Wang, H. (2009). Investigating the determinants and age and gender differences in the acceptance of mobile learning, British Journal of Educational Technology. 40(1), 92-118.

6 The Impact of Findability on Student Perceptions of Online Course Quality and Experience

David B. Robins, Bethany Simunich & Valerie Kelly, Kent State University, United States

Introduction

Findability, as defined by Peter Morville is "the degree to which a particular object is easy to discover or locate, [as well as] the degree to which a system or environment supports navigation and retrieval" (Morville, 2007, pg. 3). Or, as his more colloquial catch phrase puts it, "you can't use what you can't find." Findability is present in the concept of usability – the idea that when something is truly usable, "the user can do what he or she wants to do the way he or she expects to be able to do it, without hindrance, hesitation, or questions" (Rubin, Chisnell & Spool, 2008, pg. 4). For online students, findability is paramount – if they cannot find important course components, they cannot "use" them; having to search for assignment instructions or a course introduction may likely result in frustration, lowered motivation, and decreased self-efficacy -- all of which could impact both student learning and course attrition. Both self-efficacy and motivation have been shown to have an effect on student success in online courses (Irizarry, 2002; DeTure, 2004; Zimmerman, 2000).

There are several important course components that are imperative for students to locate early on in the course, such as instructions for getting started, a self-introduction by the instructor, and a place for student introductions. All of these components may be present and written in a clear manner, but are they easily findable? This project is a first step in determining whether this "search time", or ease of findability, impacts student learning. For example, if students need to search for course essentials, how does their frustration level impact their motivation? At what point do they stop searching? Further, "essential items" that students need early on in a course, such as the syllabus, are hard to find, how does that influence student perception of course or instructor quality? It is important to investigate the potential barrier it poses to students if they have to spend time interpreting the learning environment. Logically, if students need to spend time finding essential course components, this may result in spending less time learning the course content or engaging in course participation. Perhaps more notably, low findability and the frustration that accompanies it may not only impact student learning, but also course attrition.

Unfortunately, as noted by Fisher and Wright (2010), "...there is little research regarding the implementation of usability testing in academia, especially in online course development." While past research has shown a direct effect of "system usability" (i.e., LMS software usability) on student performance (Tselios, Avouris, Dimitracopoulou, & Daskalaki, 2001), there is a paucity of research on the effect of usability in the e-learning environment, and apparently no research on findability specifically. This study attempts to address that gap, and to investigate findability and it's relation to student perception of course quality and overall experience. The opportunity to improve online learning with such a study is substantial, as there is the opportunity to discern if best practices in user-centered design, such as findability, are specifically correlated with increased student learning.

The Study

This exploratory, theory-building study attempted to address the following research question:

RQ1: *Do findability issues impact student feelings of course quality and experience?*

Process and Procedures

For purposes of the study, two courses were selected for the control group. Both courses were English writing courses, to minimize the possible confounding variable of course discipline. Both courses underwent Quality Matters™ review by four independent Certified Peer Reviewers and met expectations. Quality Matters™ (QM) is a faculty-centered, peer review process that focuses on the design of online and hybrid courses and is intended to certified their quality. The process utilizes an extensive rubric, organized under eight general standards and 41 specific standards; the review is conducted by three Certified Peer Reviewers. The researchers used Quality Matters™ as a baseline indication of course quality, as it is a nationally recognized evaluative measure for online courses.

The two control courses, collectively labeled "Course Type 1", were then altered, in an attempt to *not* meet Standard 6.3 of Quality Matters, a standard that is concerned with ease of navigation and overall findability. All content in the course remained the same; the only difference was the layout/navigation of the course. Navigation was altered in two distinctly different ways for each course, and each type of alteration was based both on violating usability standards and also with actual course layout/design issues as experienced by one of the researchers in her role as a Certified Peer Reviewer for Quality Matters™.

For the first course, the navigation was altered such that all material originated from one central folder, labeled "Content", on the Course Home Page. To find important items (such as the syllabus) in the course, one would have to "click in" anywhere from 3 – 5 levels. Additionally, while all folders and items were named in such a way that related to their content, the names and locations were not necessarily intuitive. For example, the syllabus was found in the folder "Information". No item, however, was intentionally mislabeled or labeled something that did not pertain in some way to its content. Further, while the location of items may not have been intuitive, no items were placed in an entirely illogical place (i.e., the Syllabus was not placed in a folder labeled "Media" or "Course Calendar").

For the second course, the navigation was altered so that all material appeared in an icon and text list on the Course Home Page. Anyone in the course would have to scroll to find items, and some files were placed in folders in a non-intuitive or illogical way. For example, the Course Schedule was in an item labeled "Assignments". The four Certified Peer Reviewers reviewed these two courses, collectively labeled Course Type 2, and all independently reported that Standard 6.3 was not met in either course. Therefore, there were a total of four courses used for the study: two courses that met QM™ standards, and versions of those same two courses where the only alteration made was that the courses did not meet Standard 6.3.

Students were randomly assigned to either the eye-tracking group or the focus group, and were also randomly assigned one of the four courses. In the eye-tracking group, students used a computer with special eye-tracking software/capabilities. They were instructed to think-aloud (i.e., talk out loud about their thoughts while trying to find items in the course). Students in the focus group did not do the think-aloud portion, but did participate in a group discussion held after the session. Prior to beginning the study, students were told that they would be looking at an online course, and that the researchers might consider the course to either be well-designed or have some design issues.

Students were told that the researchers were interested in student feedback about the design of online courses and that they should actually put themselves in the scenario that the course they will be looking at was one they had signed up for and paid for, and that it is the first day of the online class. Then, students completed a list of seven "tasks", each task asking them to find 1 – 2 items in an online course. The tasks were scenario-based and items that students were asked to find were based on items that most students would be looking for in the first few days of an online course, such as the grading policy and syllabus (see Appendix 1 for the complete task list). Students were asked to highlight the item after they found it, so researchers could compare if what they found was actually the item the task was asking them to find. After each task, students were asked 3 questions: 1) Did they find the item?, 2) How difficult was it to find the item?, and 3) How frustrated were they when trying to find the item? Students were told in the introductory script that they were to give each task an honest effort, but that they could choose to move on to the next item or task if they truly felt that they could not find the item and/or would stop looking at this point if they were actually a student in the course. After completing the task list, students were asked five questions related to student perceptions of course quality and overall experience. For those in the focus group, a focus group discussion was held after all students completed the task list and answered the five "experience" questions.

Findings

Participants were undergraduate and graduate students from a mid-size, Midwestern university, and were recruited from a variety of classes and majors. Students received extra-credit form their professor in exchange for their participation. Data was collected from 81 participants -- 40 combined for the two courses in Course Type 1 (QM™ "quality" courses, with a focus on findability) and 41 combined for the two courses in Course Type 2 (low findability). Fifty-seven percent of participants were either juniors (27%) or seniors (30%), and the rest were fairly equally distributed between freshman (12%), sophomores (16%) and graduate students (15%). Most (72%) were between 18 – 22, though older/adult students were represented as well. Most (77%) had a GPA above 3.0, and most (92%) either agreed or strongly agreed that they were comfortable using a computer.

First, the researchers wanted to see if students confirmed what the Certified Peer Reviewers felt: that the Course Type 2 courses had lower findability than Course Type 1. An independent samples t-test was conducted to compare time-on-task for Course Type 1 and

Course Type 2, as time-on-task is one measure of findability. Time-on-task is quantified as the total number of seconds it took the participant to find the item. Time-on-task for all seven tasks was higher for Course Type 2. Additionally, there was a statistically significant difference between the two course types for all seven tasks. An alpha level of .05 was used for all statistical tests. See Table 1, below.

Findability was also measured using the questions that participants answered after each task, including : 1) How easy was it to find the items you were looking for in this task? (3-point Likert scale item, 1 = Easy, 2 = Neither Difficult nor Easy, 3 = Difficult), and 2) How frustrating were you when trying to find the items in this task? (5-point Likert scale item, 1 = Not at all Frustrating, 5 = Very Frustrating). Independent samples t-tests were conducted to compare difficulty level and frustration level for the two Course Types. For each question, students in Course Type 2 reported greater difficulty and higher frustration in finding the items for all seven tasks. Results were statistically significant for all tasks except Task #5. See Tables 2 and 3, below. In sum, results show that the Course Type 1 courses did indeed show higher findability (in terms of time-on-task, degree of difficult in finding items, and degree of frustration in finding items) than Course Type 2.

Table 1: Time on Task

	Mean	Std. Dev.	*t*	*p*
Course Type 1, Task 1	71.40	67.05	-3.49	.001*
Course Type 2	144.78	107.59		
Course Type 1, Task 2	87.94	56.69	-4.45	.000*
Course Type 2	171.86	98.72		
Course Type 1, Task 3	45.57	32.07	-4.91	.000*
Course Type 2	102.68	62.63		
Course Type 1, Task 4	36.80	37.82	-2.07	.042*
Course Type 2	54.16	33.26		
Course Type 1, Task 5	74.60	47.84	-1.95	.050*
Course Type 2	100.62	63.88		
Course Type 1, Task 6	64.91	41.89	-2.82	.007*
Course Type 2	102.43	68.61		
Course Type 1, Task 7	54.56	51.56	-4.21	.000*
Course Type 2	128.38	92.13		

* *denotes significant p value at* $\alpha = .05$

Table 2: Degree of Difficulty

	Mean	Std. Dev.	*t*	*p*
Course Type 1, Task 1	1.37	.646	-4.04	.000*
Course Type 2	2.03	.726		
Course Type 1, Task 2	1.17	.514	-4.59	.000*
Course Type 2	1.95	.880		
Course Type 1, Task 3	1.38	.697	-3.92	.000*

Course Type 2	2.08	.795		
Course Type 1, Task 4	1.23	.426	-2.29	.025*
Course Type 2	1.54	.691		
Course Type 1, Task 5	1.60	.695	-1.07	.285
Course Type 2	1.78	.750		
Course Type 1, Task 6	1.46	.701	-2.73	.020*
Course Type 2	1.89	.843		
Course Type 1, Task 7	1.47	.706	-3.99	.000*
Course Type 2	2.22	.854		

* *denotes significant p value at* α = .05

Table 3: Degree of Frustration

	Mean	**Std. Dev.**	*t*	*p*
Course Type 1, Task 1	1.83	1.18	-3.03	.003*
Course Type 2	2.70	1.23		
Course Type 1, Task 2	1.40	1.01	-3.75	.000*
Course Type 2	2.62	1.69		
Course Type 1, Task 3	1.41	.857	-5.69	.000*
Course Type 2	2.92	1.34		
Course Type 1, Task 4	1.23	.646	-2.80	.007*
Course Type 2	1.81	1.08		
Course Type 1, Task 5	1.94	1.06	-.835	.407
Course Type 2	2.16	1.17		
Course Type 1, Task 6	1.80	1.02	-2.63	.011*
Course Type 2	2.51	1.26		
Course Type 1, Task 7	1.59	.957	-6.07	.000*
Course Type 2	3.30	1.40		

* *denotes significant p value at* α = .05

RQ1: *Do findability issues impact student feelings of course quality and experience?*

To attempt to determine course quality and experience, students were asked five questions after completing the task list that were designed to gain an overall impression of the participants' experience, looking at five facets. The questions used a 5-point Likert scale (1 = Strongly Disagree, 5 = Strongly Agree), and were as follows: 1) It was easy to find items in this course, 2) I enjoyed my experience using this course, 3) I would recommend a course like this to my friends, 4) I feel like the instructor in this course would be a good one, and 5) I think this would be a frustrating course to take for an entire semester.

Independent samples t-tests were conducted to compare these five "experience" questions for Course Type 1 and Course Type 2. Results showed that students interacting with Course Type 1 had a better "experience" (for all five "facets"). Additionally, there was a statistically significant difference between the two course types for all five facets. See Table 4, below. In sum, students in Course Type 1 reported that items in the course were easier to find, they enjoyed their experience more than participants in Course Type 2 and were more likely to recommend the course to their friends. Additionally, students in Course Type 1 reported higher agreement that the course instructor would be good, and reported lower agreement that the course would be frustrating to take for an entire semester.

Although not asked as part of the "experience" questions, when students were asked in the focus group setting, "When you can't find something important in your online course, who do you blame?" the overwhelming response was, "the professor (instructor, teacher, etc.)". This response seemed to support student questionnaire responses that gave low ratings for whether instructors of courses with lower findability would be "good" instructors.

Table 4: Five Facets of Experience

	Mean	Std. Dev.	*t*	*p*
Course Type 1, "Easy to Find Items"	4.10	.871		
			6.08	.000*
Course Type 2	2.66	1.24		
Course Type 1, "Enjoyed the Experience"	3.75	.809		
			5.50	.000*
Course Type 2	2.61	1.05		
Course Type 1, "Would Recommend Course to Friends"	3.80	1.02		
			5.70	.000*
Course Type 2	2.49	1.05		
Course Type 1, "Course Instructor would be Good"	3.88	.911		
			5.23	.000*
Course Type 2	2.80	.928		
Course Type 1, "Course would be Frustrating to take"	2.28	1.01		
			-4.49	.000*
Course Type 2	3.44	1.31		

* *denotes significant p value at* $\alpha = .05$

Event Analysis Results

Participants were observed searching for items that, in the case of broken navigation, caused them much frustration. Besides the obvious factor of time-on-task (longer time, more frustration), participants could be observed moving their eyes across a page looking for a link. From the eye tracking data, gaze plots could be directly observed that showed participants actually fixating on links they needed to finish the task.

When the link was buried in a list of file names, however, participants had trouble distinguishing among the choices. The researchers observed fixations directly on the target link, and yet they still did not select it and would move on to another page. This problem highlights the importance of navigation design and visual design. Problems of this type may be caused by:

- Lack of chunking, (the navigation items were not grouped into logical categories so that the user can more quickly jump to the appropriate links)
- Poor labeling (in some cases using file names as labels rather than specific language)
- Poor categorization (placing needed links in non-logical locations)
- Deeply buried content (placing a syllabus, for example, in a folder four levels deep)
- Lack of visual contrast among page elements (if you want someone to see something, contrast it from the other content on a page, don't bury it visually)

Conclusion and Future Directions

This exploratory study produced some interesting results that prompt further investigation into the connection between findability and student perception of course quality, instructor quality, course experience, and the like. Future studies could focus on what design aspects most impact findability, and whether findability is of greater impact for certain items in an online course. Additionally, longitudinal studies could attempt to determine the effects of findability issues in online courses over the duration of an entire semester. Future research could also look more closely at other factors that influence student perceptions of online course quality and experience, as well as exploring the linkages between these and student learning.

This project and its findings will be useful to both designers and reviewers of online courses, and will additionally have broad implications for online students and online learning. Results of the study contribute to the currently small body of knowledge on findability in online higher education courses, and are a significant step made towards determining both the effect of findability in online courses and minimum findability standards. This project could be replicated by any other institution offering quality courses that meet QM™ standards, and would also be the first step in possibly establishing a standard measure for findability in online courses. The ease with which this study could be replicated using the developed measure would further the validity and generalizability of the study results.

References

Barnum, C.M. (2002). Usability testing and research. New York: Longman.

DeTure, M. (2004). Cognitive style and self-efficacy: Predicting student success in online distance education. The American Journal of Distance Education, 18(1), 21-38.

Fisher, E.A. & Wright, V.H. (2010). Improving online course design through usability testing. Journal of Online Learning and Teaching, 6(1), 228-245.

Irizarry, R. (2002). Self-efficacy and motivation effects on online psychology student retention. United States Distance Learning Association Journal, 16(12), 55-64.

McAuley, E., Duncan, T.E., Wraith, S. (1991). Self-efficacy, perceptions of success, and intrinsic motivation for exercise. Journal of Applied Social Psychology, 21, 139-155.
Morville, P. (2005). Ambient Findability. Sebastopol, CA: O'Reilly.
Rubin, J., Chisnell, D. & Spool, J. (2008). Handbook of usability testing: How to plan, design, and conduct effective tests. Indianapolis, IN: Wiley.
Tselios, N., Avouris, N., Dimitracopoulou, A., & Daskalaki, S. (2001). Evaluation of distance-learning environments: Impact of usability on student performance. International Journal of Educational Telecommunications, 7(4), 355-378.
Zaharias, P. & Poylymenakou, A. (2009). Developing a Usability Evaluation Method for e-Learning Applications: Beyond Functional Usability. International Journal of Human-Computer Interaction, 25(1), 75-98.
Zimmerman, B.J. (2000). Self-efficacy: An essential motive to learn. Contemporary Educational Psychology, 25, 82-91.

Appendix 1: Task List

Task 1: This is the first time you've ever logged into this course. You have no idea what to do, so you're looking for clues. See if you can find these two items that can help you get started:

1. The video entitled, "How to navigate and interact with your course"
2. The course syllabus (just find it, don't open)

Task 2: Now that you've had a little introduction to the course, you're looking for some more detailed information on what this course is all about. Find the:

1. Course schedule
2. Instructor welcome

Task 3: You now have sort of a feel for what you'll be doing in this course. Now you want to know what you'll get out of this course. Find the:

1. Learning outcomes

Task 4: Now you're ready to get started in the course. There are learning outcomes for each module in the course. Those outcomes tell you what you're supposed to have learned by the end of each module. Find the:

1. Learning Outcomes for Module 1 of the course.

Task 5: Module 1 Outcomes are spread out over three weeks. In looking at your schedule, you notice there's a great concert in New York City during the third week of the course you want to attend, so you want to get a head start. Find information on what you will be doing in Week 3 that supports the Module 1 Outcomes, specifically:

1. What you will be reading
2. What 2 assignments you will be completing

Task 6: Now that you've had a look at some of the assignments, you want to know what you have to focus on to get the grade you want. Find the:

1. Course grading policy that also includes a list of projects/activities and their associated point values.

Task 7: One of your friends just finished an online course and had some technical difficulties. Although you don't think there will be technical problems in this course, you might ask yourself, "What happens if there is one?" Find:

1. A link to technical support available to you
2. A phone number you would call in the event of a technical problem

7 The Status of Web Accessibility of Canadian Universities and Colleges: A Follow-up Study 10 Years Later

Nick Zap, Simon Fraser University & Craig Montgomerie, University of Alberta, Canada

Introduction

The accessibility to education for all individuals regardless of disability is a basic human right. The ideal of having universal access to information and education is becoming a reality as more and more institutions embrace the World Wide Web as the primary vehicle for information, instruction, and interaction. The accessibility of postsecondary institutions websites promotes greater participation and independence for those with disables to fully realize their learning potential. The challenges for those with disabilities to fully participate in postsecondary education go beyond having good grades or test scores for acceptance. The barriers of entry for those with disabilities for postsecondary education include overcoming the limitations of their disability while also addressing the physical, social, and practical challenges that come with the obstacles of dealing with non-disabled Canadians who disregard the needs of the disabled (Roeher Institute, 1996). As postsecondary institutions move more information online, the barriers of entry for those with disabilities instead of becoming transparent, are becoming more evident.

The expansion of postsecondary information, services, and resources online, directly increases a sites complexity which often leads to sites becoming progressively inaccessible (Hackett & Parmanto, 2005). With approximately 4.4 million Canadians (Human Resources and Skills Development Canada [HRSDC], 2013), and 8% of the postsecondary student aged population identified as having some form of disability (Statistics Canada, 2006), the potential of the web to provide a means for people with disabilities to particulate, contribute, and succeed in postsecondary education is a goal that must be realized. As postsecondary education is an important and necessary gateway into the workforce, the importance of individual's ability to find, access, and utilize information for the procurement of postsecondary studies is paramount.

The Canadian Government report *The Federal Disability Report: Advancing the Inclusion of People with Disabilities* (HRSDC, 2009) shows that those with disabilities are less likely to have college or university degrees. The report identifies the many obstacles prevent people with disabilities from finishing postsecondary education including 16.1% abandoning their education due to impairment and 29.8% that had to reduce their course load which slowed or halted their progress. The ability of the web to open possibilities for those with disabilities to contribute to their communities and to their own social, financial, and academic well-being cannot be understated. A major risk factor for those with disabilities wishing to continue their education and enter the workforce is in their inability to access the information, resources, and services of postsecondary institutions.

This study aims to update and review the status of web accessibility of all Canadian university and college front entry webpages in 2012, to compare this study to two previous studies in 2001 and 2002, and to review the current policies and standards that surround web accessibility. The current laws, initiatives, directives, and policies that ensure the inclusive rights for those with disabilities in Canada are also reviewed, as they may have serious legal repercussions for intuitions who do not ensure equal access and benefit to postsecondary information, services, and resources.

Canadian Laws Governing Inclusive Education for those with Disabilities

The Canadian Charter of Rights and Freedoms enacted in 1985 and the Canadian Human Rights Act of 1976, along with various provincial human rights acts, are the foundation in which the legal bases for inclusive rights for those with disabilities are ensured. Specifically, Section 15 of the Charter guarantees the equality of rights of Canadians with disabilities.

> 15 (1) Every individual is equal before and under the law and has the rights to equal protection and equal benefit of the law without discrimination and in particular, without discrimination based on race, national or ethnic origin, color, religion, sex, age, or mental or physical disability.
>
> 15 (2) Subsection (1) does not preclude any law, program or activity that has as its object the amelioration of conditions of disadvantaged individuals or groups including those that are disadvantaged because of race, national or ethnic origin, colour, religion, sex, age, or mental or physical disability

Section 15 of the Charter is the legal basis in which discrimination in any form, including those rights affecting education, can be framed, examined, and disputed (Roeher Institute, 1996). In ensuring equal protection and equal benefit of the law, Section 15 can be used to protect the educational rights for all citizens, including those with disabilities. The negligence of postsecondary institutions in not ensuring their websites facilitate the access to information, resources, and services for people with disabilities is an issue which may have legal repercussions based on the Charter of Rights and Freedoms and Human Rights acts within Canada. Although the authors have speculated that web accessibility is an issue covered under Section 15 of the Charter (see Zaparyniuk & Montgomerie, 2002, 2005), the challenge of web accessibility as a Charter issue has now been realized.

Donna Jodhan, who is blind, and earned an MBA from McGill and technical certifications from Microsoft and Novell, sued the Government of Canada in 2006 for discrimination based on Section 15 of the Charter of Rights and Freedoms (Monsebraaten, 2010). Although Jodhan is very technically proficient, she could not apply for a position posted on the federal governments website or complete the federal census due to the inaccessibility of the websites form. The government argued that their websites and forms did not have to be accessible and were not protected under the Charter because the government supplied various other accessible technologies for communication such as phone, regular mail, and in-person consultation (Baker, 2012). On November 29, 2010, the Federal Court rejected the government's arguments and found that the inaccessibility of government websites is a violation of Ms. Jodhan's Charter equality rights. The federal government subsequently appealed the decision. On May 30, 2012, the Federal Court of Appeal unanimously rejected the federal governments appeal. The Federal Court judge in the case stated that the government has a constitutional obligation to bring itself into compliance with the Charter and that 15 months was a reasonable time period to have all Government websites accessibility to visually impaired (Chester, 2010).

Although no legal cases have gone forward in Canada against universities and colleges for web accessibility, the precedent of *Donna Jodhan vs. Attorney General of Canada* case makes this challenge all the more likely.

Web Accessibility Initiatives and Directives

The World Wide Web Consortium's (W3C) Web Accessibility Initiative (WAI) is the primary source for strategies, guidelines, and support for ensuring web accessibility (Web Accessibility Initiative [WAI], 2012b). The Web Content Accessibility Guidelines 1.0 (WCAG 1.0), published on May 5, 1999, established three levels of priority for web accessibility errors (Web Accessibility Initiative [WAI], 1999).

- *Priority 1 errors* are those that seriously limit a page's accessibility. Every effort must be made by developers to ensure that these errors do not exist. Satisfying this checkpoint is a basic requirement for some groups to be able to use web documents.
- *Priority 2 errors* make the content difficult to access and should be satisfied. Satisfying this checkpoint will remove significant barrier to accessing web documents.
- *Priority 3 errors* are those that a web content developer may need to address. Otherwise one or more groups will find it somewhat difficult to access information in the document. Satisfying this checkpoint will improve access to web documents (Web Accessibility Initiative [WAI], 1999).

The W3C followed up the WCAG 1.0 with the publication of the Web Content Accessibility Guidelines 2.0 (WCAG 2.0) on December 11, 2008 (WAI, 2008). Although many of the guidelines are the same, the WCAG 2.0 guidelines aim to make the guidelines more technology independent as version 1.0 were largely based on standard web technologies such as HTML and CSS. The guidelines provide testable objective criteria to determine conformance to web design features that makes content more accessible. The guidelines have also been retooled as success conformance checks in version 2.0 instead of errors. The conformance checks allow sites to measure their conformance based on being WCAG 2.0 Level A (lowest) to AAA (highest), which align to specific guidelines.

Improvements in version 2.0 of the WCAG standards include more precisely testable criteria for automated and human evaluation of accessibility standards. The checkpoints for both standards, however, largely overlap. "Most Web sites that conform to WCAG 1.0 should not require significant changes in order to conform to WCAG 2.0, and some may not need any changes. The fundamental issues with Web accessibility are the same" (WAI, 2009).

Canadian Policies for Web Accessibility

The *Standard on Web Accessibility* (SWA) is the new Government of Canada standard effective August 1, 2011, which replaces the previous *Common Look and Feel 2.0 Standards*

(CLF) (Treasury Board of Canada Secretariat, 2011). The new standards, which adopt the WCAG 2.0, are being implemented to ensure uniformity of accessibility to all Government of Canada websites. These guidelines were established to ensure that the responsibility of design allows the widest range of technologies the ability to access information from government websites including personal computers, assistive devices, and other advanced technologies.

The websites included are those that are public facing, are pages that are accountable by government departments, or are provided by the Government of Canada. The timeline for implementation is from August 1, 2011 to July 31, 2013 to ensure all government sites meet WCAG 2.0 Level AA conformance in full. These standards however, are only policy and are not tied to any direct mandate or law to addresses web accessibility and human rights, such as Section 508 of the U.S. Rehabilitation Act of 1973 (29 U.S.C. 794d). The oversight of these standards, as an exercise in self-governance however, has not worked in the past.

The Government of Canada proposed and adopted the *Common Look and Feel Guidelines for the Internet (CLF)* in 2000, with a mandate to have all Government websites accessible by December 31, 2002. The Treasury Board Secretariat conducted a spot audit of 47 of the 146 federal departments in 2007, and found that none of their websites complied to the CLF standard (Loriggio, 2010). The Government's inability to implement and ensure its own policies, reiterates the fact that the incorporation of policies, not backed by laws, are many times not followed or implemented into practice (Whitney, 2010).

Web Accessibility of Universities and Colleges

A number of studies over the past decade have evaluated the web accessibility of postsecondary institutions and libraries around the world. A majority of these studies have found that there are serious gaps in postsecondary institutions compliance to established web standards and practices.

Thompson, Burgstahler, and Moore (2010) evaluated the accessibility of 127 university and college websites in the northwestern U.S. over a five-year period. Using manual checks the researchers found that websites generally improved from 2004-2009 in having meaningful alternative text on all images, homepages with skip navigation links, and logical structure of headings, however got worst in the area of keyboard accessibility due to dynamic menus and flash content.

Blaeser, Creedy, and Epp (2005), using a blind researcher, evaluated the web accessibility of 17 British Columbian postsecondary library websites, catalogues and databases using the JAWS screen reader to evaluate the accessibility of content and navigation. The study found that the most common problems were the inaccessibility of PDF documents, ineffective target links, missing alternative text for non-text elements, auto refreshing pages, and tables using structural mark-up for visual formatting. We note, however that software companies are constantly improving their software to be compatible with U.S. law (Section 508 of the Rehabilitation Act of 1973 (29 U.S.C. 794d)). The University of Indiana notes "with JAWS Version 5 or later, and Adobe Acrobat Version 6 or later, provided that the documents are authored correctly, most PDF files are accessable (sic) to a JAWS user (Indiana University Adaptive Technology and Accessibility Center, 2013) JAWS version 5 (released in October 2003) and Adobe Acrobat Version 6 (released in

July 2003), were released before Blaeser et al (2005) research took place (2004) but it is likely that at that time, most PDF flies had not been "authored correctly," or the researcher was using an earlier version of JAWS. Of course, software developers cannot address issues such as ineffective target links and missing alternative text for non-text elements.

Schmetzke and Comeaux (2009) evaluated academic library web sites in both the US and Canada using Bobby, comparing data from studies in 2000, 2002, and 2006. The researchers found that although accessibility has slightly improved, a majority of library sites are still inaccessible, with Bobby approval at less than 50% of sites evaluated.

Oud (2012) looked at the compliance with WCAG 2.0 of 64 Ontario university, college and public library web sites found an average of 14.75 accessibility problems per webpage. The quality of the errors, from missing ALT tags to navigational errors, suggests that accessibility is neither a priority or is even being checked.

Although this is a small sample of studies that have been completed in the web accessibility of postsecondary institutions, the trends are universal; web accessibility is largely deficient in higher learning.

In the article *University Web Accessibility Policies: A Bridge Not Quite Far Enough* (WebAIM, 2013), the authors outline how most universities fail to meet the minimum requirements for web accessibility. The lack of clearly defined policies, technical standards, compliancy policies, monitoring, and not having consequences for failure to comply with web standards, are a few of the issues. Even with a wealth of tools available to aid in the design, development, and testing of web accessibility, post secondary institutions are not addressing the rights of those with disabilities to equal access on the web.

Assessing Web Accessibility

A number of automation tools have been developed to assess the accessibility of web resources following a number of standards including WCAG 1.0, WCAG, 2.0, BITV, Stanca Act, and Section 508. Many of these tools are webpages where the URL is entered, the conformance checks are selected and the page gives the results. Other tools are standalone desktop programs or web browser plug-ins. Some of the most popular tools include A-Checker, WAVE, TAW3, and Bobby. Bobby was used in the original two studies of Canadian postsecondary web accessibility, however Bobby was discontinued in 2008.

The Testo Accesibilidad Web (TAW3) web accessibility tool developed by the Spanish Fundacion CTIC (Centre for the Development of Information and Communication Technologies), is an application for testing WCAG 1.0 and WCAG 2.0 (beta) web accessibility standards (Fundación Centre for the Development of Information and Communication Technologies [CTIC], 2013). The TAW3 Web accessibility tool comes in four versions, the *TAW3 online analyzer* on the TAW website, *TAW3 with a Click* plug-in for the Mozilla Firefox web browser, a *TAW3 Web Start* Java application, and *TAW3 standalone* application for Mac, Windows, and Linux. TAW3 was selected for this study due to it being a standalone product, it's ability to give output of the sites results with clearly identified WCAG 1.0 priority errors and conformance checks, and the ability to save the tests and the results as external files.

The Study

This study evaluated the accessibility of Canadian post-secondary top-level front entry pages using the WCAG 1.0 compliance standards. The WCAG 1.0 standards were used, as opposed to the WCAG 2.0 standards, to match the same criteria that were used in the original web accessibility studies in 2001 and 2002 (see Zaparyniuk & Montgomerie, 2005).

The TAW3 standalone automated web accessibility software was used to test each websites conformance to WCAG 1.0 Priority 1 and Priority 2 errors. No manual user checks were completed due to the size of the population in the study.

Research Methodology

A list of 393 public and private recognized and authorized post-secondary institution websites were identified from the Canadian Information Centre for International Credentials (Canadian Information Centre for International Credentials [CICIC], 2012). The list is based on information supplied by the ministries and departments responsible for education in Canada and is the only comprehensive list of postsecondary institutions recognized by the provincial and federal governments of Canada. Ten of the sites were excluded from the study due to being duplicate sites, under construction, or were not available at the time of the study. A total of 149 universities, graduate schools and seminaries, and 234 colleges and technical schools made up the list of 383 post-secondary websites that remained.

Each university and college web URL was visited and changed if it did not represent the top-level front page of the institution. If a splash page was presented that offered either an English or French version of the page, the English version was chosen to represent the top-level front page.

In November 2012, a downloadable version of TAW3 was used to evaluate each website for Priority 1 and Priority 2 errors based on the WCAG 1.0 guidelines. A report of the analysis for each site was output from the software and the results were entered into an Excel spreadsheet for analysis. TAW3 does identify manual user checks, however these checks were not completed due to time and resource constraints due to the large number of websites evaluated in the study. This practice of not completing user checks is inline with other studies that evaluate a large number of websites (e.g. Gonçalves, Martins, Pereira, Oliveira, & Ferreira, 2012; Rowland & Smith, 1999; Walden, Rowland, & Bohman, 2000). It is recognized, however, that for full compliance to WCAG 1.0 that the use of two automated tests using tools such as WAVE, A-Prompt, or TAW3, a manual check of relevant WCAG Priority checks, and a usability test using a representative test of individuals of disabilities using various assistive devices are needed (WAI, 2012b). These guidelines will serve as a roadmap for further studies on postsecondary web accessibility.

Results

Table 1 summarizes the results of the November 2012 TAW3 web accessibility evaluation for WCAG 1.0 errors. Out of the 383 post-secondary sites evaluated in the study, only 26.6% (n=102) of the university and college top-level front webpages were free of

Priority 1 errors. Approximately 1.8% (n=7) were free of Priority 2 errors, and 1.0% (n=4) were free of both Priority 1 and Priority 2 errors.

Table 1

Accessibility of Canadian Postsecondary Websites: 2012

	Number of Websites (n=383)		
	Colleges (n=234)	Universities (n=149)	Total (n=383)
Free of Priority 1 Errors	55 (23.5%)	47 (31.5%)	102 (26.6%)
Free of Priority 2 Errors	4 (1.7%)	3 (2.0%)	7 (1.8)
Free of Priority 1 and Priority 2 Errors	3 (1.3%)	1 (0.7%)	4 (1.0%)

Table 2 summarizes the results comparing the web accessibility of Canadian postsecondary websites in 2001, 2002, and 2012. In 2012 approximately 26.6% of the postsecondary pages were free from Priority 1 errors, which is a significant improvement from 19.9% in 2002 ($Chi^2=4.62$, df=1, p=0.031) and 14.9% in 2001 ($Chi^2=15.28$, df=1, p=9.27E-05). The number of websites free from Priority 2 errors fell significantly to 1.8% in 2012, compared to 9.5% in 2002 ($Chi^2=20.59$, df=1, p=5.66E-06), and 11.1% in 2001 ($Chi^2=26.97$, df=1, p=2.06E-07). The number of websites free of both Priority 1 and Priority 2 errors significantly fell in 2012 to 1.0%, from 5.5% in 2002 ($Chi^2=11.63$, df=, p=6.5E-04), but not significantly from 1.7% in 2001. The overall number of websites that contain Priority 1 errors improved to 73.4% in 2012 compared to 80.1% in 2002 and 85.1% in 2001. A comparison of the results from the studies in 2001, 2002, and 2012 (Figure 1) shows a clear trend in web accessibility improvement from Priority 1 errors.

Table 2

Accessibility of Canadian Postsecondary Websites: 2001, 2002, 2012

	Free of Priority 1 & 2 Errors	Free of Priority 1 Errors	Free of Priority 2 Errors	Containing Priority 1 Errors	Total
Accessibility of Canadian Post-Secondary Websites (2001)	6 (1.7%)	52 (14.9%)	39 (11.1%)	298 (85.1%)	350
Accessibility of Canadian Post-Secondary Websites (2002)	19 (5.5%)	69 (19.9%)	33 (9.5%)	278 (80.1%)	347
Accessibility of Canadian Post-Secondary Websites (2012)	4 (1.0%)	102 (26.6%)	7 (1.8%)	281 (73.4%)	383

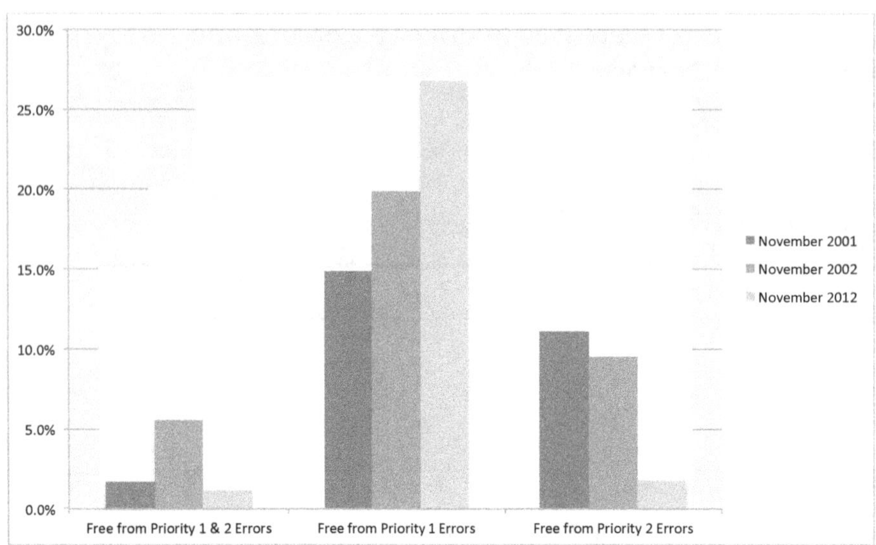

Figure 1. Percentage of Websites Free from Priority Errors in November 2001, 2002 and 2012

Discussion

Goetze and Rowland (2013) in their presentation *Cost Case Studies of Campus Web Accessibility* measure of the costs of what it takes for a postsecondary institution to make their websites accessible versus the cost of litigation for a university to be sued by a student for discrimination. Laying out the hourly cost of designers versus lawyers and compensation for a student once they win their case, addressing web accessibility becomes a cost saving measure. The financial benefit of accessible websites goes beyond the coast saving measure of litigation, web accessibility promotes many direct and indirect financial incentives for post secondary institutions to increase their accessible web presence.

The W3C article *Financial Factors in Developing Web Accessibility Business Case for your Organization* outlines the social, technical, and legal factors that contribute to a positive return on investment for organizations to develop an accessible web presence (WAI, 2012a). Some of the factors for ensuring web accessibility include, increasing the audience who can use the site, increased findability with search engines, increases in use of the site, increased usability, as well as an increased positive image of the institution for their efforts in ensuring inclusivity. Direct cost savings outlined include, decreased personnel costs for maintaining the site, server capacity and costs, site versions for different devices, cost for upgrading to new technologies, decreases for potential high legal expenses, cost for alternative formats for materials, costs of translating, and overall personnel costs. The list gives a good idea of how incorporating accessibility from the beginning can lead to financial benefits that far out weight the time and costs necessary for their execution.

As postsecondary institutions move more and more information online, the barriers to entry become more evident. This study finds that over 73% of Canadian universities and colleges still have significant web accessibility errors that limit the ability of those with disabilities to find, access, and utilize information and services for higher learning. As only the front top-level pages were evaluated to ensure consistency with the previous study, a more thorough review including the front page and level 1 pages may lead to a different picture of web accessibility of these sites. Hackett and Parmanto (2009) in a study looking at the number of pages that are needed to get a clear picture of web accessibility find that the front page, plus one level down gives a clearer representation.

Further studies evaluating the web accessibility of Canadian universities and colleges are needed to gain a better picture of the full extent of the problem. Utilizing the other standards such as the WCAG 2.0 as well as Web Accessibility Barrier (WAB) scores as a metric for measuring these sites accessibility, will lead to a different picture of web accessibility in Canada.

Conclusion

The barriers for web accessibility are clearly defined in a variety of guidelines, standards, and best practices, however the will of Canadian universities and colleges to comply is deficient. The non-compliance of university web designers to use these guidelines are not due to a lack of awareness (Lazar, Dudley-Sponaugle, & Greenidge, 2004). The WCAG 1.0 standards, published 14 years ago and the recent WCAG 2.0 guidelines published 5 years ago, are well-established guides of best practices to ensure web accessibility. Popular web development tools such as Adobe Dreamweaver and BBEdit include tools for creating accessible web content, and a number of web browsers such as Firefox and Safari have web accessibility plug-ins that can automatically check pages for errors. The excuse for having university and college front-pages not accessible to people with disabilities is, given the timeline, tools, and awareness, negligent.

The TAW3 web accessibility tool was used to evaluate the front webpages of 383 Canadian universities and colleges. Approximately 26.6% of these pages were free from Priority 1 errors in 2012, which is a significant improvement from 2001 (14.9%), and 2002 (19.9%). The number of front pages free from Priority 2 errors fell to 1.8% in 2012, compared to 9.5% in 2002, and 11.1% in 2001. The number of websites free of both Priority 1 and Priority 2 errors fell in 2012 to 1.0%, from 5.5% in 2002 and 1.7% in 2001. The overall number of websites that contain Priority 1 errors improved to 73.4% in 2012 compared to 80.1% in 2002 and 85.1% in 2001. Comparing the results from the studies in 2001, 2002, and 2012 shows a clear trend in web accessibility improvement, however the ideal of barrier free accessibility to postsecondary resources is far from realized.

The precedent of *Donna Jodhan vs. Attorney General of Canada* challenge of web accessibility as a Charter of Rights and Freedoms issue leaves Canadian post-secondary institutions open for litigation. The guarantees the Canadian Charter of Rights and Freedoms, the Canadian Human Rights Act, as well as various provincial human rights acts must be realized in the accessibility of online information. Although web accessibility is just one piece of the larger picture of disability rights, postsecondary institutions ability to ensure all students have the ability to find information, services, and resources online, moves closer to the ideal of having equal opportunity, access, and accommodation to education for everyone.

References

Baker, David. (2012). Historic Victory Makes Websites Accessible to Blind Canadians, *Press release.* Retrieved from http://www.bakerlaw.ca/contenthistoric-victory-makes-websites-accessible-blind-canadians/

Blaeser, Stephen, Creedy, Michelle, & Epp, Mary Anne. (2005). *Accessibility of British Columbia's Post Secondary Library Web Sites, Catalogues and Databases : A Preliminary Report.* Langara College. CILS. Retrieved from http://eprints.rclis.org/7250/1/Accessibility_of_BC_Library_Web_Res.pdf

Canadian Information Centre for International Credentials [CICIC]. (2012). Full list of recognized postsecondary institutions in Canada. Retrieved November 2, 2012, from http://www.cicic.ca/en/post-sec.aspx?sortcode=2.16.22&crit=1

Chester, Simon. (2010). Donna Jodhan succeeds in accessibility challenge to Federal websites. Retrieved March 21, 2013, from http://www.slaw.ca/2010/11/29/donna-jodhan-succeeds-in-accessibility-challenge-to-federal-websites/

Fundación Centre for the Development of Information and Communication Technologies [CTIC]. (2013). TAW3. Retrieved from http://www.tawdis.net/ingles.html?lang=en

Goetze, L., & Rowland, C. (2013). Cost case studies of campus web accessibility. http://ncdae.org/presentations/2013/CSUN/cost.pdf

Gonçalves, Ramiro, Martins, José, Pereira, Jorge, Oliveira, Manuel Au-Yong, & Ferreira, João José Pinto. (2012). Accessibility levels of Portuguese enterprise websites: Equal opportunities for all? *Behaviour & Information Technology, 31*(7), 659-677. doi: 10.1080/0144929X.2011.563802

Hackett, Stephanie, & Parmanto, Bambang. (2005). A longitudinal evaluation of accessibility: higher education web sites. *Internet Research, 15*(3), 281-294.

Hackett, Stephanie, & Parmanto, Bambang. (2009). Homepage not enough when evaluating web site accessibility. *Internet Research, 19*(1), 78-87.

Human Resources and Skills Development Canada [HRSDC]. (2009). *The Federal Disability Report: Advancing the inclusion of people with disabilities* Gatineau, Quebec: Human Resources and Skills Development Canada.

Human Resources and Skills Development Canada [HRSDC]. (2013). *Canadians in Context - People with Disabilities.* Retrieved from http://www4.hrsdc.gc.ca/.3ndic.1t.4r@-eng.jsp?iid=40.

Indiana University Adaptive Technology and Accessibility Center. (2013). JAWS Version 8 Frequently Asked Questions. Retrieved April 30, 2013, from http://www.indiana.edu/~iuadapts/technology/software/jaws/jaws_faq.html

Lazar, Jonathan, Dudley-Sponaugle, Alfreda, & Greenidge, Kisha-Dawn. (2004). Improving web accessibility: A study of webmaster perceptions. *Computers in Human Behavior, 20*(2), 269-288. doi: 10.1016/j.chb.2003.10.018

Jodhan v. Canada (Attorney General), 2012 FCA 161.

Loriggio, Paola. (2010). Court orders Ottawa to make websties accessible to blind, *The Globe and Mail.* Retrieved from http://www.theglobeandmail.com/news/politics/court-orders-ottawa-to-make-websites-accessible-to-blind/article1316244/

Monsebraaten, Laurie (2010). Blind woman says federal websites discriminate against the visually impaired, *The Toronto Star*. Retrieved from http://www.thestar.com/news/gta/2010/09/19/blind_woman_says_federal_websites_discriminate_against_the_visually_impaired.html

Oud, Joanne. (2012). How well do Ontario library web sites meet new accessibility requirements? *The Canadian Journal of Library and Information Practice and Research, 7*(1).

Rehabilitation Act of 1973, Section 508 (29 U.S.C. 794d)

Roeher Institute. (1996). *Disability, community and society: Exploring the links.* North York, Ontario: The Roeher Institute

Rowland, C., & Smith, T. (1999). Online distance education - "Anytime, anywhere" But not for everyone. *Information Technology and Disabilities, 6*(2).

Schmetzke, Axel, & Comeaux, David. (2009). Accessibility trends among academic library and library school web sites in the USA and Canada. *Journal of Access Services, 6*, 137-152.

Statistics Canada. (2006). *Participation and Activity Limitation Survey 2006.* (Cat. No. 89-628-XIE - No. 003). Ottawa: Statistics Canada.

Thompson, Terrill, Burgstahler, Sheryl, & Moore, Elizabeth J. (2010). Web accessibility: A longitudinal study of college and university home pages in the northwestern United States. *Disability and Rehabilitation: Assistive Technology, 5*(2), 108-114. doi: 10.3109/17483100903387424

Treasury Board of Canada Secretariat, Government of Canada. (2011). Standard on web accessibility. Retrieved March 21, 2013, from http://www.tbs-sct.gc.ca/pol/doc-eng.aspx?id=23601§ion=text

Walden, B, Rowland, C., & Bohman, P. (2000). *Year One Report: Learning anytime anywhere for anyone.* U.S Department of Education. Washington, DC.

Web Accessibility Initiative [WAI]. (1999). Web content accessibility guidelines 1.0. Retrieved March 21, 2013, from http://www.w3.org/TR/WCAG10/

Web Accessibility Initiative [WAI]. (2008). Web content accessibility guidelines 2.0. Retrieved March 20, 2013, from http://www.w3.org/TR/WCAG20/

Web Accessibility Initiative [WAI]. (2009). How WCAG 2.0 differs from WCAG 1.0. Retrieved March 21, 2013, from http://www.w3.org/WAI/WCAG20/from10/diff.php

Web Accessibility Initiative [WAI]. (2012a). Financial Factors in Developing a Web Accessibility Business Case for Your Organization. Retrieved May 6, 2013, from http://www.w3.org/WAI/bcase/fin.html

Web Accessibility Initiative [WAI]. (2012b). Web Accessibility Initiative (WAI). Retrieved March 12, 2013, from http://www.w3.org/WAI/

WebAIM. (2013). University web accessibility policies: A bridge not quite far enough. Retrieved March 21, 2013, from http://webaim.org/articles/policies/policies_pilot/

Whitney, Michael P. (2010). *The relationship between web accessibility policy and practice in postsecondary institutions.* (71), ProQuest Information & Learning, US. Retrieved from http://proxy.lib.sfu.ca/login?url=http://search.ebscohost.com/login.aspx?direct=true&db=psyh&AN=2010-99150-332&site=ehost-live Available from EBSCOhost psyh database.

Zaparyniuk, Nicholas, & Montgomerie, Craig. (2002). *The status of web accessibility of Canadian universities and colleges.* Paper presented at the EdMedia, Denver, Colorado.

Zaparyniuk, Nicholas, & Montgomerie, Craig. (2005). The status of web accessibility of Canadian universities and colleges: A Charter of Rights and Freedoms issue. *International Journal on E-Learning, 4*(2), 253-268.

8 A view into teachers' digital pedagogical portfolios showing evidence of their Technological Pedagogical Reasoning

Vicky Smart, Cheryl Simm & Glenn Finger, Griffith University, Australia

Introduction

Until recent years Australia did not have a national approach for the definition of quality teacher standards and teacher registration. Ministerial Council for Education, Early Childhood Development and Youth Affairs (MCEECDYA) rationalizes that the agreed standards "describe what teachers should know and be able to do at appropriate career stages" (2011). Australian Institute for Teaching and School Leadership (AITSL) in consultation with teachers, have defined the standards in terms of the domains of teaching including professional knowledge, practice and engagement (2011).

Parallel to this quality teacher initiative is a national policy to boost technology use in education titled the *Digital Education Revolution*. This national policy "aims to contribute sustainable and meaningful change to teaching and learning in Australian schools that will prepare students for further education, training and to live and work in a digital world" (Department of Education Employment and Workplace Relations, 2011). "Educators require the pedagogical knowledge, confidence, skills, resources and support to creatively and effectively use online tools and systems to engage students" (p.6). With these two major national policy initiatives, teachers are being encouraged to use Information and Communication Technologies (ICT).

Students are using ICT and as reported in the 2003 *Programme for International Student Assessment* (PISA), almost all participating 15-year-old students from OECD countries had experience with using computers at home and school (OECD, 2005). They suggest technology has "profound implications for education, both because technology can facilitate new forms of learning and because it has become important for young people to master technology in preparation for adult life" (2005, p. 3). The PISA results are nearly ten years old and with some of the technology innovations in the last five years, students have access to more technology and that technology is not restricted to school or home (e.g. smart mobile phones, 3G enabled tablets). In 2009, Moyle and Owens (2009) reported that over fifty percent of primary school and 84 percent of secondary students have been using technology for more than five years.

With the policy initiatives and pressures from students to use ICT, teachers need to use ICT in their teaching practices. To facilitate this at a local state level, Education Queensland (a state teacher employing authority) has developed a *SMART Classrooms Professional Development Framework* (SCPDF)(Department of Education and Training, 2012a). This framework provides a mechanism for teachers to self-assess their teaching attitudes and practices with regard to ICT use. Teachers are asked to discuss and provide evidence of their professional values, relationships, knowledge and practice in line with a series of predetermined indicators. An 'Accredited Facilitator' then accesses the portfolios before a certificate is awarded.

The *SMART Classrooms – A strategy for 2011-2014* "provides direction for harnessing the learning and business potential of ICT now and into the future" (Department of Education Training and Employment, 2012a). The strategy document provides a clear outline of the four drivers: Working Digitally; Developing Professionals; Enabling Learners; and Harnessing the Enterprise Platform. Under the 'Developing Professionals' heading, the SCPDF is outlined as a continuing strategy for teachers. "The framework is a professional learning guide that helps teachers embrace digital pedagogy" (Department of Education and Training, 2012b). As a demonstration of their ICT competency, the majority of teachers participating in the SCPDF complete an electronic portfolio. This is not stipulated in the policy but teachers have used various tools to prepare their portfolios including webpages, virtual classrooms (BlackBoard) and wikis (EdStudio). To 2010 (from a workforce of 41,000 plus teachers), 11,714 teachers have completed ICT Certificates, 2,021 had completed Digital Pedagogical Licenses and 54 had completed Digital Pedagogical License-Advanced (O'Hagan, 2010).

The objective of this paper is to report on a qualitative study carried out on the portfolios of four teachers who are part of a larger study. The research project objective is to understand of the development of Technological Pedagogical Reasoning (TPR) over a teacher's career and identify the influences on the development of TPR. "The opportunity to document the 'rich' descriptions of teachers' thinking with technology and the opportunity to uncover influences are valuable aspects of the research"(Smart, Sim, & Finger, 2012).

The literature

In exploring pedagogical reasoning embedded in digital portfolios, there are two key bodies of literature that underpin this paper. Firstly, literature on the use of portfolios in an educational setting is important, as there is strong evidence of the benefits of teachers using portfolios (Shepherd & Skrabut, 2011). This leads to the exploration of the content of the portfolios and the pedagogical reasoning embedded within this type of portfolio. The second body of literature pertains to pedagogical reasoning (Shulman, 1986, 1987) where pedagogical reasoning is developed "through the process of planning, teaching, adapting the instruction, and reflecting on the classroom experiences" (Shulman, 1987, p. 117). The SCPDF-DPLs provide a vehicle for teachers to explain their pedagogical reasoning for using ICT.

Portfolios

Portfolios have been used in pre-service education programs as part of assessment (Çimer S. Odabaşı, 2011; Davies & Willis, 2001; Napper & Smith, 2006; Ryan & Kuhs, 1993; Willis & Davies, 2002) and to prepare students in licensure with a teacher registration body (Napper & Smith, 2006). Napper and Smith (2006) suggest that portfolios completed in pre-service education programs are prepared as "evidence of meeting all of the standards for professional licensure at the entry level"(p. 2). These type of portfolios contain evidence of assessment as "lesson plans, presentations, reflections...to show how students process information and develop professional skills gleaned from their <pre-service> course" (Napper & Smith, 2006, p. 2).

Nodoye et al (2012) suggest that there is an employment portfolio which "aims to showcase a candidate's competencies for the position" (p.1). Pre-service teachers seeking employment in Queensland are required to prepare a portfolio in preparation for the application process for Education Queensland (Department of Education Training and Employment, 2012b). This portfolio is prepared based on the 'Professional Standards for Queensland Teachers (Graduate Level)' (Department of Education Training and Employment, 2012b) where pre-service teachers address each standard with evidence explained and attached to show how they meet the standard. For some applicants this is a paper-based process and for others they use an e-portfolio prepared as part of their pre-service education program.

Past graduation, portfolios can be used for planning an educational program; documenting knowledge, skills, abilities and learning; track development; job seeking; evaluating a course and monitoring and evaluating performance (Queensland College of Teachers, 2009). Though Lorenzo and Ittelson (2005) acknowledge that portfolios could be used to showcase accomplishments where Napper and Smith (2005) suggest portfolios can be used for advancement in licensure. For the teachers participating in this research project, their SCPDF-DPL portfolios are not required for licensure, do not guarantee career advancement and are not affiliated with the professional standards. The SCPDF is only promoted by one employing authority but is recognized across all employing authorities in Queensland (Education Queensland, Catholic Education and Independent School sector).

Shepherd and Skrabut (2006) acknowledge that electronic portfolios "can increase reflection, develop content and pedagogy skills and facilitate communication between teachers and administrators" (p.31) but most have a limited duration. All Queensland pre-service teachers prepare a portfolio as part of their pre-service education but there is little evidence to suggest that portfolios are updated after successful job placement. Shepherd and Skrabut (2011) explain that "research on e-portfolio retention suggests that teachers quickly abandon practices following career milestones" (p.32). Though, Rolheiser and Schwartz (2011) found that there eleven first year teachers had maintained their portfolios in their first year of teaching. Grant and Huebner (2001) found in earlier research that teachers three years after graduation were still maintaining their portfolios. No research was found to further explore this issue of portfolio retention.

The key themes on portfolio use highlight that portfolios are used extensively in pre-service education programs but there is little evidence that teachers continue to use them after graduation. There is research with evidence that portfolios are useful tools for the process of accreditation and job seeking but there has been limited research on in-service teachers using portfolios. There was no research found to support the use of e-portfolios as a tool for capturing values, relationships, knowledge and practice.

Pedagogical Reasoning

Shulman (1987) suggested a Model of Pedagogical Reasoning and Action (MPRA). There are six processes to develop the knowledge base for teaching: Comprehension; Transformation; Instruction; Evaluation; Reflection; and New Comprehension. *Comprehension* involves teachers understanding what they are going to teach. *Transformation* is about changing the content to suit the learner where Shulman suggests *Transformation* involves: Preparation; Representation; Selection; Adaptation; and Tailoring.

Instruction is the act of teaching as "organizing and managing the classroom; presenting clear explanations and vivid descriptions; assigning and checking work; and interacting effectively with students through questions and probes, answers and reactions, praise and criticism" (1987, p. 17). *Evaluation* is the check for student understanding. *Reflection* involves looking "back at the teaching and learning that has occurred, and reconstructs, re-enacts, and/or recaptures the events, the emotions, and the accomplishments" (1987, p. 17). *New comprehension* is the new understanding the teacher has gained from going through the above process. Wilson, Shulman and Richert (1987) further developed the model after studying pre-service teachers making the transition into classrooms. Wilson et al confirmed the existence of Shulman's MPRA and drew the model with linear relationships among the constructs.

This Study

The theoretical framework for this naturalistic qualitative research project is informed by Shulman's MPRA. This will be used as a theoretical lens to determine if there is evidence of TPR in teachers SCPDF-DPLs. Findings are presented as a multiple case study design where each teacher will represent one case. While conclusions drawn from this small qualitative study may lack statistical significance, the insights gained from the number of case studies will add to the growing body of literature on teachers' use of ICT. This paper concludes with suggestions for the use of portfolios by practising teachers as a way of capturing evidence of teachers' Technological Pedagogical Reasoning to help all teachers with using ICT. It adds to the current body of educational literature by presenting a new view on how teachers' reason with ICT as evidence embedded in their SCPDF-DPLs.

The research aim driving this project is to: *To investigate how teachers reason with ICT and what influences their development of technological pedagogical reasoning.* The larger study involves fifteen teachers employed in Education Queensland. The fifteen teachers have participated in video-simulated recall interviews, prepared concept maps and some have made available their SCPDF-DPLs.

The teachers

The four teachers (n=4) were experienced teachers with at least 10 years of teaching experience. They were all females and were purposively sampled by being known to the researcher. Two of the teachers were early childhood trained, one primary trained and last a secondary trained. All would be considered digital pedagogy leaders in their schools with only one of the four recognized with a part-time position of leadership. Three teachers were working in two P-12 schools and the other teacher was working in a P-7 school and all were located in South East Queensland. All portfolios have been prepared in an online secure learning management system environment where ethics approval has been obtained (from the university, their employer, their school principal and each teacher) for the researcher to be able to access the portfolios). These portfolios include the following types of data:

- Context statement (details about the school);
- Teachers belief statement for using ICT;
- Items with complete descriptions (as two items are required for submission);

- Evidence for each item including: unit overviews; assessment tasks; virtual classrooms; webquests evidence; links to learning objects; lesson plans; photographs; blogs; student work; recorded lessons; national testing data; resources; and grading;
- Individual support statement from school administration (principal or nominee); and
- Mapping of the SCPDF indicators against their evidence.

The teachers' responses were mapped against Shulman's MPRA. Data from each teacher was compared and contrasted within and across each to identify similarities and differences.

The Results

The teachers

Teachers are asked to prepare a Belief Statement that showed an influence from educational theory. Analysis of their belief statements, show they are influenced from a mix of educational theorists including Gardner, Lave, Vygotsky and Piaget. With all mentioning various educational learning theories including constructivism, connectivism and situated learning. Key messages included in their statements suggest interesting topics for learning and providing learning experiences that relate to the real world. All emphasized the importance of using digital tools for learning and were able to show evidence in their SCPDF-DPL to support this.

Teachers are asked to map their responses to Value, Relationships, Knowledge and Practice predetermined indicators. Various forms of evidence were provided and mapping to the indicators were included throughout their SCPDF-DPL portfolio. The evidence was constrained to a specific format to ensure all information for assessing the SCPDF-DPL was provided. This included: year level; item overview; reason for inclusion; development and planning; curriculum links; curriculum intent; sequence of learning; teaching and learning approach; my learning's and further reflections and information. All teachers submitted three items of evidence with supporting materials to support their discussion. From this evidence, a review of the embedded Pedagogical Reasoning was performed using Shulman's MPRA as a lens. The results are discussed in the next section.

Pedagogical Reasoning

Comprehension - In preparing a SCPDF-DPL, the teacher needed to decide to use evidence they had already taught or evidence from a unit/lesson they planned to teach. All teachers selected had used Units they had delivered in the twelve months prior to submitting their SCPDF-DPL but it is unknown if the units were purposely completed for inclusion in their SCPDF-DPL. There was significant evidence that they had developed a very detailed comprehension of their units as the required portfolio format covered many headings to explain and justify the inclusion of the item in their SCPDF-DPL.

All teachers had not decided in isolation the content for their units – the secondary teacher was following a national vocational approach with specific competencies while the other teachers had used student initiated units after negotiation with their students. The secondary teacher was using a virtual office environment that was available through a learning management system. The other teachers were using a variety of differing ICT tools available over the Internet or from within a secure web-based environment.

Transformation – All of the teachers selected have been using ICT for a many years and developed a range of lessons that included a wide variety of ICT including: websites; blogs; presentations; video conferencing; claymation animation; simulation environments; learning management systems; and virtual classrooms. Shulman describes *Transformation* as the move from "personal comprehension to preparing for the comprehension of others" (1987, p. 16). Transformation "requires some combination or ordering of the following processes: Preparation, Representation, Selection, Adaption and Tailoring" (Shulman, 1987, p. 16). As all teachers had been teaching at the same level for multiple years, there was evidence of previous *New Comprehensions* to aid in their Preparation, Representation, Selection, Adaption and Tailoring practices. For Teacher A, the students creating their own story was important but adding ICT to that *in classroom* event meant it could be captured on the video camera to extend on the classroom experience. Not only did it add further evidence for assessment but it 'triple-coded' the experience (real life, books and Internet) for the students. There was little evidence of Tailoring to suit individual learners needs except as an option for extension work or providing alternative ICT options for students with learning support issues.

Instruction – The SCPDF-DPLs held rich evidence of teachers' instructional activities including photographs, professional observations, examples of student work and lesson recordings. Many unit plans were included but there were not lesson plans to be able to assess the full level of instruction. As part of this research project, these teachers were videoed in the classroom to show their instructional practices with using ICT. Although not discussed in this paper, this data will be used in the final research thesis.

Evaluation - As evidence of checking for student understanding, photographs and examples of student work were included. Teacher A used checklists to capture evidence of student understanding, while Teacher M was able to track student use in the virtual classroom. Teacher K used the lesson to capture evidence of competency with online recording using BlackBoard Collaborate (one of Education Queensland's available online tools).

Reflection – Teachers were asked to evaluate how they used ICT in each evidence item. The following questions were offered as a guide:

- What worked?
- What didn't work?
- What would I change?

There were technological issues highlighted with student use of ICT and failure of the ICT devices. However, teachers commented that it helped build their confidence in using new devices, it allowed opportunities for families to see inside and be better connected to the classroom and that students enjoyed using ICT.

New Comprehension – The SCPDF-DPL asked a question relating to the skills that have been developed with implementing their evidence item. All teachers added that they had developed better understanding of using ICT in their teaching. All comments related to the new understanding they had gained from using ICT in the classroom not solely related to learning a new ICT tool.

Is this Technological Pedagogical Reasoning (TPR)?

There was evidence of Shulman's MPRA as the SCPDF-DPL evidence could be mapped to the model, as shown in data presented in Appendix A. Each element of the model was evident in all four SCPDF-DPLs. Because the focus of the SCPDF-DPL was on teachers using ICT and this could be mapped to the MPRA, could this be termed Technological Pedagogical Reasoning? Or could MPRA with technology be redefined as TPR? In Shulman's original work there were many references and examples to teachers' work that do not reflect the current use of ICT. Shulmans work was published over twenty-five years ago when ICT did not have a great impact on the practice of teachers. The SCPDF-DPLs do not provide a 'full' picture of the process of TPR, as some aspects of *Transformation* could not be captured in SCPDF-DPLs as it was not the purpose to capture those details in these portfolios. There was also little evidence of *Instruction* unless the teacher was able to capture a recording of the lesson, one teacher did have recordings but the nature of the captured lessons via distance education would not assist in defining TPR for classroom-based teachers.

Other themes identified

The portfolios showed many items of evidence of where students were involved in curriculum decision-making for early years learning (Teacher A, Teacher M). This student-negotiated curriculum was driving the teachers' ICT choices, not innovative ICT driving the curriculum choices. Teachers were making ICT decisions based on their students and how they could engage them in the learning. This was reflected in their Belief Statements where these teachers talked about Constructivism and Vygotsky's Social Development Theory. The second major theme highlighted in this research is the use of ICT in the early years of learning – students aged 4-5 years old. Some evidence items used by teachers show that early years learners are capable of using ICT to make movies, use email, photography, Claymation and using a virtual classroom. Even at this early age, these students were capable of using ICT and that teachers can develop *New Comprehensions* of what is possible with that age range.

Conclusion

This paper has been prepared to report on part of a qualitative study currently being completed. This paper reports on the use of digital portfolios of four experienced teachers. The research project objective is to understand the development of Technological Pedagogical Reasoning (TPR) over a teacher's career and identify the influences on the development of TPR. The research project will look into SCPDF-DPLs, teachers' thoughts about TPR and teachers interpretations of their teaching with ICT. This paper has been prepared to discuss initial analysis thoughts of SCPDF-DPLs.

The research has collected the voices of four experienced teachers as represented in the SCPDF-DPL online portfolios. The objective of the SCPDF-DPL is to capture evidence of teachers using ICT purposefully and for that to be professionally recognized by their employer. With some modification (some extra questions) a new ICT focused MPRA could be embedded into the SCPDF-DPL to provide a theoretical base. A new framework could provide the basis for a national approach for recognizing ICT using teachers within the teaching profession. This could influence the definition and development of the career stages in the National Professional Standards and that more emphasis is placed on a digital portfolio to be used as evidence for the move from proficient to highly accomplished and to lead teacher. As there is no connection between the SCPDF-DPL and the pre-service teacher digital portfolio, this framework could influence the development of a pre-service digital portfolio that moves to a in-service digital portfolio and is used across a teacher's career rather than being separate requirements. This emphasizes the "role pre-service portfolios can play in creating a base for professional growth"(p. 16) as suggested by Shulman in 1987.

Not all teachers use ICT and as the SCPDF-DPL is not mandatory students will have teachers using ICT and the next year teachers that do not use ICT. These disruptions in ICT learning will be noticeable by students and their parents. Parents that want their children to use ICT will lobby for their children to be placed in ICT-using teachers' classrooms. This novelty factor will continue as fewer teachers are using ICT but this will change as more teachers complete their SCPDF-DPLs and use ICT in their teaching, though the completion of SCPDF-DPL offers no tangible reward or benefits for teachers. This will need to be reviewed to increase the number of teachers completing their SCPDF-DPLs.

This research has focused on Shulman's MPRA as separate to its role in creating Pedagogical Content Knowledge (PCK). Further work will be completed as part of this research project to understand the implications on MPRA and TPR in the development of Technological Pedagogical Content Knowledge (TPACK) (Koehler & Mishra, 2009).

Appendix A

Pedagogical Reasoning with ICT = Technological Pedagogical Reasoning

			Teacher 1			Teacher 2			Teacher 3		Teacher 4		
			Early childhood (P)			Early childhood (P-3)			Early childhood		Secondary		
Shullman's Model of Pedagogical Reasoning and Action		**DPL Heading**	**Item 1** **Plants**	**Item 2** **Medieval**	**Item 3** **Communication**	**Item 1** **Welcome to my class**	**Item 2** **Data conferencing**	**Item 3** **Scientist for a day**	**Item 1** **Claymation**	**Item 2** **GXXXX Virtual Classroom (VCR)**	**Item 1** **Paricipate in OHS processes**	**Item 2** **Work effectively with others**	**Item 3** **Using meetings**
		ICT Approach used	Interactive whiteboard (IWB) Digital photgraphy	Created movie	Email	PowerPoint with digital photographs, video, voice and hyperlinks	Data conferencing Teleconferencing	Digital storytelling	Claymation animation	Virtual classroom - This wasn't a specific unit but rather an extra for the classroom	Virtual office Web conferencing Learning management system	Virtual course Web conferencing Wiki Learning management system	Web conferencing Email
Comprehension - Understand what is to be taught		Item description Curriculum links	Early maths Language learning	Language and communication Active learning process Health and physical learning Early Maths Social and personal learning	Social and personal learning Health and physical learning Language learning and communication Early maths Active learning processes	English SOSE	Language learning and communication Early maths Fine motor Social and personal learning	English Science	Science	Provide a safe and secure environment	Competency based requirements Virtual office already designed with applicable content Situated learning	Competency based requirements Virtual classroom with applicable content Constructionist learning	Competency based requirements Discovery learning approach
Transformation - taking subject matter and understanding student minds and motivations	**Preparation - examining and critcally interpreting the materials**	How this task was developed Central focus of the student learning Teaching and learning approach used and why	Student initiated idea Student negotiated curriculum Play based Intellectual quality Connectedness	Idea student initiated Student negotiated curriculum Play-based Whole language Triple coding Connectedness	Teacher initiated Knowledge integration	Teacher initiated Multimodal text	Teacher initiated Distance teaching approach	Teacher initiated Natural world investigation	Student negotiated curriculum		Teacher developed materials to assist students in gaining competency	Teacher developed materials to assist students in gaining competency	Teacher developed materials to assist students in gaining competency
	Representation - thinking alternative ways of teaching	Why this is in my portfolio Evidence provided for this item	Display large images on IWB Triple code - real life, internet and books	ICT became whole learning experience Used ICT to solve problems eg costume consistency	ICT an avenue for students to use a range of communication tools	Students opportunity to communicate and share Learning by doing Planning and making	New approach on old paper based way to communicate	ICT to record experiement to be able to show parents and future students	Student engagement in a topic Ability to communicate work		Using virtual office and web conferencing through distance learning	Using virtual classroom and web conferencing through distance learning	Using email as a communication method to simulate an office communication Web conferencing to simulate an office meeting
	Instructional Selection - teaching strategy	Item description Teaching and learning approach used and why	Research Labelling plants and seeds Science experiement	Research Electronic storyboarding Costume capture Movie making Editing Premiere invitations Premiere showing	Roleplay Communication wall of fame Travelling pet Email	Intel teach to the future module - Creating student multimedia presentations	Data conferencing Teleconferencing	Experiement Digital video Digital photography Software editing	Video Digital photography Voice recording Story plan	Online strategy	Online strategy	Online strategy	Virtual work environment
	Adaption - fitting material to students	When this item was implemented Year level and student context	2006	2007	2007	2006	2006	2006	2008	2008	2011	2011	2011
	Tailoring - To suit individual students							Photo Story used as extension for some students and support for others		VCR provides content as an extension to classroom learning VCR allows for different lerning styles	ASD student issues addressed through Task Planning Sheet	ASD student issues addressed through Task Planning Sheet	
Instruction - the act of teaching		Evidence provided for this item	Unit plan Photographs - student work	Unit plan Student work Movie Photographs of work Invitations	Unit plan Email tasks Photographs Comminication wall of fame	Powerpoint template and examples Student work	Meeting examples Video of lesson	Teacher instruction Student experiement	Clamation video Video Story plan Photo Open day photo	Online access	Online access	Online access Web conferencing	Email Web conferencing
Evaluation - checking for understanding		How as this item assessed	Observing child with ICT Photgraphs as evidence of professional observations	Observing child participating in Movie creation Photgraphs as evidence of professional observations Checklist for specific tasks	Observation Reflect with students individually Digital photos Checklist for letter recognition	PowerPoint presentations Feedback from student	Observations Listening to students	Written and verbal recall of information, material and process	Observations Photographs Interview	Able to track student usage	Competency demonstrations	Competency demonstrations	Competency demonstrations
Reflection - looking back at teaching and learning		Why was this item worth doing: 1. what worked 2. what didn't work 3. what I would change Further reflection or other information	Revisit work completed Use of camera difficult for students Time to test equipment Use photography more More PD	Learnt software use Confidence of using IWB Costume making and consitency was a problem Technological problem with video camera	Communication wall of fame Linking families with the class Blog idea was not suitable Email addresses for parents collected at start of year	Intel Teach to the Future - Module on creating student presentations Use a VCR to share online	Learnt how to use NetMeeting Design lessons in on online environment	Software use	More understanding of MovieMaker Better understanding of doing claymation Good for students Good to communicate students work to others	Opens lines of communication with families	Students enjoy the virtual work space Relationships with developers and other users	Detailed planning best for successful students Students liked the activity Students questioned the time to complete the activity	Pleased with realism of meeting and students approach Students motovated to participate
New Comprehensions - learning from experience		Skills I developed by doing this item	Extension topics Use digital camera more	Software use Use of video cameras by students	Email communication with parents	Using Powerpoint with students	Students learnt the technology very quickly	Use of digital storytelling for experiments	Peoples interest in children using technology	VCR use for teaching	Using a virtual office for teaching competencies	Organising student into effective teams Virtual classrooms	Realistic student experiences

References

Australian Institute for Teaching and School Leadership. (2011). National Professional Standards for Teachers. Canbera: AITSL.

Çimer S. Odabaşı. (2011). The effect of portfolios on students' learning: student teachers' views. *European Journal of Teacher Education, 34*(2), 161-176. doi: 10.1080/02619768.2011.552183

Davies, Mary Ann, & Willis, Elizabeth. (2001). Through the looking glass ... preservice professional portfolio's. *The Teacher Educator, 37*(1), 27-36. doi: 10.1080/08878730109555278

Department of Education and Training. (2012a). eLearning Frameworks. Retrieved 25/10/2012, from http://education.qld.gov.au/smartclassrooms/developing-professionals/elearning-frameworks/index.html

Department of Education and Training. (2012b). SMART Classrooms - A strategy for 2011-2014. Retrieved 25/10/2012, from http://education.qld.gov.au/smartclassrooms/strategy/index.html

Department of Education Employment and Workplace Relations. (2011). Digital Education Revolution. Retrieved 5/10/2011, from http://www.deewr.gov.au/Schooling/DigitalEducationRevolution/Pages/default.aspx

Department of Education Training and Employment. (2012a). About the strategy. Retrieved 25/10/2012, from http://education.qld.gov.au/smartclassrooms/strategy/index.html

Department of Education Training and Employment. (2012b). Professional Folio. Retrieved 25/10/2012, from http://education.qld.gov.au/hr/recruitment/teaching/pro-folio.html

Koehler, Matthew, & Mishra, Punya. (2009). What is Technological Pedagogical Content Knowledge (TPACK)? *Contemporary Issues in Technology and Teacher Education, 9*(1), 60-70.

Lorenzo, G., & Ittelson, J. (2005). An overview of e-portfolios. *EDUCASE Learning Initative, Çevrimiçi sürüm, 9*, 2011.

Ministerial Council for Education Early Childhood Development and Youth Affairs (MCEECDYA). (2011). Release of national standards for initial teacher education programs [Press release]. Retrieved 25/10/2012, from http://www.aitsl.edu.au/verve/_resources/MCEECDYA_-_Initial_Teacher_Education_-_Media_Release.pdf

Moyle, K., & Owens, S. (2009). *Listening to students' and educators' voices: The views of students and early career educators about learning with technologies in Australian education and training.* Canberra: Department of Education Employment and Workplace Relations, Retrieved from http://www.deewr.gov.au and http://www.aictec.edu.au.

Napper, Vicki, & Smith, R. Mike. (2006). *e-Reflecting Through a Portfolio Process*. Paper presented at the World Conference on E-Learning in Corporate, Government, Healthcare, and Higher Education 2006, Honolulu, Hawaii, USA. http://www.editlib.org/p/23791

Nodoye, A, Ritzhaupt, A.D., & Parker, M.A. (2012). Use of ePortfolios in K-12 Teacher Hiring in North Carolina: Perspectives of School Principals. *International Journal of Education Policy and Leadership, 7*(4), 1-10.

O'Hagan, D. (2010, 5/11/2012). *Smart Classrooms journey: Past, present and future.* Paper presented at the eLearning Innovation Expo 2010, Brisbane.

OECD. (2005). Are Students Ready for a Technology-Rich World? What PISA Studies Tell Us. Paris: OECD.

Queensland College of Teachers. (2009). *Professional Standards for Queensland Teachers (Graduate Level): A guide for use with preservice teachers.* Brisbane: Retrieved from http://www.qct.edu.au/standards/documents/PSQT_GradLevel_v3_Web.pdf.

Rolheiser, Carol, & Schwartz, Susan. (2001). Pre-Service Portfolios: A Base for Professional Growth. *Canadian Journal of Education / Revue canadienne de l'éducation, 26*(3), 283-300.

Ryan, Joseph M., & Kuhs, Therese M. (1993). Assessment of preservice teachers and the use of portfolios. *Theory into Practice, 32*(2), 75-81. doi: 10.1080/00405849309543578

Shepherd, CraigE, & Skrabut, Stan. (2011). Rethinking Electronic Portfolios to Promote Sustainability among Teachers. *TechTrends, 55*(5), 31-38. doi: 10.1007/s11528-011-0525-5

Shulman, L.S. (1986). Those Who Understand: Knowledge Growth in Teaching. *Educational Researcher, 15*(2), 4-14.

Shulman, L.S. (1987). Knowledge and Teaching: Foundations of the New Reform. *Harvard Educational Review, 57*(1), 1-21.

Smart, V., Sim, C., & Finger, G. (2012). *ACEC2012- It's Time To Technological Pedagogical Reason*. Paper presented at the ACEC2012: ITs Time Conference, Perth. http://acec2012.acce.edu.au/its-time-teachers-technological-pedagogical-reason

Willis, Elizabeth M., & Davies, Mary Ann. (2002). Promise and Practice of Professional Portfolios. *Action in Teacher Education, 23*(4), 18-27. doi: 10.1080/01626620.2002.10463084

Wilson, S.M, Shulman, L.S., & Richert, A.E. (Eds.). (1987). *150 Different ways of knowing: Representations of knowledge in teaching*. Sussex: Holt, Rinehart, & Winston.

9 Pre-Service Mathematics Teachers' Growth in Incorporating Technology into their Teaching Practices

Barbara Ann Swartz & Joe Garofalo, University of Virginia, United States

Introduction

The National Council for Teachers of Mathematics (NCTM, 1991; NCTM, 2000) presents a vision for school mathematics that mathematics educators believe reflects high-quality mathematics instruction. In the *Professional Standards for Teaching Mathematics,* NCTM (1991) presents six standards for teaching mathematics that highlight the creation of worthwhile tasks, the teacher's role in discourse, the student's role in discourse, tools for enhancing discourse, and the learning environment. The NCTM's (2000) *Principles and Standards for School Mathematics* includes six *principles* advocating for educators to set high expectations and provide support for *all* students, to create coherent challenging curricula and appropriate assessments that support learning with understanding, as well as to integrate technology in order to enhance students' mathematical thinking. Their *Technology Principle* states that "Technology is essential in teaching and learning mathematics; it influences the mathematics that is taught and enhances student learning" (NCTM, 2000, p. 24), and furthermore, the Council advocates that "teachers should use technology to enhance their students learning opportunities by selecting or creating mathematical tasks that take advantage of what technology can do efficiently and well – graphing, visualizing and computing" (p. 25). Similarly, the Association of Mathematics Teacher Educators' TPACK Framework (AMTE, 2009) calls for teachers to: (1) combine their knowledge of technology, pedagogy, and content to design and develop technology-enhanced mathematics learning environments and experiences; (2) integrate technology to maximize mathematical learning and creativity; (3) assess and evaluate technology-enriched mathematics teaching and learning; and (4) enhance their technological pedagogical content knowledge through ongoing professional development (p. 1). Furthermore, the International Society for Technology in Education (ISTE) *National Technology Standards for Teachers* (2008) advocates that "Teachers use their knowledge of subject matter, teaching and learning, and technology to facilitate experiences that advance student learning, creativity and innovation… (p. 1). The Mathematical Sciences Education Board and National Research Council (MSEB & NRC, 1990) also affirm the benefits of using technology in the mathematics classroom.

In order to be prepared to teach well with technology, the Association of Mathematics Teacher Educators (AMTE) believes that pre-service mathematics teachers should have: "(1) a deep, flexible, and connected conceptual understanding of K-12 mathematics that acknowledges the impact of technology on what content should be taught; (2) a research-based understanding of how students learn mathematics and the impact technology can have on learning; (3) a strong pedagogical knowledge base related to the effective use of technology to improve mathematics teaching and learning; and (4) appropriate experiences during their teacher preparation program in the use of a variety of technological tools to enhance their own learning of mathematics and the mathematical learning of others" (AMTE, 2009, p. 1). The Mathematical Association of America (MAA) and the Committee on the Mathematical Education of Teachers (1991) list "Using Technology" as a standard for the preparation of mathematics teachers, and the Conference Board of the Mathematical Sciences (CBMS, 2001) asserts that prospective teachers need to understand that technology can be used to eliminate complicated computations allowing students to focus more on mathematical thinking and problem solving.

Studying changes in pre-service secondary mathematics teachers' (PSMTs) teaching practices can help identify ways in which teacher preparation programs can better serve these future teachers by helping them develop into high-quality teachers. Juersivich, Garofalo, and Fraser (2009) found that two cohorts of PSMTs who frequently used a variety of technology to both do mathematics and practice teach mathematics in their pre-student teaching course and field experiences regularly used technology in their student teaching to facilitate their pupils' conceptual and procedural understanding. Fraser (2010) subsequently found that those same PSMTs continued to teach with technology when they became novice teachers, largely because they had extensive experience teaching with technology prior to their student teaching. These findings are evidence that it is possible to successfully prepare pre-service mathematics teachers to effectively utilize technology in their instruction. This present study focuses on the growth of pre-service teachers' use of technology in their pre-student teaching experiences.

Research Question

This paper reports on data taken from a larger study of the growth of pre-service teachers' (PSMTs) quality of teaching practices during a yearlong secondary mathematics pedagogy course that is consistent with the NCTM vision (Swartz & Garofalo, under review). The course included peer-teaching with feedback and a concurrent pre-student teaching field placement. That study examined PSMTs' overall growth in standards-based mathematics teaching practices, as measured by M-Scan (Berry, Rimm-Kaufman, Ottmar, Walkowiak, Merritt, & Pinter 2012). This particular report focuses on the evolution of the PSMTs' teaching practices related to their use of technology. The specific research question addressed in this paper is: *To what degree did the PSMTs' incorporation of technology into their teaching practices improve over the course of an academic year?*

Design and Methodology

Site and Participants

The setting of this study was a two-semester secondary mathematics pedagogy course taught at a mid-Atlantic state university. The eight students in the course were enrolled in a five-year teacher education program that leads to a BA in mathematics and an MT in education at the end of the program. During their fourth year of study, students complete this yearlong mathematics pedagogy course taught by the second author prior to their student teaching, which takes place in the first semester of their fifth year. These eight students are all white, from the United States, and in their early twenties, with all but one being female.

Course and Teaching Assignment Overview

The two-semester secondary mathematics pedagogy course is consistent with the NCTM's *Principles and Standards for School Mathematics* (2000). Throughout the entire year, the course emphasizes problem solving and mathematical behavior (Polya, 1945; Schoenfeld, 1992), conceptual understanding (Hiebert & Lefevre, 1986), applications of mathematics, and use of technology to generate multiple representations and perform calculations not otherwise feasible (Garofalo, Drier, Harper, Timmerman, & Shockey, 2000). The course addresses the development of teaching strategies to facilitate students' mathematical sense making and ability to apply mathematics; it also includes peer-teaching episodes and is coupled with a year-long field experience in which PSMTs observe and teach lessons at a local public middle or high school. In essence, one goal of the course and field experience is to help PSMTs develop mathematics TPACK (Mishra & Koehler, 2006).

Course Activities

Every week the PSMTs are assigned homework tasks and readings. The tasks are typically non-routine problems, which elicit different problem solving strategies and contextual tasks which involve application of mathematics. Applications of mathematics explored in class or assigned for homework often involve different types of functions and usually include modeling. These tasks address topics from astronomy, earth science, business, economics, political polls, projectile and periodic motion, etc. Many tasks require the creation of technology files. These tasks are meant to help the PSMTs further develop and utilize their content knowledge, develop better problem solving strategies, think about pedagogy, and use technology effectively. For samples of course activities, see Garofalo et al. (2000), Garofalo & Trinter (2012), Garofalo & Trinter, (in press), and Trinter & Garofalo (2011). When completing these tasks, PSMTs are often prompted to revisit some mathematics content they may have forgotten, never fully understood, or never applied.

Technology experiences emphasize the use of *content-focused technology applications*, including both content-specific technologies (e.g., graphing calculators, dynamic geometry, math-specific applets) and more generic technologies used in content-specific situations (e.g., Excel, digital cameras). PSMTs are exposed to *model lessons* incorporating appropriate technologies to enable them to see the potential of technology and develop a vision for their own technology uses. These experiences include *multiple opportunities* to explore mathematics concepts and applications with technology and to practice teaching mathematics with technology. Throughout the pedagogy course and student teaching,

PSMTs have *ready access* to technology to gain experience in planning, implementing, and evaluating technology use.

Teaching Episodes

Over the course of the academic year, the PSMTs created and taught four video-recorded lessons to their peers in the pedagogy course, and they averaged about two hours a week in their field experience observing, assisting the classroom teacher or teaching lessons. For the peer-teaching episodes, each PSMT created a full-period lesson, but were only asked to teach a portion of it to the other PSMTs in the pedagogy course and authors of this study. They set up their teaching episode by telling the class "who they were supposed to be" (i.e. an eighth-grade geometry class), and then, after teaching their lesson, explained how they would complete the lesson when their timed portion ended. After each peer-teaching episode, the PSMTs were asked to evaluate themselves on their lesson plans and teaching actions and discuss what changes they would make to improve their lessons. Other PSMTs in the class then offered their feedback, along with the authors of this study. The PSMTs also received written comments as a condensed and formal version of the feedback provided to them during the debriefing discussion that immediately followed his or her teaching episode. After their third peer-teaching episode, PSMTS were assigned, as homework, to watch the videos of all three of their lessons, review the written feedback for each of them, and then revise the lesson plan for their third episode, with the feedback and what they observed in their videos in mind. They were asked to incorporate what they learned from this assignment into their teaching of subsequent lessons.

Data Collection Methods and Procedures

This study focused on the *four* lessons the PSMTs taught to their peers in the pedagogy course and the *one* lesson taught out in their field placement. The four peer-teaching episodes were taught over the course of the year, with the first and second teaching episodes in November and February (10-15 minutes), and the third and fourth ones at the end of March and April, respectively (20-25 minutes). Between the third and fourth peer-teaching episodes, each PSMT created and taught a full-period lesson to the pupils in their public school field placement.

The peer-teaching lessons taught in the pedagogy course were observed by the researchers and were also videotaped. The lessons taught in the field were not observed live, but were videotaped and submitted by the PSMTs. The four live observations allowed the researchers to experience the lessons first-hand and give feedback on each. In the semester subsequent to the end of the course, the videos of all five lessons of each PSMT were coded, in no particular order, using M-Scan (described below) by the first author. The first author was certified as an M-Scan master coder prior to the commencement of the study. To become an M-Scan master coder, the first author attended an M-Scan training workshop that consisted of a full week of reading relevant literature, practice coding sessions, and discourse with M-Scan authors to ensure reliable baseline coding. Then she coded eight videos of mathematics teaching and satisfied the required criteria of scoring within one point of the master codes at least 80% of the scores and within two points 90% of the scores, for each dimension for all videos (for more details on the reliability process see Berry, Rimm-Kaufman, Ottmar, Walkowiak, Merritt, & Pinter, 2012). The coding of the videos provided numerical scores on each of the nine dimensions of M-Scan for each of the lessons.

Mathematics Scan (M-Scan)

M-Scan is a multi-dimensional observational measure developed specifically to focus on standards-based mathematics teaching quality after an exhaustive search of existing instruments to measure quality mathematics instruction (Berry et al., 2012). It is made up of nine dimensions and its format is based on of the Classroom Assessment Scoring System (Pianta, LaParo, & Hamre, 2005) with identical scoring: "a seven-point scale that is divided into three sections: low (1–2), medium (3–5), and high (6–7)" (Walkowiak et al., in press, p. 20). It uses key word descriptors to characterize the three levels of performance.

The nine dimensions measured by M-Scan are the *Structure of a Lesson*, the teacher's and students' use of *Multiple Representations*, the *Students' Use of Mathematical Tools*, the *Cognitive Demand* of the activities in the lesson, the *Mathematical Discourse Community* in the classroom, the *Explanation and Justification* of the students' mathematical thinking, *Problem Solving* by the students, *Connections and Applications* of the mathematics taught to other mathematics topics and to the real world, and the *Mathematical Accuracy* in which the teacher presents the material (Berry et al., 2012). These dimensions measure the quality of mathematics teaching, as they are based on NCTM's *Principles and Standards* and also because researchers in mathematics education have identified their importance (NCTM, 2000, 2007; Walkowiak et al., in press; Weiss & Pasley 2004). M-Scan has an inter-coder reliability coefficient of 0.84 and was validated by content experts (Walkowiak et al., in press).

> The experts agreed that the dimensions of the M-Scan represent components of mathematics instructional quality. After the experts determined whether each coding guide descriptor was indicative of low, medium, or high mathematics instructional quality, their responses were analyzed for matches to the coding guide. The mathematics educator matched 79.7% and the university mathematician matched 82.7% of the descriptors. (Walkowiak et al. p. 27, in press).

The dimensions of *Multiple Representations* and the *Students' Use of Mathematical Tools* most directly correspond to the PSMTs' use of technology in their lessons because many PSMTs used Geometer's Sketchpad, TI Smartview, PowerPoint or Smart Notebook to create representations of mathematical content, and/or had students use an interactive whiteboard, graphing calculator, or Geometer's Sketchpad as a tool. *Connections and Applications, Problem Solving* and *Cognitive Demand* are also related to the PSMTs technology use, but not as strictly, for some utilized the technology to incorporate real-world data or connections in their lessons but the activities posed did not always utilize technology.

Results

The results are reported in two sections. The first section provides a brief glimpse of PSMTs' technology implementation issues in their first three peer-teaching episodes, along with the types of feedback they were given. In the second section, M-Scan scores are presented to demonstrate improvements in the PSMTs' technology use in their lessons over the course of the academic year.

Technology Use in PSMTs' First Three Teaching Episodes

Here we briefly comment on PSMTs' technology use in their *first three* peer-teaching episodes, because it is important for the reader to get a feel for the kind of mistakes they made in their initial teaching practices and the feedback they received. We believe this feedback helped them improve in their teaching practices over the course of the year. The PSMTs exhibited some quality teaching practices such as good overall planning of lessons, posing good questions, trying to engage all students, bringing in some useful representations and applications of the content, and using appropriate technologies. However, they also demonstrated what the authors refer to as "rookie" mistakes, with and without technology, some of which pertain to implementation difficulties.

Most of the PSMTs *did not incorporate technology in their first* episode, even though they had access to technologies that could have been used to enhance their lessons. Prior to that first teaching episode, PSMTs had several course sessions, which included work with graphing utilities, spreadsheets, dynamic geometry, and digital images, but they still did not incorporate any of these technologies. Feedback given to one PSMT illustrates one type of implementation issue each of them had when trying to represent the mathematics content without using available technology: "You can use the grid feature in Geometer's Sketchpad and the interactive whiteboard to plot points accurately." Later, when they began to incorporate technology, all had *difficulties with implementation at one time or another.* Sample comments to PSMTs about their use of technology included: "The interactive chart was good, but you should refer back to it during the discussion." "Pictures were confusing – use Geometer's Sketchpad to create accurate figures" and "The PowerPoint slide was too wordy…" The PSMTs had good intentions for different representations of mathematics content, but they did not utilize them well. The comments provided individualized feedback and suggestions for how to improve their lessons and use of technology to generate representations.

Improvements in PSMTs' M-Scan Scores Over Time

The increase in PSMTs' M-Scan scores provide empirical evidence that their teaching with technology improved over the academic year. Table 2 displays the average scores the eight PSMTs earned for their first and last teaching episodes in the *Multiple Representations* and *Students' Use of Mathematical Tools* dimensions, the numeric gain from first to last episode, and how many PSMTs had improved by two or more points in each dimension.

M-Scan Dimensions	First	Last	Gain	PSMTs with Gain ≥ 2
Multiple Representations	2.75	4	1.25	3
Students' Use of Mathematical Tools	1.25	3.75	2.5	6

Table 1: Average Growth in M-Scan Dimensions for the 8 PSMTs from their First to Last Teaching Episode

All PSMTs started out with low to medium scores in the *Multiple Representations* dimension, and ended with a range of medium scores. Seven out of the eight gained at least 1 point, with three gaining at least 2. Almost all PSMTs started with low scores in the *Students' Use of Mathematical Tools* dimension, but showed considerable growth in this dimension, with 6 PSMTs gaining at least 2 points and the other two gaining 1 point. Tables 2 and 3 below show how many PSMTs scored at each point-value in their first and last teaching episodes.

Multiple Representations

M-Scan Score	1	2	3	4	5
Number PSMTs scoring for first episode	0	3	4	1	0
Number PSMTs scoring for last episode	0	0	1	6	1

Table 2: Number of PSMTs receiving each score for *Multiple Representations* Dimension

In their first peer-teaching episodes, three PSMTs (Lauren, Jordan, and Dana) received a low score of 2, four PSMTs (Sara, Liz, Nicole, and Chelsea) received a low-medium score of 3, and Margaret had a medium score of 4 in the *Multiple Representations* dimension. All of these PSMTs used at least *two* traditional representations (i.e. hand-drawn or computer-generated figures on the white board, hand-written or typed algebraic equations, or hand-drawn graphs) during their first teaching episodes, but they did not particularly plan for the use of different representations of the mathematics addressed in their lessons. Several of them incorporated three traditional representations, and/or brought in physical shapes, inserted charts or inserted images to provide context for the lesson into a SMART Notebook or PowerPoint presentation file.

By the last episode, all of the PSMTs scored between a low-medium and a high-medium on this dimension. Lauren received a high-medium score of 5, Liz received a low-medium score of 3, and the rest received a medium score of 4. Each PSMT used at least *three* representations. All PSMTs prepared and taught their final lessons using SMART Notebook with a SMART board, and they took advantage of some of its features to bring in different representations of mathematics. Seven of them utilized software like Geometer's Sketchpad and/or specific SMART Notebook features for displaying accurate geometric figures and written notes. They brought in physical shapes, and/ or embedded video, images, three-dimensional figures, and/or maps. Jordan utilized the interactive ability of SMART Notebook and a SMART board to instantly create bar graphs to display data pupils collected in the lesson.

Students Use of Tools

M-Scan Score	1	2	3	4	5
Number PSMTs scoring for first episode	7	0	1	0	0
Number PSMTs scoring for last episode	0	1	3	1	3

Table 3: Number of PSMTs receiving each score for *Students' Use of Tools* Dimension

In their initial teaching episodes, only one PSMT, Margaret, used any type of tool to help illustrate mathematical concepts and she received a score of 3 on the *Students' Use of Tools* dimension; each of the other PSMTs received the lowest possible score (1). During these lessons, many PSMTs simply told the class the mathematics they needed to know, and thus did not plan for students' active engagement in the lesson.

However, by their final teaching episodes, seven of the eight had their pupils use some type of tool. Four of them received a medium or high-medium score in this dimension. Both Margaret and Dana used a combination of physical manipulatives and embedded three-dimensional figures in her SMART Notebook file to teach lessons on volume. Nicole created a Geometer's Sketchpad file that her pupils could manipulate to investigate the relationships between individual data points and the mean and standard deviation of the data set. This dynamic sketch displayed data both numerically and graphically. Lauren combined an interactive Geometer's Sketchpad diagram, with pupils measuring of triangles, in a lesson exploring trigonometric ratios. Only Liz maintained a "low" score (2) in this dimension because her lesson did not provide the students an opportunity to use the tools; she, as the instructor, was the only one to use any tools.

Figure 1 below shows line graphs of the eight PSMTs' average score in the *Students' Use of Mathematical Tools* and *Multiple Representations* dimensions over each of the five teaching episodes to illustrate their growth trajectories in these dimensions of their technology use.

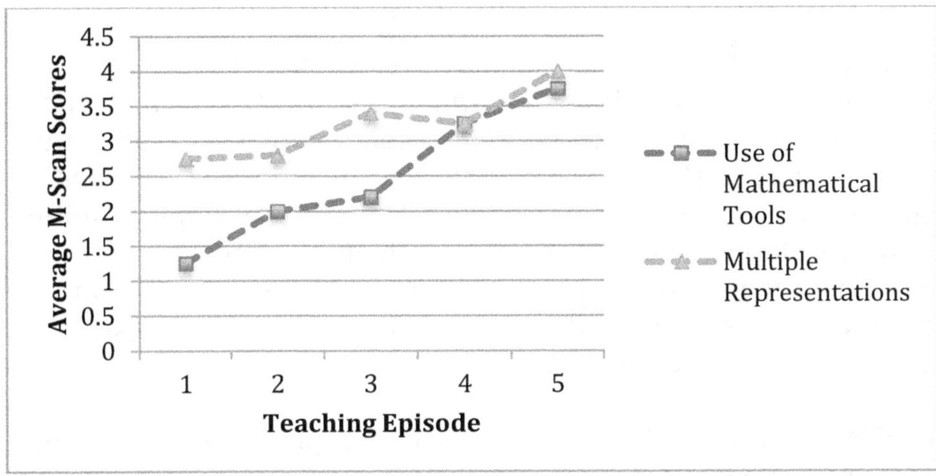

Figure 1: Average Growth by M-Scan Dimensions

In the graph, the growth in scores in the two dimensions is not monotonic, but has upward trends. The graph also depicts the non-linear and non-uniform increases in individual scores, which suggests a potential complex process of incorporating lessons learned from the activities in class and the constructive feedback given to them over time.

Discussion

The increase in the *Multiple Representations* dimension scores can be attributed to many of the activities in the pedagogy course. Regularly, the PSMTs created and worked with multiple representations of concepts for many activities and assignments. They experienced how such representations helped them better understand mathematics concepts and procedures and thus were motivated and able to incorporate such into their own lessons.

The *Students' Use of Mathematical Tools* dimension had a large average increase from the first teaching episode to the last over the eight PSMTs. The growth is not surprising since PSMTs learned to use tools to do mathematics throughout the course, to solve problems and explore applications. PSMTs often commented that using tools to do mathematics gave them new insights and helped them better understand mathematics. When asked what this implied to them, they often mentioned that they would have their own students use tools to learn as well. Clearly by the end they attempted to do this, even when teaching conditions were not conducive (i.e. the final scores could have been depressed due to the short duration of lessons since there was not enough time to fully utilize many tools).

The PSMTs development in these two dimensions is not only due to the course experiences, but also to the feedback that each was given after each teaching episode relative to their implementation of technology. In response to this ongoing feedback, they incorporated more representations, utilized them more effectively, and had students using tools in their lessons.

It is important to note that when the course was taught the researchers did not anticipate using the M-Scan measure on the PSMTs. The course reflects the *Principles and Standards* of NCTM and so does M-Scan, resulting in the congruency between the activities and foci of the course and the researchers' lens for which they evaluated the lessons and gave feedback. The pedagogy course is centered on multiple problem solving opportunities for the PSMTs and focuses on developing understanding of mathematics and its applications. This is achieved with cognitively demanding tasks, making connections and showing the applications of the content, representing the content in multiple ways, and utilizing tools to help develop students' understanding.

Overall, the lessons the PSMTs developed for their final teaching episodes demonstrated a better understanding of appropriate planning for technology use for their pupils' development of mathematical understanding. They utilized technology to generate and incorporate a variety of representations to help illustrate the mathematics concepts to be learned in their lessons. The PSMTs were also able to provide richer problem-solving, discourse opportunities for their pupils, successfully enacted small group work, and had students explain their work and thought processes.

Conclusion

The *Principles and Standards* defined by NCTM (2000) have created a descriptive model for high-quality mathematics teaching including the use of technology to create mathematical tasks and representations. It is important to notice that explicit instruction can help improve pre-service teachers' teaching practices to help them achieve NCTM's vision. Santagata, Zannoni, and Stigler (2007) advocate that pre-service teachers need to practice what they learn in teacher education programs, and activities such as teaching lessons to their peers is just the sort of activity that provides necessary practice for pre-service teachers' developing TPACK. The immediate feedback and opportunities to "re-do" a lesson helped the pre-service teachers practice revising and improving their lessons while simultaneously impelling them to reflect upon what worked in the lesson, what did not, and why. The course also required the PSMTs to write reflection papers on what it means to teach mathematics and to be an effective teacher of mathematics. Activities like these help the pre-service teachers to solidify their own conceptions of teaching mathematics with technology, so they can apply it to their lesson planning and instructional practices.

An important finding to highlight is that *teacher education can help PSMTs improve their teaching and technology incorporation through a combination of classroom activities and practice teaching with feedback.* It also shows that the more time spent on practice teaching, the greater improvements there were in the PSMTs' teaching dimensions. This study suggests that true improvements in teaching practices and technology incorporation do not materialize after a few short weeks, but can take the entire academic year. Teacher preparation programs can incorporate opportunities for PSMTs to practice teaching with technology, coupled with direct feedback, so that these PSMTs are better prepared to take advantage of technology. This will help them develop TPACK and incorporate it in their teaching.

References

Association of Mathematics Teacher Educators. (2009). *Mathematics TPACK (technological pedagogical content knowledge) framework.*

Berry, III, R. Q., Rimm-Kaufman, S. E., Ottmar, E. M., Walkowiak, T. A., Merritt, E. & Pinter, H. H. (2012). The Mathematics Scan (M-Scan): A Measure of Mathematics Instructional Quality. Unpublished measure, University of Virginia.

Conference Board of the Mathematical Sciences. (2001). *The Mathematical Education of Teachers.* Providence RI and Washington DC: American Mathematical Society and Mathematical Association of America.

Fraser, V. (2010). The use of technology-generated representations in mathematics instruction: A study of novice teachers' practices. Doctoral dissertation, University of Virginia.

Garofalo, J., Drier, H., Harper, S., Timmerman, M. and Shockey, T. (2000). Promoting appropriate uses of technology in mathematics teacher preparation. *Contemporary Issues in Technology and Teacher Education, 1*(1), 66-88.

Garofalo, J. & Trinter, C. P. (in press). Using Simulations to Foster Pre-Service Mathematics Teachers' Self-Assessment, Learning, and Reflections on Teaching. *The Mathematics Teacher.*

Garofalo, J. & Trinter, C. P. (2012). Tasks That Make Connections through Representations. *The Mathematics Teacher, 106,* 302-306.

Hiebert, J., & Lefevre, P. (1986). Conceptual and procedural knowledge in mathematics:An introductory analysis. In J. Hiebert (Ed.), *Conceptual and procedural knowledge: The case of mathematics* (pp. 1-27). Hillsdale, NJ: Lawrence Erlbaum Associates.

Juersivich, N., Garofalo, J. & Fraser, V. (2009). Student Teachers' Use of Technology-Generated Representations: Exemplars and Rationales. *Journal of Technology and Teacher Education, 17*(2), 149-173.

Mathematical Association of American & the Committee on the Mathematical Education of Teachers. (1991). *A call for change: Recommendations for the mathematical preparation of teachers of mathematics.* Washington, DC: MAA.

Mathematical Sciences Education Board & National Research Council. (1990). *Reshaping School Mathematics: A Philosophy and Framework for Curriculum.* Washington, DC: National Academy Press.

Mishra, P. & Koehler, M. J. (2006). Technological pedagogical content knowledge: A framework for teacher knowledge. *Teachers college record, 108*(6), 1017-1054.

National Council of Teachers of Mathematics. (1991). *Professional standards for teaching mathematics.* Reston, VA: NCTM.

National Council of Teachers of Mathematics. (2000). *Principles and standards for school mathematics.* Reston, VA: NCTM.

Pianta, R.C., La Paro, K., & Hamre, B. (2005). *The classroom assessment scoring system, Pre-K manual.* Unpublished manuscript, University of Virginia.

Polya, G. (1945). *How to solve it.* Princeton, NJ: Princeton University Press.

Santagata, R., Zannoni, C., & Stigler, J. W. (2007). The role of lesson analysis in pre-service teacher education: An empirical investigation of teacher learning from a virtual video-based field experience. *Journal of Math Teacher Education, 10*, 123-140. DOI: 10.1007/s10857-007-9029-9.

Schoenfeld, A. H. (1992). Learning to think mathematically: Problem solving, metacognition, and sense-making in mathematics. In D. Grouws (Ed.), *Handbook for Research on Mathematics Teaching and Learning* (pp. 334-370). New York: MacMillan.

Swartz, B. A. & Garofalo, J. (under review). Documenting changes in pre-service mathematics teachers' instructional practices.

Trinter, C. P. & Garofalo, J. (2011). Exploring non-routine functions algebraically and graphically, *Mathematics Teacher,* 104 (7), 508-513.

Walkowiak, T., Berry, R.Q., Meyer, J.P., Rimm-Kaufman, S.E., & McCracken, E.R. (in press). Introducing an observational measure of mathematics instructional quality: Evidence of validity and score reliability. *Educational Studies.*

Weiss, I. R. & Pasley, J. D. (2004). What is high-quality instruction? *Educational Leadership, 61*(5), 24-28.

10 TPACK: Exploring a Secondary Pre-service Teachers' Context

Petrea Redmond, University of Southern Queensland, Australia & Jennifer Lock, University of Calgary, Canada

Introduction

Pre-service teachers have difficulty finding appropriate information and communication technology (ICT) integration models both within their professional experience placements in schools and in their university courses. Without a robust model or framework, they struggle to develop the knowledge, skills and practice in relation to technology management, content, and pedagogies in conjunction with discipline content and pedagogy.

Further, Niess (2008, 2011) argued that teacher preparation courses need to emphasize the understanding of learning design skills to provide teaching and learning experiences for a diverse range of learners with differing learning needs in a technology-mediated classroom. As teacher educators, our role is to provide pre-service teachers with the knowledge, skills and experiences to be able to design and teach in today's and tomorrow's technology-enhanced learning environments. For pre-service teachers to be able to be designers of learning in these technology-enabled environment, Niess (2008) suggested effective experiences that can be integrated in courses include "exploring students' thinking and understanding when learning with technology" (p. 228).

ICT in classrooms can no longer be viewed as being an "option or a fun activity that is added to daily work" (Redmond & Lock, 2008, p. 4295). Rather, Redmond and Lock (2008) argue for a shift from ICT being viewed as "cute (e.g., something new or different) to being convenient (e.g., increase productivity) to being complementary (e.g., additional) to being core (e.g., integral and necessary to extend and enhance learning)" (p. 4295). The shift in thinking in terms of ICT in teaching and learning being *core* requires a change in how teachers and pre-service teachers view and value digital technology in their personal and professional lives. It also requires them to develop the necessary knowledge and skills in digital technology used, teaching with digital technology, technology supporting the pedagogy, and using technology to support the teaching and learning of content. It is important that the professional development and educational opportunities for teachers and pre-service teachers are not 'technocentric' (Harris, 2005) emphasising the tool rather than how it can support effective learning and teaching.

Koehler and Mishra (2008) described traditional pedagogical technologies as being characterized by *specificity, stability, transparency of function* and *transparency of perception*. The ever changing nature of digital technology may result in teachers feeling a lack of expertise and confidence in the use of emerging technology for teaching and learning. As such, "[l]earning to become flexible, creative educators who can transcend functional fixedness and other barriers is an ongoing and complicated process and must be confronted at both pre- and in-service levels" (Koehler & Mishra, 2008, p. 9). No longer can teacher educators and pre-service teachers see the use of ICT as being the domain of some other educational professional (e.g., ICT lead teacher, computer teacher or ICT technician).

Rather, it is for them to develop the capacity to meaningfully integrate digital technology to support teaching and learning in knowledge creation environments.

Designing and facilitating rich learning within technology-enabled learning environments is complex. Harris, Mirshra, and Koehler (2009) argued:

> Understanding that introducing new educational technologies into the learning process changes more than the tools used – and that this has deep implications for the nature of content-area learning, as well as the pedagogical approaches among which teachers can select - is an important and often overlooked aspect of many technology integration approaches used to date (p. 395).

In today's teacher preparation programs, teacher educators are confronted with the challenge of how to design learning experiences for pre-service teachers that give them the experience of developing content, pedagogical, and technological knowledge through the integration of technology in their teaching practice. This paper reports on the learning experience *with* technology resulting from secondary pre-service teachers self-reporting on their TPACK competencies early in their program and prior to completing an ICT required course.

TPACK

Shulman (1986) introduced the concept of pedagogical content knowledge (PCK). He advocated that effective teachers need to integrate multiple domains of knowledge in the areas of pedagogy and content. He identified the following three distinct content knowledge categories: "(1) subject matter content knowledge, (b) pedagogical content knowledge, and (c) curricular knowledge" (p. 9). The complex nature of teaching and learning has been further complicated by the introduction of new and emerging digital technologies.

Mishra and Koehler (2006) built on Shulman's (1986) PCK concept in the development of TPACK (initially TPCK). "TPACK emphasizes the connections among technologies, curriculum content, and specific pedagogical approaches, demonstrating how teachers' understandings of technology, pedagogy, and content can interact with one another to produce effective discipline-based teaching with educational technologies" (Harris et al., 2009, p. 396). TPACK is an evolving construct to frame the complex and dynamic nature of learning and the knowledge required for teaching in technology enhanced learning environments (Doering, Veletsianos, Scharber, & Miller, 2009). Effective technology integration requires the intersection among the three key interdependent knowledge areas: pedagogical content knowledge, technology content knowledge and technological pedagogical knowledge. At the intersection of all these knowledge areas is technological pedagogical content knowledge (Koehler & Mishra, 2008). The TPACK framework provides an approach "to examine a type of knowledge that is evident in teachers' practice when they transform their own understanding of subject matter into instruction in which technology and pedagogies support students' understanding and knowledge creation" (Kinuthia, Brantley-Dias, & Clarke, 2010, p. 647).

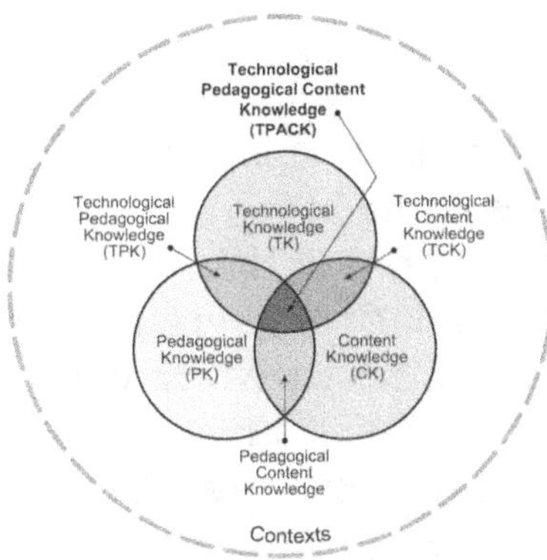

Figure 1. The TPACK Framework and Its Components. (http://www.tpck.org/)

Context

Internationally, there has been greater an emphasis placed on how ICT is being used to support and enhance learning and teaching in all educational contexts. Within Australia, the Federal Government funded the *Teaching Teachers for the Future* (TTF) project which is designed to enable all pre-service teachers "to become proficient in the use of ICT in education" (Australian Government, n.d.). The project included all 39 Australian teacher education institutions and involved capacity building activities for pre-service teachers and teacher educators. As part of this work, the TPACK framework was used to track and report on pre-service teachers' development of knowledge in using ICTs to transform teaching and to provide new ways to engage learners. In addition to this national project, the Queensland and Australian Professional Standards for Teachers have clearly articulated explicit expectations that support the need for pre-service teachers to develop strong understandings of ICT integration. For example, teachers need to "Use ICT safely, responsibly and ethically" (Australian Institute for Teaching and School Leadership, 2012) and "use teaching, learning and assessment strategies and resources in which ICT is embedded" (Queensland College of Teachers, 2006).

In this study, the participants (*N*=55) were secondary pre-service teachers in their second year of a four year program or in their first semester of a one year after-degree graduate diploma program at a regional university in Australia. At the end of the semester, the pre-service teachers completed their second professional experience placement in schools. Further, the participants were enrolled in a curriculum and pedagogy course for Middle Years learners. The course was designed to model the integration of digital technology to support self-directed and collaborative learning. While inquiring into the issues for middle years learners and investigating curriculum and pedagogy for middle years learner, pre-service teachers participated in an international online collaborative activity to explore issues related to today's diverse and digital classroom, for example, inclusivity, Indigenous perspectives, cyber bullying, ESL and ICT integration. The course was offered in face-to-face, blended and online modes.

Method

Towards the end of the semester, pre-service teachers were asked to complete the online TPACK survey. The survey was modified from earlier studies found at http://www.tpack.org/. The survey originally had an elementary focus rather than secondary. It was modified to include a range of disciplines that secondary pre-service teachers could teach beyond Social Studies, Mathematics, Science and Literacy which were included the initial survey. The following disciplines were added: Languages other than English (LOTE), Computing, The Arts, and Health and Physical Education (HPE) and Business. Given the secondary pre-service teachers were required to teach in two different disciplines, this enabled them to self-report in two discipline areas.

It was a three-part survey: Part A elicited demographic information (10 questions); Part B was related to specific components of TPACK; and Part C included open ended questions regarding ICT for teaching and learning (6 questions). In Part B the questions asked pre-service teachers to self-rate their competency related to TPACK and the six other sub-elements of the TPACK construct (i.e. technology knowledge, content knowledge, pedagogical knowledge, pedagogical content knowledge, technological content knowledge, technological pedagogical knowledge) and also explore where they see models for TPACK in their teacher education program and while on field experience. The survey used a 5-point Likert scale (1 – Strongly Disagree to 5 – Strongly Agree). The survey was selected because the original survey had been revised based on previous research and included reliability score for each TPACK domain.

Findings and Discussion

Fifty-five (N=55) pre-service teachers completed the online survey. Forty-two percent who completed the survey were male and 58% were female. The majority of the participants (51%) were between the ages of 32 – 50. The next highest group was aged between the ages of 18 – 22 (22%); with 13% between the ages of 27-32; 11% between the ages of 23 – 26; and only 3% were over 50 years of age. The secondary disciplines represented within the study included: English, Mathematics, Sciences, Social Sciences, Computing, LOTE, HPE, The Arts and Business. In Queensland, high school teachers must select two disciplines to teach in. The most number of participants for the study were in the Sciences and Mathematics disciplines, followed by the Social Sciences and Business. Further, 67% of the participants were in the first semester of a one year graduate diploma program and 33% were in their second year of a four year Bachelor of Education. None of the participants had yet to complete a course related to integration of digital technology and learning and only 31% had participated in any professional development or other learning opportunities to assist them with the integration of ICTs in teaching and learning. Table 1 presents the mean rating and standard deviation data for the seven inter-related TPACK components for this study based on the survey responses.

TPACK Components	Mean Rating (M)	Std Dev (SD)
Content Knowledge (CK)	4.31	0.62
Technology Knowledge (TK)	3.66	0.75
Pedagogical Knowledge (PK)	3.89	0.68
Pedagogical Content Knowledge (PCK)	4.24	0.52
Technological Content Knowledge (TCK)	4.13	0.71
Technological Pedagogical Knowledge (TPK)	4.02	0.51
Technological Pedagogical and Content Knowledge (TPACK)	4.10	0.71

Table 1: Mean and Standard Deviation Score Responses for TPACK Components

Overall, the pre-service teachers self-reported confidence in their knowledge in all seven components of TPACK with limited variance. The highest confidence was in their CK (M = 4.31, SD = 0.62). In the CK component those pre-service teachers who had Social Sciences as a teaching area had the highest confidence levels (M = 4.48, SD = 0.57) and HPE had the lowest (M = 4.00, SD = 0.82.). This is a similar result to Lee, Chai and Koh (2012) whose research found in the pre-service teachers first teaching area that CK was the component with the highest value of self-report.

In this study, the pre-service teachers' self-report indicated that their lowest confidence was in TK (M = 3.66, SD = 0.75) from a 5 point scale. This result aligns with the research outcomes of Schmidt, Baran, Thompson, Mishra, Keohler and Shin (2009) who found that TK had the second lowest level of confidence at 3.82 (SD = 0.57). In contrast, Lee, Chai and Koh (2012) found that PCK had the lowest mean and TK was rated mid-range across the seven TPACK components. Pre-service teachers reported they were confident in their abilities to learn to use technology with 82% reporting at the combined agree and strongly agree score. On the other hand 24% of them did report that they did not frequently play with technology and did not know about a lot of different technologies.

Pedagogical knowledge (PK) had the second lowest mean of the seven TPACK components (M = 3.89, SD = 0.68). Again, Schmidt et al., (2009) had lower levels of self-reporting (M = 4.0, SD = 0.44). The survey question where they had the lowest confidence was in their ability to identify common student understandings and misconceptions. All other question responses had a combined confidence (agree and strongly agree) at or above 79% with 96% self-report for their ability to adapt their teaching based on what students currently understand or do not understand.

Pedagogical Content Knowledge (PCK) had the highest mean in the self-report at 4.24 (SD = 0.52) within a five point scale. Those pre-service teachers who had LOTE as a teaching area had the lowest levels of comfort in PCK, with 32% of them suggesting they would have difficulty selecting effective teaching approaches to guide student thinking and learning in LOTE. The highest confidence in PCK was in the discipline of Business with over 80% agreeing or strongly agreeing they can select teaching approaches to guide student thinking and learning. The next highest were in Math, English and Social Science all with over 70% agree and strongly agree responses. Although the LOTE pre-service teachers did not report a low confidence in their content knowledge when combined with pedagogical knowledge they self-reported much lower than all of the other disciplines.

The pre-service teachers self-reported a Technological Content Knowledge (TCK) mean of 4.13 (*SD* = 0.71). Again the LOTE pre-service teachers reported lowest in their confidence to know about technologies that can be used to enhance understanding in their discipline (33%). HPE pre-service teachers also reported low with 21% unsure about technologies for their discipline. The low TCK is not unexpected given they reported the lowest mean for CK. The disciplines with the highest levels of confidence with TCP were Business and Computing having over 70% with a combined agree/strongly agree self-rating. This should not be unexpected given high levels of technology in both disciplines.

The mean for Technological Pedagogical Knowledge (TPK) was 4.02 (*SD* = 0.51). The self-report from pre-service teachers in the Schmidt et al, (2009) study was 4.3 (*SD* = 0.48). The weakest element the pre-service teachers reported was in their confidence to provide help to others in TPK. All other components of TPK had a combined agree and strong agreement at over 80%.

The participants mean score for Technological Pedagogical and Content Knowledge (TPACK) was 4.1 (*SD* = 0.71). Figure 2 below provides the percentage responses for all nine disciplines for each of the five response options.

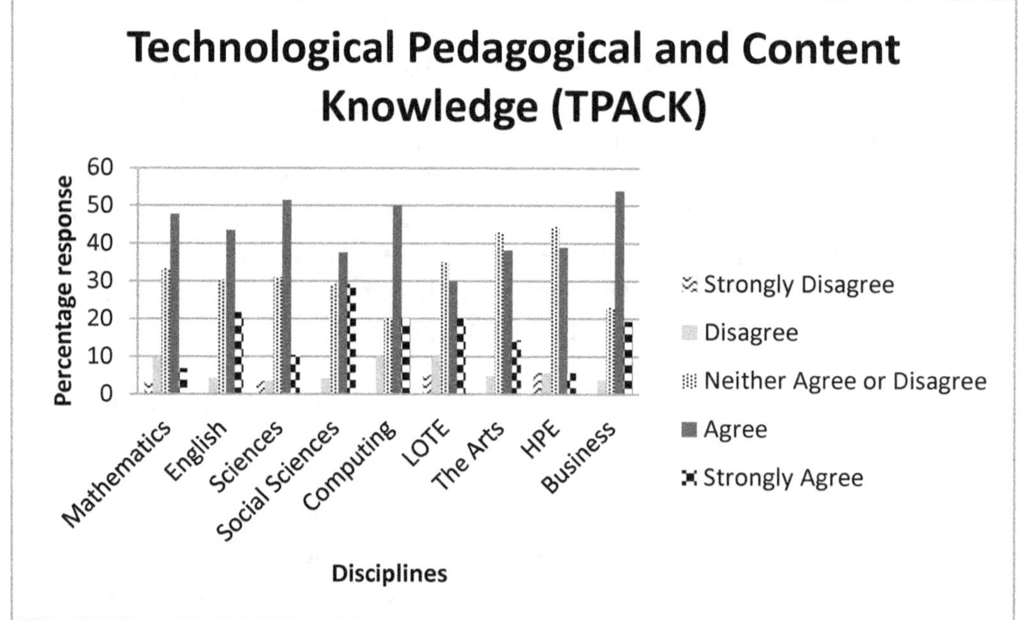

Figure 2: Self report TPACK according to disciplines

As indicated in Figure 2, the lowest level of confidence in TPACK was for pre-service teachers in the Mathematics discipline and the highest levels of strong agreement was in English (21.7%) and Social Sciences (29%). The highest level of agreement was for Business (53.8%). In all disciplines there were low levels of disagreement and strong disagreement about their TPACK confidence.

Pre-service teachers acknowledged strong support of modelling of TPACK by both their faculty instructors and their mentor teachers. More than 65% of the pre-service teachers indicated that their instructors in foundation courses and curriculum and pedagogy courses modelled various approaches of teaching and learning *with* technology. In open ended responses, the pre-service teachers explicitly provided examples from a range of courses that demonstrated the TPACK model by making the following statements: "In [course name] we used SimSchool. We were taught about differentiating tasks for students"; and "[course name] consistently focused on the combination of teaching strategies alongside of ICTs and content. Every lesson that was taught by her was sufficiently detailed and acted as an excellent reminder for the implementation of these areas into our planning and teaching".

The percentage of modelling was lower (45%) for instructors in other faculties. This is concerning because the majority of pre-service teachers will have 43% of their courses for the four year program completed in other faculties as they gain their content knowledge for their teaching areas. During their professional experience placement, 75% of the pre-service teachers indicated that their mentor teacher provided modelling of TPACK. The majority of pre-service teachers provided examples that went beyond the traditional use of PowerPoint, Internet searching and students using MS Word. They shared many examples of online collaboration, and the use ICT devices such as interactive whiteboard, iPods, probes, and graphic calculators used in various disciplines. Disappointingly several pre-service teachers commented that they did not see any modelling of TPACK during their professional experience with one pre-service teacher stating "No mentor has modelled any IT".

The majority of pre-service teachers self-reported high levels of comfort with regard to using and teaching with digital technology. One pre-service teacher stated "I'm quite comfortable using ICTs within my classes, as long as I've had time to play around with it and understand its functions". They were able to provide an example of how they have already done so on one of their professional experience placements. Most of the examples were discipline specific which positively emphasised the relationship between content, pedagogy and technology. For example, when "teaching natural disasters in SOSE I combined theory with a virtual national geographical natural disaster survival game"; and "I was teaching a senior art class and we used an Interactive whiteboard and located websites, images (artworks) and virtual tours of galleries".

What was disappointing was that it appeared from the data they have limited knowledge of what is possible using ICT for teaching and learning beyond what has been demonstrated or modelled to them within their teacher education program or on professional experience. For example, when they are asked to collaboratively create a wiki as part of assessment within their teacher education program and then on professional experience they have their students do the same. There was an acknowledgement by one pre-service teacher that

> "What is possible only relates to what is available in the school and class. To learn a bunch of technologies you are never going to use is disheartening and time consuming. This course teaches that knowledge is evolving and so my current knowledge of what is possible in terms of teaching with ICT depends on what is available".

However, within teacher education, as well as during their professional experience, pre-service teachers need to explore possibilities of how they can use ICTs beyond duplicating what they have already seen. This is affirmed by Harris and Hofer (2011) whose research suggest that professional development should not focus on the affordances of hardware and software but provide opportunities for exploring and sharing technological possibilities and consider "how best to select and combine them to match the student's standards-based learning needs" (p. 228). One pre-service teacher commented "Many things are possible with ICT and as technology continues to expand so does the numerous opportunities to integrate ICT in student learning. It is clear that ICTs can be used in all subject areas and enhance them".

Implications

Teacher education programs strive to create rich learning experiences and model effective practices using technology to enhance teaching and learning. Irrespective of location, the mandate to integrate technology to enhance learning and teaching requires teachers to have strong content knowledge, pedagogical knowledge and technological knowledge and practice. In the Queensland (Australia) context the recently funded *Teaching Teachers for the Future* project placed additional pressure on Australian teacher education providers to further develop the knowledge and experience of both teacher educators and pre-service teachers in the area of technology enhanced learning. The National and Queensland professional standards for teachers demand pre-service teachers demonstrate levels of knowledge and practice in this area also.

The pre-service teachers' self-perceptions of their confidence of the TPACK elements were high not only at the individual content, pedagogical and technology levels but also improving learning at the TPACK level. The course provided a lived experience of working in a technology-enhanced environment to develop content, pedagogical and technological knowledge and skills that pre-service teachers can draw from for their professional practice and was supported by learning in other courses and their professional experience placements. Further, pre-service teachers were able to provide specific examples from different courses where TPACK was effectively modelled for them and this is prior to them completing a specific course focusing on ICT integration.

Although this paper reports on a snapshot of data from one course within teacher education, working in a TPACK framework has a number of consequences for educators at all levels.

1) Teaching teacher educators. "[T]houghtful pedagogical uses of technology require the development of a complex, situated form of knowledge" (Mishra & Koehler, 2006, p. 1017). Teacher educators often see themselves as content experts or even pedagogical content experts. Very few would consider themselves technological pedagogical content experts. As such, teacher education programs require the right mix of experts and expertise to speak to content, speak to pedagogy, speak to technology, and to speak to TPACK.

2) Modelling and exploring options. Angeli and Valanides (2008) recommended that "teachers need to be explicitly taught how tool affordances can be used to transform content into powerful pedagogical forms" (p. 19). Practicing teachers and teacher

educators need to provide these models and also opportunities for exploration and implementation of innovative learning experiences for pre-service teachers to integrate technology as part of their everyday teaching practices.

3) Designing for TPACK learning experiences. When designing learning experiences, teachers guide their thinking and decision-making based on their theoretical knowledge, contextual knowledge, epistemological beliefs, and practical experiences. In preparing to design TPACK experiences in teacher education, it must take into account teachers' current knowledge but also extend their knowledge about how to teach with technology (Angeli & Valanides, 2008).

4) Knowledge and context impact on practice. Doering et al, (2009) remind us that in terms to TPACK "teachers do not use all three of the knowledge domains equally" (p. 336). The level of content, pedagogical or technological knowledge used in practice is related to the individual context at the time and also an educator's personal knowledge of each domain. "[C]ontext influences both teacher knowledge and practice. In turn, teacher knowledge influences practice, and practice influences which types of knowledge are used more in the classroom" (p. 336).

Limitations and Conclusion

A limitation of this study was that the data were limited to one course in one regional university in Australia. This limits the ability to generalise beyond the initial context. A second limitation is that the data were collected through pre-service teachers self-rating their competencies for each of the elements of TPACK. Data collected through self-rating is subjective, although the impact of this is reduced through the use of a previously validated survey instrument. A third limitation is the fuzzy boundaries related to TPK, TCK and PCK. Researchers have difficulty articulating the boundaries around these areas (Graham, 2011) and it may be that the pre-service teachers similarly had difficulties distinguishing between these components and the questions related to them in the survey may be misleading. Future research in this area could include a longitudinal study tracking pre-service teachers over time. Further, the use of pre- and post-test within a course or over a program would provide additional information with regard to growth and change areas.

TPACK is a "unique body of knowledge that is constructed from the dynamic interaction of its constituent knowledge bases namely knowledge of content, pedagogy, learners, context, and technology" (Angeli & Valanides, 2008, p. 16). It provides a framework to build learning opportunities to enhance both the individual components of TPACK and TPACK overall. This paper forms part of an ongoing dialogue around the use of TPACK as we explore and embrace new possibilities of teaching and learning *with* technology. Specific teaching and modelling is required so that pre-service teachers adopt and use TPACK as part of their repertoire of practice, as well as, for teacher educators to be able to design and implement such a framework within their course contexts.

Teacher education programs can no longer teach basic technology skills in isolation from content and pedagogical contexts. The development of TPACK in teacher educators, practising teachers and pre-service teachers is a messy and ill-structured problem. The content, pedagogy and technology knowledge of teacher education are dynamic, complex and interrelated. The complexity of developing the next generation of teachers is compounded with the infusion of technology in both homes and in classrooms. TPACK provides a framework to unpack and repack the parts and the whole so to design and facilitate meaningful learning and teaching *with* technology. Our challenge as teacher educators is to design and model robust learning experiences using TPACK as a way to provide pre-service teachers with a lived experience to best inform their professional practice.

Bibliography

Angeli, C., & Valanides, N. (2008). *TPCK in pre-service teacher education: Preparing primary education students to teach with technology.* Paper presented at the Annual Meeting of the American Educational Research Association, New York City, NY.

Australian Government. (n.d.). Teaching Teachers for the Future. Retrieved October 15, 2012, from http://www.ttf.edu.au/

Australian Institute for Teaching and School Leadership. (2012). National Professional Standards for Teachers - Graduate Teachers. Retrieved October 15, 2012, from http://www.teacherstandards.aitsl.edu.au/CareerStage/GraduateTeachers/Standards

Doering, A., Veletsianos, G., Scharber, C., & Miller, C. (2009). Using the technological, pedagogical, and content knowledge framework to design online learning environments and professional development. *Journal of Educational Computing Research, 41*(3), 319-346.

Graham, C. R. (2011). Theoretical considerations for understanding technological pedagogical content knowledge (TPACK). *Computers & Education, 57*(3), 1953-1960.

Harris, J. (2005). Our agenda for technology integration: It's time to choose. *Contemporary Issues in Technology and Teacher Education, 5*(2), 116-122.

Harris, J., & Hofer, M. J. (2011). Technological pedagogical content knowledge (TPACK) in action: A descriptive study of secondary teachers' curriculum-based, technology-related instructional planning. *Journal of Research on Technology in Education, 43*(3), 211-229.

Harris, J., Mishra, P., & Koehler, M. (2009). Teachers' technological pedagogical content knowledge and learning activity types: Curriculum-based technology integration reframed. *Journal of Research on Technology in Education, 41*(4), 393-416.

Kinuthia, W., Brantley-Dias, L., & Clarke, P. A. J. (2010). Development of pedagogical technology integration content knowledge in preparing mathematics preservice teachers: The role of instructional case analyses and reflection. *Journal of Technology and Teacher Education, 18*(4), 645 – 669.

Koehler, M., & Mishra, P. (2008). Introducing TPCK. In AACTE Committee on Innovation and Technology (Ed.), *Handbook of Technological Pedagogical Content Knowledge (TPCK) for Educators* (pp. 1-29). New York, NY: Routledge.

Lee, K. S., Chai, C. S., & Koh, J. H. L. (2012). *Fostering Pre-service Teachers' TPACK Towards Student-centered Pedagogy.* Paper presented at the Society for Information Technology & Teacher Education International Conference.

Mishra, P., & Koehler, M. J. (2006). Technological Pedagogical Content Knowledge: A Framework for Teacher Knowledge. *Teachers College Record, 108*, 1017-1054.

Niess, M. L. (2008). Guiding preservice teachers in developing TPCK. In AACTE Committee on Innovation and Technology (Ed.), *Handbook of Technological Pedagogical Content Knowledge (TPCK) for Educators* (pp. 223-250). New York, NY: Routledge for the American Association of Colleges for Teacher Education.

Niess, M. L. (2011). Investigating TPACK: Knowledge growth in teaching with technology. *Journal of Educational Computing Research, 44*(3), 299-317.

Queensland College of Teachers. (2006). Professional Standards for Teachers. Retrieved October 15, 2012, from https://www.qct.edu.au/Publications/ProfessionalStandards/ProfessionalStandardsForQldTeachers2006.pdf

Redmond, P., & Lock, J. (2008). *Investigating Deep and Surface Learning in Online Collaboration.* Paper presented at the Society for Information Technology & Teacher Education 19th International Conference Las Vegas, Navada.

Schmidt, D., Baran, E., Thompson, A., Koehler, M., Punya, M., & Shin, T. (2009). *Examining preservice teachers' development of technological pedagogical content knowledge in an introductory instructional technology course.* Paper presented at the Society for Information Technology & Teacher Education International Conference.

Shulman, L. S. (1986). Those who understand: Knowledge growth in teaching. *Educational Researcher, 15*(2), 4-14.

11 How Online Teacher Educational Backgrounds, Student Satisfaction, and Frequency of Teacher-Student Interactions Relate to Completion Rates for Two Critically Needed Courses Statewide

Bonnie Swan, University of Central Florida, Michael Hynes, University of Central Florida, Beth Miller Florida Virtual School, Jaime Godek, Florida Virtual School, Kristopher Childs, University of Central Florida, Xuan-Lise Coulombe-Quach, University of Central Florida, Yan Zhou, University of Central Florida, United States

Purpose

The purpose of this study was to examine the relationship between course completion rates and the educational practices and backgrounds of 75 Algebra I and 45 General Biology online distance education teachers in Florida who taught at Florida Virtual School in 2010-2011. By examining the educational practices and backgrounds of a statewide workforce of distance teachers in a large virtual school—and examining how these factors relate to student satisfaction and course completion—the authors aim to add to the existing knowledge that guides important policy decisions intended to address improvements in this area.

Introduction

Recent technology is vastly changing the way we communicate and learn, and one result is a huge growth in virtual schooling. The National Center for Education Statistics (Queen & Lewis, 2011) revealed that for 2009-2010, 55 percent of public school districts reported having students enrolled in distance education courses, which is up from 37 percent a few years earlier, in 2004-2005. Because of this increase, there is a strong need to examine issues related to virtual schooling in order to inform policymakers who are considering how to use it to expand and improve on teaching and learning (Picciano, & Seaman, 2008). Growth is even more pronounced in Florida, where the Digital Learning Now Act (2011) now requires all upcoming Florida high school graduates—beginning with 9th graders in 2011-12—to complete an online course as part of the 24 credits required for graduation.

Many believe a teacher has more impact on student learning than any other factor, yet little is known about the population of K-12 online distance education teachers and their pedagogical practices (Carpenter, 2011). The objective of this study was to investigate which practices and backgrounds are associated with effective online teaching. Another focus is to compare the most to the least effective online distance education teachers as identified by student satisfaction, instructional leader perspectives, and course completion rates in two of Florida's most critical courses: Algebra I and General Biology.

Florida Virtual School (FLVS) is a learning community where students learn without limitations: *any time, any place, any path,* and *any pace*. The free, accredited, online public school, has served over half a million K-12 students since its inception in 1997. Right now over 120 different virtual courses are being offered by FLVS to Florida school children and others around the world. The school is massive with over 1,800 highly-qualified teachers and 148,000 students.

FLVS students are encouraged to contact the teachers when there is a need of any kind. Teachers are available between 8 a.m. and 8 p.m. daily, including weekends. Teachers and students interact through email, voice mail, telephone conversations, text messages, and instant messaging. The program emphasizes the importance of student-content and student–instructor interactions, with less emphasis on student-student interactions. Students can enroll at any time during the calendar year.

Data Sources and Methods

This research study uses a comparison descriptive research design using purposive sampling. The research questions asked are:

- What are the average course completion rates for these courses?
- How do different aspects of online distance education teachers' qualifications (experience, certification, and degree level) relate to course completion rates?
- Does the number of professional development hours that teachers experience over the year relate to their course completion rates?
- What do instructional leaders report differentiates the most and least effective distance online teachers?
- Is there a difference in student satisfaction ratings for teachers with high versus low completion rates?
- How does the frequency of teacher-student interactions relate to course completion rates?

Courses being investigated include Algebra I and General Biology at FLVS for the 2010-2011 academic year. The study was conducted by researchers at the University of Central Florida and an administrator at FLVS (the investigators). The work engaged multiple perspectives and used qualitative and quantitative methods. Over several months, investigators engaged in conversations almost weekly to help frame perspectives about the research activities and what was learned, and guide the process.

The electronic facet of online learning provides a wealth of opportunity to collect data on teacher performance. Since FLVS already logs many of the variables being investigated, much of this research involved careful mining of existing data sets with the assistance of FLVS research and assessment staff, including student end of course survey results, course enrollment/completion numbers, teacher contact logs, and number of hours of professional development hours teachers had completed. Other data were obtained by investigators using interviews with the teachers' ILs.

Because it is believed that the quality and frequency of human interactions is vital to students' success, the nature of the communications of key individuals involved and the level that has been achieved during each course were studied and described. This investigation will help capture and understand the importance of how the teachers interact with students using available tools promoted by FLVS, including the following: Elluminate sessions, including virtual tutoring and other; email; text messaging; instant messaging; telephone calls, including discussion-based assessments; and others.

Examples of existing data gleaned from student end of course surveys were explored, including students' ratings of the quality and frequency of communications, length of time for the teacher to respond, length of time to resolve issues, perceptions about how well the teacher demonstrated an interest in their success as a student, etc. Structured interviews with the teachers' ILs were done by telephone using a standard set of open- and closed-ended questions so that data could be aggregated to gather their perceptions about what makes an effective online distance education teacher.

Descriptive statistics were used to inspect the distribution of key variables and to identify data patterns and organize data for presentation purposes. T-tests and other appropriate methods were used to examine the mean differences. Procedures were used to verify that common violations of assumptions were not made to limit the possibility of reaching the wrong conclusions. Other data, for example with assessing the effectiveness of the services, information collected from program records, and interviews, were analyzed via content analysis.

Results

This study included 75 Algebra I and 45 General Biology teachers at FLVS who taught both segments in 2010-2011. For Algebra I, at the time of this study 20 percent are no longer employed at FLVS. Eighty-five percent of Algebra I teachers were female and 15 percent were male. For General Biology teachers, 11 are no longer employed at FLVS. Ninety-three percent of the General Biology teachers were female and seven percent were male.

For each course, in some portions of this study, teachers were divided into tertiles based on their adjusted course completion rate. Those that fell in the top third became the upper tertile and those in the bottom third were in the lower tertile.

Course Completion

When evaluating the effectiveness of online distance education programs, course completion rates are an important factor. Especially for courses like Algebra I and General Biology, which are both difficult for many to successfully complete and are required for high school graduation in Florida. For this study, 43 percent of the students in Algebra I and General Biology in 2010-2011 were enrolled for grade forgiveness—meaning these students were working on replacing a grade of "D" or "F". Analysis revealed the average course completion rate for Algebra I teachers was 68 percent, meaning that this proportion of the students enrolled in the class completed with the grade of a D or higher. For Biology this rate was higher at 83 percent. This rate was calculated after deducting the "non-starters" from those admitted to a course. Non-starters are defined as the sum of those who are either not activated or do not complete any assignments beyond the fourth week—they are considered dropped, and not assigned a grade by FLVS.

Teacher Attributes

Teacher Seniority (Experience)

Teacher seniority was defined as the length of time, in months and in completed years, a teacher had served both at FLVS and prior to FLVS. Despite the categorical differences, the average years of experience were equal for Algebra and Biology teachers, at 2.5 years. The average years of experience prior to becoming employed at were almost equal, averaging 6.8 for Algebra and 6.7 for Biology.

This investigation basically showed that for these teachers seniority did not make a difference with how many of their students completed the course with a passing grade in either course. More specifically, for years at FLVS and course completion rates, Pearson product-moment correlation revealed almost no correlation between the two variables for Algebra [r=-.025, n=75, p=.832] or Biology [r=-.03, n=45, p=.847]. To see if having teaching experience prior to working at FLVS made a difference, the same test, revealed a small negative correlation between the two variables [r=-.208, n=75, p=.073] for Algebra. After removing the three potential outliers for over 27 years of experience before FLVS even less correlation between the two variables [r=-.012, n=72, p=.919] exists. Results for Biology, revealed almost no correlation [r=-.047, n=45, p=.761].

Teacher Certification

Teacher certification types were categorized as Mathematics 6-12, Middle Grades General Mathematics 5-9, Middle Grades Integrated Curriculum, Biology 6-12, or Middle Grades General Science 5-9. Fifty-nine percent of the Algebra teachers were certified 6-12; and 41 percent were certified for Middle Grades 5-9. For Biology, 91 percent were Biology 6-12 and 9 percent were Middle Grades General Science 5-9.

Independent-samples t-tests were conducted to compare the course completion rates for teachers. For Algebra there was no significant difference in the adjusted course completion rates for Mathematics 6-12 (M=65.9, SD=10.10) and Middle Grades 5-9 with General and Integrated numbers combined [M=70.4, SD=8.99; t(73)=1.98, p=.052]. The magnitude of the differences in the means was small (eta squared=.051). The test for Biology teachers certification also revealed almost no difference in the mean course completion rates between Biology 6-12 (M=83.1, SD=6.73) and Middle Grades General Science 5-9 [M=81.8, SD=9.69; t(43)=.346, p=.731]. The magnitude of the differences in the means was small (eta squared=.002).

Teacher Degree Level

About 42 percent of the Algebra and 47 percent of Biology teachers had earned advanced degrees. It is unknown what content area these degrees of these are in. No information was available for what content area these degrees are in so having a degree "in the subject area" may have revealed differently.

For Algebra, findings from an independent-samples t-test revealed no significant difference for those who had earned only a bachelors (M=69.23, SD=9.59) versus those who had earned an advanced degree [M=65.82, SD=10.01; t(73)=1.98, p=.760]. The magnitude of the differences in the means was small (eta squared=.057). There was also no significant difference in the scores for Biology teachers who had earned a bachelors (M=82.01, *SD*=7.88) compared to those having earned an advanced degree (M=84.09, *SD*=5.59).

Teacher Professional Development Hours

The average number of hours was slightly higher for Biology teachers (102 hours) than for Algebra teachers (97 hours). An investigation using Pearson product-moment correlation coefficient into the relationship between the number of PD hours and course completion rates, revealed almost no correlation between the two variables [*r*=.054, *n*=75, p=.648] for Algebra. After removing an outlier with over 400 hours, Pearson revealed a small correlation [*r*=.232, *n*=75, p=.047]. For Biology, the same test revealed almost no correlation between the two variables [*r*=.022, *n*=45, p=.884].

Instructional Leader (IL) Interviews

According to the FLVS job description, Instructional Leaders (ILs) assist in managing the school and provide evidence of effective instruction that result in student achievement. The IL is also to support instructors in personal and professional growth. Requirements for the position include a master's degree and a valid professional Florida certificate in Educational Leadership, as well as three years of successful teaching experience and demonstrated experience in supervision, training, and development of teachers.

Nine out of ten ILs agreed to participate in the structured telephone interviews, which focused on their experience working with teachers at FLVS, specifically for mathematics and science teachers. Topics included: what roadblocks virtual teachers face; what makes an effective online teacher; what effective online teachers do to prevent student attrition; and what advice they would give teachers wanting to teach online. Major themes, drawn from the analysis are organized under each topic from most to least prevalent.

Characteristics of the Most- and Least-Effective Online Instructor

When asked what they perceived differentiated the most effective teachers from the least effective for Algebra and Biology. Overwhelmingly their responses focused on soft skills. For example having effective organization and time management skills, having a good balance between personal with work time, building positive relationships with students, being proactive about student success, and constant and effective communication in ways that caused them to be more approachable, were all important for being effective. One also mentioned that having strong content knowledge was essential.

Organization/Time Management

- "Where I see less effective teachers, is where they try something for a week and then try something different and that doesn't work... It's having that specific routine of reaching out to students who aren't working and following that routine—putting a student on a student success plan. It's just having a routine for all aspects of the job and doing that same routine every week."
- "I'd say for the least effective teachers, typically the barriers that they face is that they have an inability to structure their day to provide the highest *work smarter, not harder* type of day for themselves. So often times they're always playing catch-up: trying to complete monthly calls, get caught up on monthly calls, with their grading."
- "I think one of the things that <the most effective instructors do>, is to develop a time management system that is extremely organized, where they chunk their time effectively to where they can allow for purposeful phone calls to occur, to where they allow a certain percentage of their day to providing exceptional feedback because that is really where the teaching occurs."
- "I think another indicator is level of organization, a balance of time, that sort of thing."

Balancing Work and Personal Time

- "In our environment it's really difficult in the beginning to balance your family or your personal life with your professional life. Unlike in the classroom where you close the classroom door and go home, in our world that computer is always there."
- "So we have to train our teachers how to put themselves on a schedule and how to shut down and walk away and refresh and rejuvenate.... It's finding the balance and establishing that schedule."
- "They're able to organize their lives and balance sort of personal stuff, family stuff, and work stuff and they're effective."
- "A lot of times when teachers are at home, their family are at home as well and there's a difficulty there.... It's hard for some teachers to shut down and walk away from the computer because it's at home and they're not leaving it in the classroom... . That is a huge indicator between the most and least effective teachers. Being able to block off time and being able to use it for what you've blocked it off for."

Building Relationship with Students

- "Where I think a lot of my least effective teachers lose focus .... They're so caught up in 'Well I have to grade so I can't meet with that student' or 'I have to return all these emails so I can't meet with that student'. They're losing the big picture of why we do what we do."
- "Ability to build relationships and rapport with their students."

- "So least effective would be . . . they don't really build a relationship with a kid and don't start out that relationship asking how they're doing, you just go straight to the business."

Proactive About Student Success

- "I'd say that a more effective online Algebra instructor would be proactive in recognizing not only that the student is struggling or may not be engaged. . . . Being proactive in doing any form of a reach out is typically is the best way in order to engage them into the learning. Coaching them to attend a tutorial session on the topic that they're struggling with instead of waiting for the failed exam."
- "Being positive and being an advocate for students. Those are the things that make our most effective teachers as effective as they are."
- "Oh the least effective teachers... in the business world you'd say I'm a 9 to 5 person and I shut down at 5. . . . They have more of a laissez faire practice for 'You either do the work or you don't and if you don't you're going to fail.'"

"Constant" and Effective Communication

- "I think the most effective... <has a> culture of openness, acceptance, nurturing environment, and those are established through the telephone calls, the welcome calls, making sure the email communications are looked at, read, re-read to ensure that as little misperception can occur when you're reading a document and not hearing a person deliver the message. I think those are what make the more effective math teachers see a greater number of students complete their course than the least effective is that relationship."
- "So least effective would be if you just call at random times that don't make any sense and you just leave generic messages..."
- "<For the most effective,> being able to communicate effectively with students and parents and being able to organize their time around that."

Job Expectations

- "I think what makes an effective teacher in our environment too is the notions that they come into this job with."
- "So often times, our least effective teachers have come in with a different mindset for what online teacher is and so then they're not engaged and learning the best way to do the job so they fail."

Preventing Student Attrition

Like at any other school, having students successfully complete Algebra and Biology is important, and unfortunately, it is often a struggle. ILs were asked to reflect on what strategies effective teachers use to limit attrition. They all described two major factors, including being able to build a positive relationship with their students and being approachable. Others included a need for teachers to have "constant" communication and being available for students' questions, as well as for effectively collaborating with other teachers.

Relationship Building

- "That's what I see as some of the best teachers that are able to limit their student attrition is they've built good relationships."
- "It's all about that relationship that they build with the kids. They hook them from the beginning and a student that believes that you care about them will almost always be more successful than a student that doesn't feel like the teacher had a vested interest in their success."
- "So really just that rapport that they're able to build from the students from the very beginning is what really dictates success and the ability to keep a student engaged and completed in the class."
- "Letting them know you're still there, having that relationship, letting them know that you still care."

Constant and Effective Communication

- "I think what I said about letting them fall off the radar, not keeping those students in that routine of their monitoring, and talking to that student this week and saying, 'Oh you need to turn in three assignments this week,' but then not following up with them the second week and then the third week goes by and oh they didn't turn in the work, so if that teacher would have called them that second week and been on top of them and had that constant communication, that student might have been more successful."
- "I think communication is really important and constant communication with students, with parents as well, to kind of keep them in the loop and keep them moving through the course."
- "I think it really goes back to celebrating successes and knowing the kids strengths and harnessing that. It really comes down to that communication."

Response Time and Availability

- "They've made themselves available to their students and the students are aware of that availability and then they make use of the availability."
- "The reason is they really stay on top of the kids and the kids know if I call I'm going to get help immediately. I don't have to wait 24 hours. The least effective teachers if they know they have 24 hours to return a call which is our policy, they might wait 24 hours. My most effective teachers don't."

- "The least effective ones will take their time. Saying, 'I'll call them back tomorrow or whatever'. Where the more effective teachers will hop right on it and get the student while the student is engaged with the curriculum because if they took the time to call, then they've got an issue that needs to be resolved now."

Friendly Disposition

- "If you feel from the teacher that they really love what they're doing and that they just care about you and what you need, you don't have a problem picking up the phone and saying, 'Hey I'm struggling with this Edgar Allen Poe poem' or 'I don't know how to solve two-step equations, can you help me with that'. Whereas from the very beginning if you have that boring, not so engaged conversation for your welcome call you might feel turned off from that teacher and not feel so open and wanting to call them when you're struggling."
- "It is to me again being positive and having that nurturing nature and the friendly voice. So being positive and again being an advocate for students that's what our best teachers do best."

Advice for Teaching Online

ILs shared what advice they give to people who want to teach online. Responses were focused on the job expectations, specifically the ability to manage their time and being well organized while having a good home/work balance. There was also the need to be passionate about helping students and being able to build strong relationships with students. Almost all of them stressed the importance of having accurate knowledge and expectations of what the job requires.

Understanding and Meeting Job Expectations

- "So just forewarn them of that time expectation. Many people come here with a false sense of I'm going to come here and I'm going to have babies and I'm going to work from home and I don't need a nanny and I can just do it all and be super mom, and then they realize that you're not going to eat dinner with your family."
- "Working from your home means work is always there. . . . So setting that expectation up front is usually what I try to do for anybody that wants to know."
- "I think it's difficult for teachers that we don't set expectations for when they come in. So as long as we as an organization do our part and letting teachers know that this is a very different environment than what they've experienced for the last 8 to 10 years."

Be Well Organized

- "The main thing is that the teachers here have to be extremely organized with their time and also all their different dashboards and information they have to keep track of. They really have to be flexible so they can rearrange things to be accessible to their students. The key thing is that accessibility. Students need to be able to get ahold of their teachers when they have questions. So in most of our teachers cases, that means that dinner time with your family may get interrupted about 20 times by a phone call from a different student and you have to be okay with leaving the table and answering that call because that's when our students are working and that's when they need help from their teachers."
- "The other thing is self-motivated. You need to be organized."

Maintain a Good Home/Work Balance

- "You have to actually build it into your day and build it into your week. The folks that take that to heart end up staying here and absolutely loving it. Those folks that can't step away and can't be okay with one email or a voicemail for a couple of hours then they don't last. They end up going back to the traditional classroom."
- "I would definitely talk about the work life balance and how difficult it is to shut it down. Although the job does offer flexibility, you still have to be in it for the right reasons."
- "If they're looking for more one-on-one interaction with students which is what you're going to get with an online environment, then you're going to have to adjust your schedule. You're going to have to be extremely flexible as far as how you want to do this with your family and letting them know that you might take a call for 15 minutes at 6:30 at night. You might take a five minute discussion based assessment question at noon on a Saturday."

Have Passion for Helping Students

- "Well they've got to be somebody that's student focused. We know that there are teachers, why are you teaching history? Well, I love history and I love the content. Okay, I could care less. I don't need you in my school. I need the teacher that loves kids and that will do anything they can to help this student be successful."
- "I want to hear people that are frustrated with not being able to give students the individual time that they need to be successful because that class has to leave and another class has to come in. Those are the teachers I'm looking for, the ones that are frustrated with the constraints in the brick and mortar world that will thrive in our environment which is more flexible."

Build Relationships with Students

- "Being able to build those relationships, being personable, being the self-motivated type-A personality, and then being aware of the hours. It's not a 7 to 3 job. It's much more than that. It's a lifestyle basically."
- "I would say you will have an opportunity to interact directly with students and you'll be able to see the impact each and every day. The keys to success also come down to your own personal leadership development and your own ability to manage time because our school doesn't end."

Other

- "I think our teachers can be most effective when we get out of their way and let them do what they do best and that is to teach kids."
- "Watching a kid do an equation on paper and then asking them to explain to you how they were able to do that equation is two different things, right? So discussion based assessment is crucial in understanding really the depth and breadth of their knowledge. That's why we have them so frequently and that they're such a crucial integral part of what our teachers do every day so they can kind of figure out where a kid is and what their levels are."

Student Satisfaction Ratings for Teachers with High versus Low Completion Rates

Students who were enrolled and completed at least 60 percent of the course were invited to complete an end of course questionnaire administered by FLVS. Students were asked about the quality, frequency, and type of interactions with their teacher and other students in the course, as well as their teachers' interest in their academic success. Comparisons in this section, because of the large number of surveys (2,618 for Algebra and 1,880 for Biology), were made between survey responses for the upper versus lower tertile by completion rates.

Quality and Frequency of Interactions

For both courses students in classes with the higher completion rates rated the quality of teacher-student and student-student communications positively versus those in classes where completion rates were lower (90% vs. 84% for Algebra I, respectively; and 96% vs. 90% for General Biology).

Higher proportions of students in the classes with higher completion rates indicated that their teacher responded within 48 hours for a) providing feedback/grades when they submitted assignments (83% vs. 75% for Algebra I, respectively; and 88% vs. 81% for General Biology); and b) responded to questions they asked about course content (81% vs. 76% for Algebra I, respectively; and 85% vs. 82% for General Biology).

About the same number of students indicated that their online teacher(s) demonstrated an interest in their success as a student in the highest versus lowest tertile by completion rate for both courses (98% vs. 96% for Algebra I, respectively; and 99% vs. 98% for General Biology). Using a scale for the level of interest could produce more definitive results.

It should also be mentioned that overall ratings for the quality of interactions were slightly higher for General Biology than they were for Algebra I.

Relationship between Frequency of Teacher-Student Interactions and Course Completion Rates

According to Moore (1989) there are three kinds of learner interactivities that may affect learning in distance learning environments: learner-content interaction, learner-instructor interaction and learner-learner interaction. In this study we focus on learner-instructor (or in this case teacher-student) interactions.

To help capture and understand the importance of how these teachers interact with students using available tools promoted by FLVS teachers' contact logs for their interactions with students were investigated. This included 355,366 logs for Algebra I and 217,102 logs for General Biology. Of the 19 types of contacts listed in the log, 15 were teacher-student interactions. The other four were initiated by FLVS or a call center. Of those teacher-student interactions, e-mail was used most frequently, with an average (SD) of 1,753 *(1,317)* emails per year sent per teacher for Algebra I and 1,778 *(1,172)* for Biology each year, followed by monthly phone calls with averages (SD) of 777 *(380)* and 871 *(364)*, respectively. Results reveal a small, positive correlation between the number of teacher-student interactions and course completion rates for both Algebra I and General Biology, with higher completion rates associated with more teacher-student interactions.

Limitations

There are limitations. The foremost of which are the representativeness of the samples and that the study is non-experimental and does little to control for extraneous factors. Other limitations, inherent to most survey and interview research, are that it relies on self-reporting. Finally, looking at whether an advanced degree in-field, rather than in any-field might yield different results.

Significance

"Many school districts continue to have concerns about quality, student readiness, and staff development related to online education" (Picciano & Seaman, 2008, p. 26). Furthermore, many believe a teacher has more impact on student learning than any other factor. Still, little is known about the population of K-12 online distance education teachers and their pedagogical practices. These issues are becoming more pronounced as the quickly growing realm of K-12 online distance education is gaining on education experienced in "brick and mortar" classrooms. This study adds to the existing knowledge base for how educational practices and backgrounds of a workforce of critically needed distance teachers relate to student and parent satisfaction and course completion. It could be used to help guide important policy decisions intended to address improvements in this area.

References

Carpenter, J. K. (2011). *An exploratory study of the role of teaching experience in motivation and academic achievement in a virtual ninth grade English I course.* University of Florida). ProQuest Dissertations and Theses, Retrieved from http://ezproxy.lib.ucf.edu/loginurl=http://search.proquest.com/docview/922398697?accountid=10003

Clark, T., Hibbard, L., Kennedy, K., LaFrance, J., Oliver, K., & Swan, B. (in press). Working Title: *A Winning Formula: Lessons from RTT-D Round 1 Winners, Resources for Round 2 Applicants.* Report published by iNACOL (International Association for K-12 Online Learning).

Gall, M. D., Borg, W. R., & Gall, J. P. (2007). *Educational research: An introduction* (8th ed.). New York: Longman.

Moore, M.G. (1989). Three types of interaction. *American Journal of Distance Education, 3*(2).

Picciano, A. G., & Seaman, J. (2008). *K–12 Online Learning: A 2008 Follow-Up of the Survey of U.S. School District Administrators.* NY: The Sloan Consortium. Retrieved October 28, 2011, from http://sloanconsortium.org/publications/survey/pdf/k-12_online_learning_2008.pdf

Queen, B., & Lewis, L. (2011). *Distance education courses for public elementary and secondary school. students: 2009–10 (NCES 2012-008).* U.S. Department of Education, National Center for Education Statistics. Washington, DC: Government Printing Office.

U.S. Department of Education, (2010). *Evaluation of Evidence-Based Practices in Online Learning: A Meta- Analysis and Review of Online Learning Studies.* Office of Planning, Evaluation, and Policy Development. Washington, D.C. Retrieved October 26, 2011 at http://www2.ed.gov/rschstat/eval/tech/evidence-based-practices/finalreport.pdf

Acknowledgements

This study was made possible through funding provided by the Morgridge Family Foundation (MFF).

12 Do 21st Century Learning Environments Support Self-Directed Learning? Middle School Students' Response to an Intentionally Designed Learning Environment

Christopher Fahnoe & Punya Mishra, Michigan State University, United States

21st Century Frameworks and Self-Directed Learning

Self-directed learning is a concept present in many of the current frameworks on 21st Century Learning and has often been regarded as critical part of individualizing learning experiences (Caffarella, 1993). The P21 Framework Life and Career Skills (2010) included "Initiative and Self-Direction", the ISTE Standards for Students (2007) specifically called for students to be able to "plan and manage activities to develop a solution or complete a project", the AASL Standards for the 21st Century Learner (2009) noted that learners should "pursue personal and aesthetic growth", and the enGauge 21st Century Skills (2003) Inventive Thinking section included "adaptability, managing complexity, and self-direction." Although the research on self-directed learning has been around for several decades, the context has changed with online learning, greater access to technology, opportunities for more personalized learning experiences, and connection to information and resources that were not previously available. Schools are recognizing the importance of self-directed learning as a necessary skill needed for the 21st century as well as the need for teachers to "enhance students' abilities for accessing self-directed learning" (Chou, 2008). Self-directed learning remains a relevant life skill and requires a new examination under the current educational contexts and the opportunities provided by access to new technologies for learning.

Along with the standards and frameworks, concepts related to self-directed learning are prevalent in educational technology and leadership discussions as a way to differentiate learning, change the role of learner and teacher in the classroom, alter the time/place of learning, and potentially alter the structure of traditional schooling. New developments in 21st Century educational landscape such as online learning opportunities, shifts in pedagogy, and Internet-connected mobile device put additional expectations on all learners (not just adult learners) to take more initiative in their own learning (Teo, 2010). Similarly innovations such as Khan Academy (www.khanacademy.com) or the Flipped Classroom (vodcasting.ning.com/video/the-flipped-classroom) have sparked intrigue about the value of self-directed learning in elementary schools and consequent changes in the role of the traditional classroom teacher. In these models additional class-time is not needed for direct instructional purposes and the teacher is more available to address questions and individualize instruction. In such flipped classrooms students must be able to manage resources, demonstrate independence and be capable of self-discipline in order to be successful.

Despite this emphasis on SDL, in these frameworks and other writing, there are some significant limitations to the existing scholarship in this area. For instance, a majority of research on SDL has centered solely on adult learning – with little attention to elementary and middle school students. Moreover, much of the work has been theoretical in nature with the consequence that there are few instruments and measures for researchers to use. Finally, despite a significant level of agreement about the how technology can change the learning context, there is little work on how innovative 21st century, technology-rich classrooms can influence the development of SDL.

The remainder of the article summarizes the research on the relevance and value of 21st century learning environments to enhance the SDL of younger students. The next section focuses on the design of the study in particular describing the methods and instruments used, as well as a description of the two learning environments. Subsequent sections describe the data and analysis of both the quantitative and qualitative data collected and the findings of the analysis.

Self-Directed Learning and the Learning Environment

Current research on the development of SDL has focused both on the internal characteristics of the learners as well as the broader context the learners are situated within. For instance, Guglielmino (1977) commented that certain learning contexts are more effective at promoting self-directed learning. Confessore (1998) concluded from existing research that there is "evidence that the characteristics used to describe the learning organization are necessary ingredients for SDL to flourish." The emerging learning environments of the 21st century combine different pedagogies and technologies and provide ample reason to reexamine the opportunities for self-directed learning.

Candy (2004) suggested, that self-directed learning "provides a more direct route into understanding the actual dynamics of and relationship(s) between learning and technologies." Technology can constrain direction and focus allowing for a user to quickly seek and record relevant yet it also can be a distracting environment leading to inefficiency or reduced motivation. Technology affords incredible access for learners to connect with others, explore topics of interest, and participate in opportunities they might not otherwise engage in. In addition, technology provides vast amounts of resources in terms of information and people to serve as material for further inquiry. These affordances can also be detrimental as the vastness of resources can reduce the ability to select relevant materials or stay on target for the learning activity. The connected era creates a new need for learners to be knowledgeable about resource selection as well as the ability to manage the collection, management, and use of relevant information (Lankshear, 1997). Current digital technologies also allow for newer ways of configuring classrooms, allowing for greater flexibility to students in selection of topics to study as well as approaches to studying them (individually, collaboratively and so on). Clearly these have significant implications for the development of SDL. All this said, there has been little research and discussion of the direct impact of technology, and the manner in which it can afford and constrain SDL, particularly for younger learners. In this context, utilizing appropriate assessment tools (customized to the age and developmental level of the population of interest) based on clear definitions of self-direction can help better understand the impact of technology on self-directed behavior and skills. Focusing, in particular, on intentionally designed environments that broadly support SDL principles (such as a modified schedule to allow for longer times for projects and collaboration, pervasive access to technology, problem-solving content design, and intensive professional development for the teachers) could be informative to both theory and practice.

Research Design – Methods and Procedures

This study used a mixed-method non-equivalent group design examining the relationship between the perception of self-direct learning by students and the design of their learning environment in a middle school setting.

Site & Participants

The research centered on a new model of instruction at a high achieving middle school in a mid-to-high socioeconomic suburb northwest of Chicago, Illinois. The total population of the school exceeds 900 students and serves grade 6-8.

The new model, called Sigma team, consisted of a two-teacher instructional team serving 30 students at 6th grade. The parents of the students opted into this team after a brief overview of the structure and goals of the model. The core subjects for all teams included mathematics, language arts, science, and social science. Two staff members volunteered to take on this project and their selection was approved by the building administration. One constraint on the selection process was that the students had to choose between Spanish or Chinese as their language instruction.

The staff in this model had a lot of latitude and flexibility when it came to scheduling and grouping students. Further, the students had constant access to technology (enough laptops and iPads for each student) and Internet (with limited filters intended for supporting learning and engaging in the content). The staff members had the opportunity for professional development prior to the beginning of the school year including a national conference focusing on educational technology and specific training on understanding the TPACK model (Koehler & Mishra, 2008). One goal of this model was to leverage the flexibility to individualize learning experiences supported by technology. Specifically, the foundation of the Sigma Team was an environment that leverages technology to provide students with alternative ways to connect, collaborate, discover, engage, and reflect throughout the learning process. The opportunity for students to have constant Internet access, personal devices, flexible schedules, and a variety of experiences can lead to more self-directed learning opportunities. These opportunities were supported by connections to experts in the field, time for deeper exploration, technology tools to collect and manage information, and ability to extend the learning beyond the traditional school periods. Further, the staff members were committed to the idea that students should have an integral role in the learning process. The teachers also received significant training on both 21st century learning tools and methods in increase their technology pedagogical knowledge. The combination of teacher preparation, learning environment design, access to technology, and foundation on student ownership of learning could certainly generate meaningful self-directed choices for students to explore their interests and passions not available in other settings.

The remaining participants (in what can be called the traditional or control condition) came from the two additional teams (Alpha & Beta) at the 6th grade. Each of these teams consisted of between 140-160 students and 6 staff members. This model was a traditional team set-up at the middle school level in the school district. Each teacher was responsible for specific subject/curricular area, times of classes are fixed (38-42 minutes), and students move from once class to the next. Technology was available for these students in the form of laptop or iPad carts for checkout and access to a computer lab but not constantly with each student in each classroom. Students on these teams did not have a choice of placement on one team or the other. Similarities existed between the two environments. The same curriculum standards, assessments, materials (besides technology), general content areas and district expectations were in place for both teams. The main difference between the two team configurations was the instructional constraints such as timed class periods focused on a particular content area with more restricted access to technology. Further, the teachers in these classes had not received the same type of focused professional development experiences or time to explore related resources. Due to these factors, student did not have the same opportunities to explore areas of interest on their own, move away from a traditional scope and sequence within a topic, or spend the necessary time collaborating on the learning experiences that can proceed without the direct intervention or planning from a teacher.

Further examination of the teachers in these two environments is important in order to provide a more complete understanding of their background and past performance. Although the recent training opportunities differ, the teachers that volunteered and were selected for these roles had similar outcomes as their peers when examining prior student performance on standardized tests. In order to account and appreciate the possibility that the two teachers may inherently provide a more robust or successful educational experience regardless of environment, Measures of Academic Progress (MAP) and Illinois State Achievement Tests (ISAT) data were examined at the classroom level for the past 4 years. The teachers were thoughtfully selected based on their willingness to explore alternatives, grow professionally, and their past strong performance with students. Clearly there are numerous differences between teachers and their effects cannot be discounted. However, the dimensions outlined indicate a strong level of uniformity between the teachers in both environments.

Statement of Purpose

The described learning environment (the Sigma classroom) offers unique characteristics and design elements that distinguish it from a typical middle school classroom (The Alpha and Beta classrooms). The alternative configuration of the Sigma classroom, with a focus on 21st Century skills, alternative schedule, and increased presence of technology can provide self-directed learning opportunities and experience for students that would not take place in a traditional setting. Therefore, this study examined the relationship between the design of the learning environment (configuration, lesson design, presence of technology) and the self-directed learning perception of students.

It was anticipated that after time in the learning environment designed for 21st century learning, the students experiencing the environment would show a larger increase on the Self-Directed Learning with Technology Scale (SDLTS) than the remaining members of the 6th grade team.

Demographics

Information from the district student management system (SMS) was used to collect demographic on all sixth grade students involved in the research. The demographic data included gender, ethnicity, IEP status, gifted status, and LEP status. This information was collected to identify any distinct characteristics that differ between the team configurations (for example, much higher percentage of LEP students on team or another) that may have an impact on the interpretation of the results or observations.

Demographic data are displayed below for each of the teams. These data indicate several areas of consistency between the teams including the percentage of LEP (Limited English Proficiency), gifted, and ethnic breakdown. However, there are noticeable differences in the composition of the teams including the percentage of males and females and students with an IEP (Individualized Education Plan). The differences must be considered in all discussion of implications and generalizability.

Table 1. Demographic Information by Team Membership

Team	% Male	%Female	%IEP	%LEP	%Gifted	%White	%NonWhite
Sigma	62%	38%	0%	0%	10%	79%	21%
Alpha/Beta	49%	51%	16%	1%	9%	81%	19%

Instruments: The Self-Directed Learning with Technology Scale (SDLTS)

The majority of scales related to measuring self-directed learning focus on adult learners (Guglielmino, 1977; Oddi, 1986; Stockdale & Brockett 2010). Further, the scales generally do not specifically include technology as component in the measurement tool. Researchers from the National Institute of Education at Nanyang Technological University in Singapore developed and tested a scale that is more appropriate for younger learners and recognize the presence of technology in learning (Teo, 2010). The Self-Directed Learning with Technology Scale (SDLTS), a 6-item, two-factor was piloted and validated in their study. The two factors in the scale measure the self-management and intentional learning perception of students. This scale is relevant to this research not only because of the focus on younger learners and the inclusion of technology but also because "the results from this scale may also assist teachers in promoting a learning climate that fosters student autonomy and mutual responsibility." Overall, this measure is best suited to gather the information for the population in the current study due to the inclusion of technology and the intentional development for young students.

Data Collection and Analysis

Data collection was a three-step process to gather various information about the performance and perceptions of the learner as well as observations about the learning environment and activities.

> Step 1: Demographic information about students in the 6th grade was collected in the summer prior to the beginning of school as were the performance information based on past assessments for the 6th grade teachers. Students in the 6th grade filled out the self-directed learning with technology scale (SDLTS) in September at the beginning of the school year.
>
> Step 2: The self-directed learning with technology survey (SDLTS) was re-administered for 6th grade students for both team models in January of the same school year.
>
> Step 3: After the follow-up survey was completed, interviews were conducted (Appendix B) with six students, three on the Sigma team and three students on the Alpha/Beta teams in February. The students were selected based on their responses on the SLDTS. Two students were randomly selected from one standard deviation from the mean, two from one standard deviation above the mean, and two from one standard deviation below the mean. This selection provided a more accurate reflection of the team experience than concentrating solely on the high or low end.

Non-Equivalent Group Studies

For this study, a non-equivalent group design was used to attempt to understand the relationship between the team environment and self-directed learning. This design is very common in educational research and includes an existing group of participants who receive a treatment (Sigma team) and another existing group of participants to serve as a comparison group (Alpha/Beta members). Since the students in the Sigma group were able to opt-in, the participants were not randomly assigned to the teams (non-equivalent), but rather received different experiences, or treatments, with the others in their existing group. The goal of the Sigma team was not specifically to improve self-directedness however it must be considered whether the selection process is directly related to the outcomes on the self-directed survey. Although this is similar to correlational design with a lack of manipulation of variables and important cautions when interpreting results, the non-equivalent group design strives to compare two groups as similar as possible. In this case the students are from the same school and grade with relatively comparable demographic and achievement characteristics. Despite many similarities, it is important to understand that the groups may be different and those differences may affect outcomes.

Quantitative Data

A one-way analysis of covariance (ANCOVA) was conducted for the study. The independent variable, team membership, includes two options: Sigma and Alpha/Beta. The dependent variable was the post-test results on the SDLTS and the covariate is the pre-test results on the SDLTS (See Table 2 for summary of responses). For each question on the measurement, the interaction effect between team membership and the pre-test scores was assessed to rule out a violation of regression homogeneity assumption. Then, an ANCOVA was conducted to determine whether the post-test results on the SDLTS for the team membership groups differed after adjustments for pre-test differences. A summary of these evaluations is listed below by questions and an alpha level of .05 was used for all statistical tests. Note, a lower score means a higher degree of use.

Table 2. Student perception of self-directedness as measured by the Self-Directed Learning with Technology Survey (SDLTS)

Team	Q1		Q2		Q3	
	Pre	Post	Pre	Post	Pre	Post
	M (SD)	*M (SD)*	*M (SD)*	*M (SD)*	*M (SD)*	*M (SD)*
Sigma	5.06 (1.39)	4.70 (1.53)	4.61 (1.54)	4.26 (1.65)	3.29 (1.29)	2.83 (1.42)
Alpha/Beta	5.16 (1.38)	5.29 (1.37)	5.19 (1.30)	5.38 (1.21)	3.82 (1.52)	3.78 (1.53)

Team	Q4		Q5		Q6	
	Pre	Post	Pre	Post	Pre	Post
	M (SD)	*M (SD)*	*M (SD)*	*M (SD)*	*M (SD)*	*M (SD)*
Sigma	3.00 (1.26)	2.39 (1.38)	3.58 (1.75)	3.43 (1.36)	3.77 (1.65)	3.13 (1.57)
Alpha/Beta	3.97 (1.74)	3.83 (1.82)	4.02 (1.32)	4.44 (1.41)	4.41 (1.64)	4.23 (1.76)

Quantitative Summary

For all six questions on the SDTLS, the homogeneity-of-regression assumption is met. On five of the six questions, the null hypothesis that students on the Sigma team will score the same on the SDLTS than students on the other 6th grade teams is rejected based on the information from the ANCOVA. Therefore, the after the adjusting the group means for the pre-test performance, team membership proves significant in five of the six questions on the SDLTS. The only question where this was not significant was "6. I use the computer to get ideas from different websites and people to learn more about a topic." This may be a result of significant technology access throughout the school and several experiences using the computer to do research for various assignments in both team environments. However, the 5 remaining questions were statistically significant and indicated that the Sigma team went online to connect with their teachers outside of school time more often than the Alpha/Beta team. The results also indicated that the Sigma students were more inclined than the Alpha/Beta Team to share their ideas using the computer. Examples from the student interviews included multiple opportunities for blogging and posting work on the team Web page. The Sigma students also went to the Internet as a resource for their school work more often than the Alpha/Beta Team and were more likely to use the computer to further work with the information from their lessons or units. Although the exact use for the computer is not defined, this shows the possible extension from the content lessons to more integrated or technologically extended experiences for Sigma students. The Sigma team indicated a higher use of the computer to further develop skills of interest than the Alpha/Beta Team. Sigma teachers provided several experience based on student choice (this was recognized in the student interviews as well). This opportunity for selected interests for exploration in school may be directly related to the results of this question.

These results strongly suggest that such an open-ended technology-rich environment (as provided by the Sigma team) supports the development of self-directed learning attitudes and behaviors in middle school students. The environment was not specifically designed to increase self-directedness, *but the study shows that students in the Sigma team were more likely to connect with their teachers online and after-school, share their work and ideas online, conduct information searching to solve their own problems, and initiate skill development on topics of interests.*

Qualitative Data

The quantitative analysis showed that the Sigma team results indicated statistically significant differences in their perception of self-directed learning (for 5 of the 6 questions). This however, does not provide insight into why this happened or the nature of the student experience in each of these team settings. Additional qualitative data provided a deeper understanding of the process by which this happened. To gather more information, six students (3 from the Sigma team and 3 from the Alpha/Beta Team) were interviewed. These interviews focused on their perceptions of their experiences in the classroom, about the work they were asked to do, the relationship between teachers and students, and the use of technology. This process provided important insight that go beyond the numbers in the scale. Although they represent a small portion of the study, the comments were an important source of student viewpoints.

Quantitative Summary

The objective of recording and cataloging the interview with the students was to determine the categories that formed the students' view of the experience in the classroom. In this stage, terms were identified from the transcripts and a close examination of conceptual linkage led to a set of core concepts. Four major themes emerged from their accounts of the classroom experience of the Sigma group and the Alpha/Beta group: choice, work style, work type, and technology. The Sigma team respondents generally felt that there was plenty of choice for students including picking topics, deciding whom to work with, and alternative forms of output. These students indicated an even representation of group work and individual work, several longer-term, high interest, project-based learning experiences and constant availability to technology. The responses from the Alpha/Beta team students showed a feeling of limited options for choice noted by the students. All students commented that the teacher directed the lessons and activities. All three students noted some group work but the majority of the examples were isolated lessons or single units that students worked on individually. Finally, the students all indicated that technology was available when needed either in the room or in the computer labs. All three indicated that most of their work with technology took place in the school.

Discussion

The quantitative results indicated that after 6 months, students in the intentionally designed 21st century classroom were more self-directed on 5 of the 6 categories evaluated by the survey than the equivalent students in the traditional classroom. These categories include: online connection with teachers, increased utilization of technology throughout the process as a resource, increased self-management and intentional learning. Although both environments have strong teachers and similarly performing students, the perception of self-directed learning was strong in the environment where teachers allowed for more choice the topics, provided constant technology access, engaged in more project-based learning, and had a variety of group and individual of experiences. Not one of these factors would reasonably be used to explain the difference in performance based on this study. However, they do account for a different type of experience for both the student and the teacher. The interviews revealed a noticeable difference in assignment types, online experiences, and collaboration between students. The composition and expectations of the Sigma team design were distinct from the Alpha/Beta Team and the professional development supported those areas of focus. The qualitative and quantitative results show that a purposefully structured technology-rich learning environment can provide students with great opportunities and abilities to be self-directed in their learning.

Appendix

Items on the Self-Directed Learning with Technology Scale (SDLTS)

SDLTS is a 6-point scale, ranging from 6 for 'All the time', and 1 for 'Not at all' with two factors – self-management and intentional learning.

<u>Self-Management</u>

1. I go online to ask my teachers questions on my lessons when I am not in school.
2. I use the computer to share my thoughts and ideas about my schoolwork (e.g., through multimedia storytelling, voice-recording, blogs).

<u>Intentional Learning</u>

3. I find out more information on the Internet to help me understand my lessons better.
4. I use the computer to work with information for my learning.
5. I use the computer to become better at a skill that I am interested in e.g., learn a language.
6. I use the computer to get ideas from different websites and people to learn more about a topic.

Appendix B
Questions for Student Interviews

What types of projects did you work on in class? Types of technology?
Did you ever work on your projects outside of school? How?
Who decided what types of projects/activities you worked on?
What types of projects did you work on individually? How did you like those?
What types of projects did you work on in groups? How did you like those?
How much did the teachers tell you to do before you started a project?
What would you do if you got stuck during your work and didn't know how to move forward?
What were your favorite projects/activities so far and why?

References

Arnold, H.J., & Feldman, D.C. (1981). Social desirability response bias in self-report choice situations. *Academy of Management Journal, 24*, 377-385.

Bandura, A. (1986). *Social foundations of thought and action: A social cognitive theory.* Englewood Cliffs, NJ: Prentice-Hall.

Bartlett, J. E., & Kotrlik, J. W. (1999). Development of a self-directed learning instrument for use in work environments. *Journal of Vocational Education Research, 24*(4), 185-208.

Brockett, R. G., & Hiemstra, R. (1991). *Self-direction in adult learning: Perspectives on theory, research, and practice.* New York, NY: Routledge.

Brookfield, S. (1985). *Self-Directed Learning: From Theory to Practice.* San Francisco, CA: Jossey-Bass.

Candy, P. C. (1991). *Self-direction for lifelong learning: A comprehensive guide to theory and practice.* San Francisco, CA: Jossey-Bass.

Candy, P.C. (2004). *Linking thinking. Self-directed learning in the digital age.* Canberra: Australian Government, Department of Education, Science and Training. Retrieved from http://www.dest.gov.au/research/publications/linking_thinking/default.htm

Caffarella, R. (1993). Self-directed learning. *New Directions for Adult and Continuing Education, 57*, 25-35.

Chan, D. (2009). So why ask me? Are self report data really that bad? In Charles E. Lance and Robert J. Vandenberg (Eds.), *Statistical and methodological myths and urban legends: Doctrine, verity and fable in the organizational and social sciences* (309-335). New York, NY: Routledge.

Chou, P.-N., & Chen, W.-F. (2008). Exploratory study of the relationship between self-directed learning and academic performance in a web-based learning environment. *Online Journal of Distance Learning Administration, 11*(1).

Confessore, S. J., & Kops, W. J. (1998). Self-directed learning and the learning organization: Examining the connection between the individual and the learning environment. *Human Resource Development Quarterly, 9*(4), 365-375.

DeFreitas, S., & Oliver, M. (2006). How can exploratory learning with games and simulations within the curriculum be most effectively evaluated? *Computers & Education, 46*(1), 249-264. doi: 10.1016/j.compedu.2005.11.007.

Donaghy, R. C. (2006). "It permeates the whole fabric of your life": The experience of scholars who have studied self-directed learning. (Doctoral dissertation, The University of Tennessee, Knoxville, 2005). *Dissertation Abstracts International, 66* (7), 2462.

Ertmer, P. (1999). Addressing first- and second-order barriers to change: Strategies for technology integration. *Educational Technology Research and Development. 47*(4). 47-61.

Field, L. (1989). An Investigation Into the Structure, Validity, and Reliability of Guglielmino's Self-Directed Learning Readiness Scale. *Adult Education Quarterly, 39*(3), 125-139. doi: 10.1177/0001848189039003001.

Finestone, P. (1984). A construct validation of the Self-Directed Learning Readiness Scale with labour education participants (Doctoral dissertation, University of Toronto, 1984). *Dissertation Abstracts International, 46*, 5A.

Fischer, G., & Scharff, E. (1998). Learning Technologies in Support of Self-Directed Learning. *Journal of Interactive Media in Education, 98*(4), 1-32.

Fisher, M., King, J., & Tague, G. (2001). Development of a self-directed learning readiness scale for nursing education. *Nurse education today, 21*(7), 516-25. doi: 10.1054/nedt.2001.0589.

Gall, M. D., Borg, W. R., & Gall, J. P. (2002). Educational research: An introduction (7th ed.). White Plains, NY: Pearson/Allyn & Bacon.

Gibbons, M. (2002). *The self-directed learning handbook: Challenging adolescents to excel.* San Francisco, CA: Jossey-Bass.

Greene, J., & Azevedo, R. (2010). The measurement of learners' self-regulated cognitive and metacognitive processes while using computer-based learning environments. *Educational Psychologist, 45*(4). 203-209.

Gardner, H. (2008). *Five minds for the future.* Boston, MA: Harvard Business School Press.

Garrison, D. R. (1997). Self-directed learning: Toward a comprehensive model. *Adult Education Quarterly, 48*(1), 18-33.

Graeve, E. A. (1987). Patterns of self-directed learning of registered nurses (Doctoral dissertation, University of Minnesota, 1987). *Dissertation Abstracts International, 48*, 820.

Greene, J., & Azevedo, R. (2010). The measurement of learners' self-regulated cognitive and metacognitive processes while using computer-based learning environments, *Educational Psychologist, 45*(4), 203-209.

Guglielmino, L, M. (1977). Development of the self-directed learning readiness scale. Doctoral Dissertation. Athens, Georgia: University of Georgia.

Hassan, A. J. (1981). An investigation of the learning projects of adults of high and low readiness for self-direction learning (Doctoral dissertation, Iowa State University, 1981). *Dissertation Abstracts International, 42*, 3838A-3839A.

Hoban, D., Lawson, S., Mazmanian, P., Best, A., and Seibel, H. (2005). The self-directed learning readiness scale: A factor analysis study. *Medical Education. 39*(4), 370-379.

Hmelo-Silver, C. E. (2004). Problem-based learning: What and how do students learn?. *Educational Psychology Review, 16* (3), 235–266.

Koehler, M. J., & Mishra, P. (2008). Introducing TPACK. In J. A. Colbert, K. E. Boyd, K. A. Clark, S. Guan, J. B. Harris, M. A. Kelly, & A. D. Thompson (Eds.), *Handbook of Technological Pedagogical Content Knowledge for Educators* (pp. 1-28). Routledge.

Knowles, M. S. (1975). *Self-directed learning: A guide for learners and teachers.* New York, NY: Association Press.

Lankshear, C., Gee, J., Knobel, M., & Searle, C. (1997). *Changing literacies.* Great Britain: St Edmundsbury Press.

Miller, R. B., & Brickman, S. J. (2004). A Model of Future-Oriented Motivation and Self-Regulation. *Educational Psychology Review, 16*(1), 9-33. doi: 10.1023/B:EDPR.0000012343.96370.39.

Oddi, L. F. (1986). Development and validation of an instrument to identify self-directed continuing learners. *Adult Education Quarterly. 36*(1), 97-107.

Pink, Daniel H. (2009). *Drive: the surprising truth about what motivates us*. New York, NY: Riverhead Books.

Presser, S., Couper, M., Lessler, J., Martin, E., Martin, J., Rothgeb, J., et al. (2004). Methods for testing and evaluating survey questions. *The Public Opinion Quarterly, 68*(1), 109-130.

Stockdale, S., & Brockett, R. (2011). Development of the PRO-SDLS: A measure of self-direction in learning based on the personal responsibility orientation model. *Adult Education Quarterly, 61*(2), 161-80.

Rothenham, A., & Willingham, D. 21st century skills: The challenges ahead. *Educational Leadership. 67*(1), 16-21.

Shin J., Haynes R., & Johnston M (1993). Effect of problem-based, self-directed undergraduate education on life-long learning. *CMA, 148*(1), 969-76.

Schunk, D. H. (1985). Self-efficacy and classroom learning. *Psychology in the Schools, 22*(2), 208-223.

Spear, G. E., & Mocker, D. W. (1984). The organizing circumstance: Environmental determinants in self-directed learning. *Adult Education Quarterly, 35*(1), 1-10.

Teo, T., Tan, S. C., Lee, C. B., Chai, C. S., Koh, J. H. L., Chen, W. L., et al. (2010). The self-directed learning with technology scale (SDLTS) for young students: An initial development and validation. *Computers & Education, 55*(4), 1764-1771.

Tough, A. M. (1967). *Learning without a teacher.* Toronto, CA: Ontario Institute for Studies in Education.

Zhao, Y. (2009). *Catching up or leading the way: American education in the age of globalization*. Alexandria, VA: ASCD.

Zsiga, P., & Webster, M. (2007). Why should secondary educators be interested in self-directed learning*? International Journal of Self-Directed Learning, 4*(2), 58-67.

13 Helping or Hindering? Technology's Impact on Secondary Students' Self-Regulated Learning

Prue Salter, University of Technology Sydney, Australia

Introduction

Zimmerman (2002) explains that self-regulated learning (SRL) relates to the degree to which students are metacognitively, motivationally, and behaviourally active participants in the learning process. There is widespread agreement that self-regulatory processes are an important factor influencing levels of student achievement (Zimmerman & Martinez-Pons, 1986, 1988). There is also consensus that self-regulation is not a specific personality trait that students either do or do not possess. Nor is it a mental ability or particular academic performance skill. Instead it is a selective use of strategies by which learners transform their mental processes into academic skills adapted to individual learning tasks (Zimmerman, 2002).

The focus of self-regulation research has been on defining and measuring SRL, and subsequently, exploring experimental targeted in-class interventions to foster SRL. However, there is little understanding of how, or indeed if, contemporary secondary schools are approaching SRL development from a broader whole-school perspective.

In Australia there is no nationwide 'self-regulated learning curriculum' or a policy on how schools should approach the development of self-regulation skills. The Australian Government Department of Education, Employment and Workplace Relations website covering school education states "Australia's future depends on a high quality and dynamic school education system to provide students with foundation skills, values, knowledge and understanding necessary for lifelong learning, employment and full participation in society" (Commonwealth of Australia, 2010). However, foundation skills are not defined and, while there are policies for Numeracy and Literacy, 'learning-to-learn' or self-regulation skills are not addressed. As there is not a consistent policy in Australian secondary schools towards the development of these skills, approaches taken by schools vary widely with a notable lack of school-wide procedures. This means that there is no guarantee that the needs of students who enter secondary schools without the necessary 'learning-to-learn' skills will be met. Zimmerman (2002) discusses the increased demands facing students in high school and states "many students respond to these increasing demands for self-regulation by adopting effective learning strategies, but a significant number of students do not adopt them" (p.3).

Technology and Self-Regulated Learning

SRL has been described as one of the key competencies contributing to maintaining life-long learning skills (EU Council, 2002). Almost two decades ago, Weinstein (1996) raised the point that self-regulation is becoming increasingly important as we move towards technologically driven self-directed learning environments where greater amounts of autonomous learning are necessary. There has been much exploration into the changing nature of the skills needed for students to achieve their academic potential at school given modern curriculum changes, new understandings about the learning process, and the increasing use of technology for learning both at school and home (Palfrey & Gasser, 2009). Anderson and Balsamo (2007) advocate that today's students "require new literacies: cultural, technological, social, and epistemological" (p.245). This suggests that the self-regulated learning strategies needed by today's students may be different from the traditional skills focused on in previous decades.

Anderson and Balsamo (2007) paint a picture of a possible 2020 classroom and pose the question: "How should these institutions change to address this generational disposition?" (p.245). For example, the skills needed to be 'organized' will be very different for a student using papers and folders, as opposed to a student now using a laptop or tablet for their notes. This leads to the question as to whether current approaches to meeting the needs of students as self-regulated learners are still valid.

Previous thinking was that the nature of a self-regulated learner was essentially solitary. Entwistle and McCune (2004) explain that much greater prominence is now being given to collaboration, particularly using Web 2.0 technologies. Indeed, Sharples, Taylor and Vavoula (2007) see education in the mobile age as a way to extend the support of learning beyond the boundaries of the classroom.

Challenges faced by students have also undergone transformation. The incompatibility of (modern) achievement values and (post-modern) well-being values in a post-industrialized society, and the limited opportunities for students to integrate these values (Fries & Dietze, 2007), result in increasing conflicts for students: to do schoolwork or engage in leisure activities. With a wider range of potential distractions available, as well as less parental supervision and control, well-developed self-regulation skills are vital for this generation.

The Study

This doctoral study explores, through the lens of SRL, the whole-school approach of an Australian secondary school to improving student learning outcomes. The study examines stakeholders' attitudes, beliefs, and experiences of SRL in contemporary secondary education and analyzes the role of the school in developing self-regulated learners. The main research questions were:

1. How can secondary schools embrace a whole-school practice approach to developing self-regulated learners?
2. What can we learn from stakeholders' attitudes, beliefs, experiences and perceptions around the development of SRL?
3. How is technology impacting students' self-regulated learning skills development?

This paper focuses on data addressing research question 3.

A social cognitive perspective was deemed to be appropriate for this research, underpinned by Bandura's (1986) view of SRL as a triadic model of personal, behavioral and environmental processes. Secondary school settings provide a suitable social learning environment for investigating these processes.

A mixed-methods methodological approach was used in this interpretive study. This approach allowed the school strategies and attitudes to SRL development to be examined in context, leading to a richer, deeper understanding of the phenomena (Denzin & Lincoln, 2005) while also benefiting from the insights available from quantitative analysis.

Data was obtained across two phases. Phase 1 was an initial online survey of Years 7-12 schools in the Sydney metro region to aid in preliminary data collection and to facilitate case selection. Findings relating to the data obtained by the 54 schools that completed the Phase 1 online survey are reported in Salter (2012). Phase 2 was a case study and the focus of this paper. The case school was selected as a purposeful sample (Patton, 2002) due to the interesting and proactive approaches taken by the school to fostering SRL.

To obtain multiple perceptions and verify interpretations (Stake, 2005), the case study research for Phase 2 used the following methods: online questionnaires for students, parents and teachers, semi-structured interviews of teachers and school executives, observations and document gathering. The data collection was spread across the 2012 school year in order to allow time to incrementally analyze the data and let each stage inform the next (Merriam, 2009). Data was analyzed thematically.

This paper focuses on findings emerging from analysis of the Phase 2 case study online survey data, exploring student and parent perceptions of how technology is impacting the area of SRL. From a student body of 950, 256 (27%) students (age range 12-18) voluntarily completed the online anonymous survey of five open-ended questions and 59 parents also participated. As part of this 5 item online survey, participants were asked: "How do you think technology is impacting the area of self-regulated learning?". A pilot survey was implemented to test the rigor of the survey instruments and feedback led to the following explanation being added to this question: "Some of the areas to consider might be: Is technology changing the skills needed for students to be self-regulated learners? Can technology be used to support the development of self-regulated learning skills? Is technology impacting on any other areas of self-regulated learning for students?".

Case Background

Students at this co-educational school have traditionally been perceived by teachers as having low self-efficacy and low motivation for their academic studies. Six years ago a new Principal began to instigate widespread changes across the school. For the first time in 2011, the school reached State average in their overall Year 12 Higher School Certificate results and teachers are noticing positive changes in student approaches to learning.

In terms of technology the school has around 600 Mac laptops (for a student body of 950) with laptops being assigned to teachers who then use them with their classes. In addition to this many students bring their own laptop or tablet to school. While a number of teachers have embraced technology in their classroom with, for example, the creation of Apps, exploring iBook authoring, or the use of Wikis or robotics work, many have not or are using technology in more traditional ways such as Powerpoint presentations. The school overall is becoming more relaxed and accepting of the use of personal devices, for example allowing students to take photos of the board with their phone in class. All teachers have had to become competent in the use of Engrade, an online database where parents and students can see student markbooks, comments and attendance information. Engrade also acts as a learning management system, with chat and email facilities that students and parents can use to contact teachers.

Findings

Findings emerging from analysis of the online survey data demonstrated that while the majority of the student and parent respondents expressed positive perceptions of the impact of technology on SRL, students are not leveraging technology to its potential as a learning tool. The majority of students viewed the impact of technology as a speedier and more convenient research tool, with few students taking advantage of the opportunities available in existing and emerging technologies for communication and new approaches to studying. Students and parents were concerned about how much of a distraction from studies technology had proven to be, while parents also had a myriad of other concerns from the loss of handwriting skills to technology dependence. By understanding student and parent perspectives, educators can provide the support needed to ensure students can make informed decisions about their technology use as a learning tool.

Students' Perceptions of the Impact of Technology on SRL

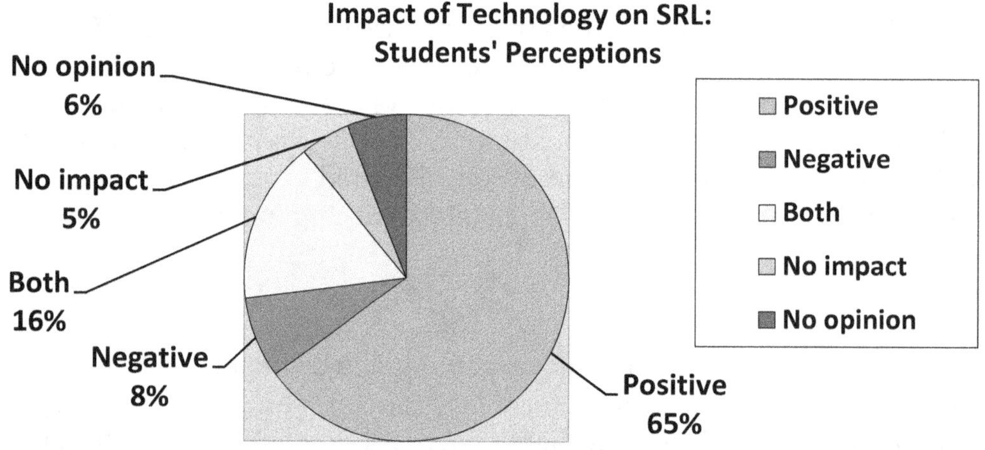

Figure 1: Students' perceptions of the impact of technology on SRL

Of the 256 students who responded to the survey, 65% expressed only positive viewpoints on the way technology was impacting on them as self-regulated learners, while 8% outlined only negative impacts. A number of students could see both sides with 16% expressing both positive and negative responses. A small number, 5% only, stated they did not believe technology has any impact on the area of SRL. The remainder, 6%, did not express an opinion.

Students' Perceptions of Negative Impacts

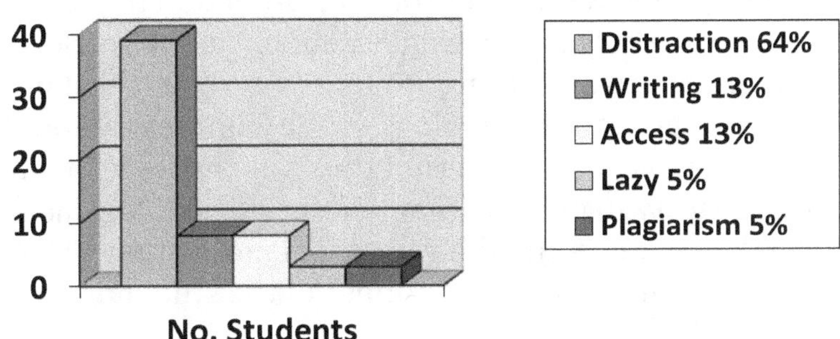

Figure 2: Students' perceptions of the negative impact of technology on SRL

There was a range of reasons expressed as to why students believed that technology was having a negative impact on the area of SRL, however common themes emerged. A few students (5% of the negative responses) stated that technology "is making me lazy". Other students (5% of the negative responses) raised the issue of plagiarism, explaining that "some students just 'copy and paste' rather than putting it in their own words". Some students (13% of the negative responses) were concerned about the inequity that could arise due to unavailability of technology for all students or students with poor technological skills. Two typical responses were: "These days if you don't have the Internet you are at a huge disadvantage" and "some students are not confident in using technology". A student explained that submitting work online "can be daunting for others if they are not tech savvy" and "problems always occur with sending and compatibility with other computers".

The effect on handwriting skills was a concern raised by a number of students (13% of the negative responses). The loss of handwriting skills was seen to be an issue for the external examinations in the final year of school. Students saw handwriting skills to be critical, ensuring they can write neatly and quickly for the examinations that contribute to their university entrance rank. One student explained: "Many have become dependent on technology way too much, which is impacting on their writing skills, spelling, grammar, punctuation and research skills". Another student pointed out the shorthand text abbreviations used by students, viewing this as detrimental to their writing skills. Zimmerman (2002) explains that self-regulated learners select and create environments to optimize learning, and from these student responses it seems students see handwriting skills as an important component of the learning environment.

Despite this range of concerns, the overwhelming response (64% of the negative responses) indicated that technology was perceived as a distraction from students' studies, making it challenging for students to work effectively as self-regulated learners. While many students simply stated blankly that technology was a major distraction (often with added emphasis!), some students discussed their addiction to technology and how it was preventing them from concentrating and focusing on their work, both at school and in the classroom. For example, one student explained: "Students only think about technology". Social networking was frequently mentioned as leading to procrastination and students moving off task: "It is affecting our marks because of Facebook" and "technology does impact my learning as social networking websites have become an addiction to the routine of someone in my age group". The school's policy of blocking Facebook on the school network was pointed out by one respondent to be helping students who abuse technology. There was an awareness that it was not inherently technology or the "limitless amounts of entertainment and leisure activities" available on the Internet that was the issue. It was interesting that one student had the maturity to observe that whether technology has a negative impact on SRL "depends on the students and their personal motivation". The following response captures the predominant feeling of a number of the students:

> For me personally, and I'll be honest, technology has gotten in the way of my learning at school. Sometimes I don't get to do my homework or assignments until later on because technology has greatly distracted me. It's a hinder and a blessing in one, to be honest.

Students' Perceptions of Positive Impacts

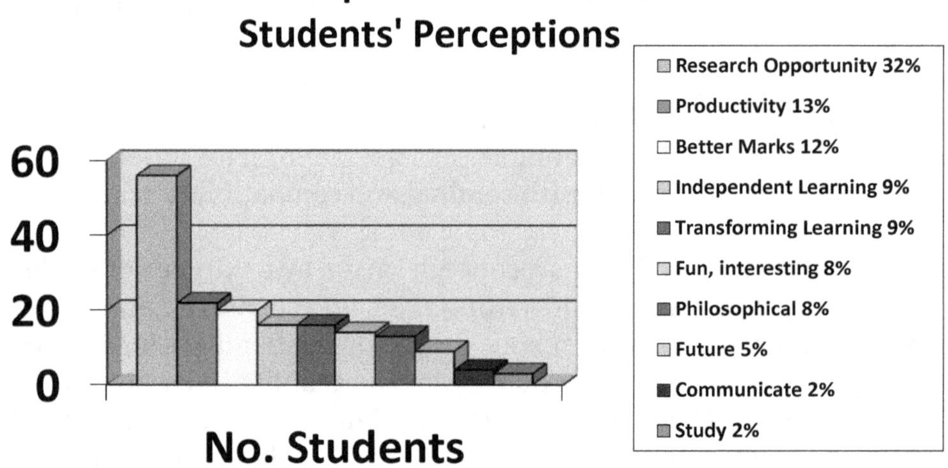

Figure 3: Students' perceptions of the positive impact of technology on SRL

Despite the strong evidence that many students struggled with the distracting elements of technology, the positive responses told a different story:

> I believe that the use of technology has had a good effect on me personally because I find myself working much better. The teachers may have noticed

> that technology is keeping a lot of the students more on task most of the time.

Yet another student could see the opportunities to become a more self-regulated learner: "By learning to ignore such distractions, most notably Facebook, I believe one builds a stronger self-regulating learning routine in turn benefiting one in the long run".

'Ease of research' and 'timely access to information' were commonly reported benefits (32% of the positive responses). One student explained: "Technology allows us to have better access to information that in turn will help speed up the process of learning, communicating and sharing".

Students looked beyond the compulsory work for school, viewing technology as allowing them to access further knowledge on topics of interest: "The Internet if used correctly can be a big asset of our daily learning. It allows us to seek more in-depth explanations and knowledge". Without technology, this research would be more difficult and time-consuming, likely requiring a trip to the library, and thus, most likely, not undertaken. One student explained a perceived benefit: "Technology allows us to research our own topics independently allowing us to scout our own information".

The ability to work independently with technology was only a minor theme (9% of the positive responses) with students explaining "it teaches us to learn for ourselves and to become more independent". Students liked that they could discover and learn on their own "without the teacher spoon-feeding you", encouraging students to "develop work in our own way". They also liked the flexibility, students could "continue learning within our homes" and use it wherever they were with minimal assistance. One student pointed out that "much of the classwork is going online which is good as it can be easily accessed at home at any given time".

The value to productivity was also highlighted (13% of the positive responses), with students citing the speed and ease at which they could retrieve information and also use technology to be more organized, for example putting due dates into their phone. One student observed: "Technology is impacting SRL because our generation does heavily rely on it to keep us updated and remind us about certain things".

Surprisingly few students (8% of the positive responses) mentioned the value of technology was that it was fun or engaging or more interesting. It seems students can look beyond technology as a toy and see the value for learning. Most responses indicated that the value of technology being 'fun' was that "the use of laptops and projectors have made learning easier and transformed from a boring way to a fun and more practical way" keeping students interested in what they were learning.

A smaller number of students (5% of the positive responses) were aware of the possible benefits in their future of mastering present day technology with one student explaining the benefits: "Learning how to work through a new set of skills which will benefit us in the future". Students viewed the use of technology as training them for skills they may need later in life or in the workplace explaining: "It is helping us keep up with the developing world and allows us to expand our horizons to see more".

Students also recognized that technology had transformed the way they experience their classes at school, for example: “Teachers are able to broaden their teaching activities”. Videos and images and interactive activities were given as examples of ways students could now better understand what is being taught or gain a different perspective on concepts. There were a number of comments (9% of the positive responses) indicating that technology “has changed the learning environment at our school”.

While a number of students (12% of the positive responses) referred to technology as helping them get better marks, there was no explanation as to how technology was providing this benefit. Perhaps students simply assumed it was obvious and no explanation necessary? Interestingly a few students stated it would decrease marks (due to being a distraction).

Unexpectedly few students (2% of the positive responses) mentioned the benefits of technology as a communication tool allowing them to find assistance if they need it. One student mentioned that “it is giving students the option to contact friends about work” but none of the students discussed contacting teachers, despite there being an online mechanism in place at this school (Engrade) to allow students to do so. Similarly only a few students (2% of the positive responses) mentioned that they now use technology to help them study for a test “we now can use our laptop at lunch time to study for up-coming tests”.

Some students (8% of the positive responses) answered the question with statements about their belief around the role of technology, for example: “Technology is not changing the skills I need, it helps me to improve on my skills by being another way to learn things” and “technology allows people to present their work in new, creative ways and also to learn in new ways”.

While many could see both positive and negative aspects, the majority of students had firm and decided opinions. There were only a small number of students who seemed indifferent in their opinions.

Parents’ Perceptions of the Impact of Technology on SRL

Comparison of Parents' and Students' Perceptions
of the Impact of Technology on SRL

80
60
40
20
0

% of Students
% of Parents

Positive
Negative
Both
No impact
No opinion

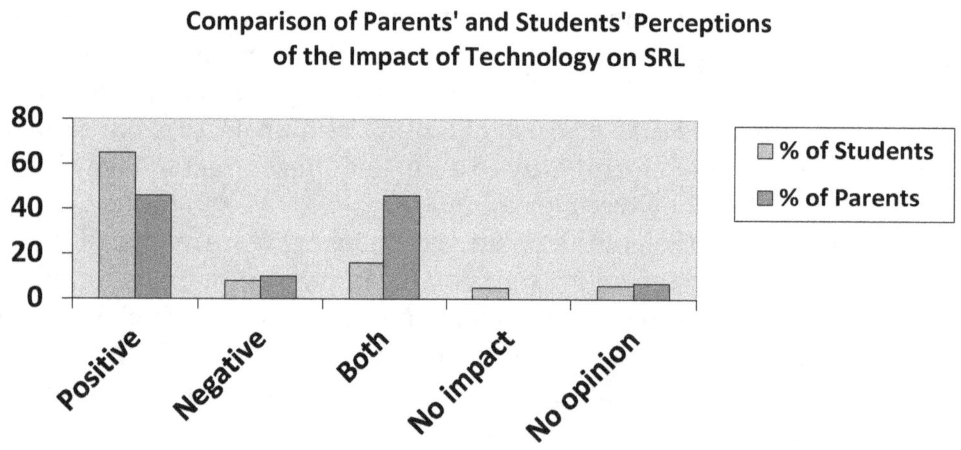

Figure 4: Comparison of parents’ and students’ perceptions of the impact of technology on SRL

A similar percentage of parents, 10%, (compared to 8% of students) expressed reservations that technology was having a negative impact on SRL, while 46% (compared to 65% of students) expressed a positive view and 7% of parents either did not express a view or stated that they did not know ("absolutely no idea"). Over double of the parents 37% (compared to 16% of students) could see both positive and negative impacts. While most students had a definite opinion, parents were often unsure or divided in their opinion of the impact of technology on SRL, and more able to see both sides of the issue, for example one parent stated: "The use of technology in the educational system is a double edged sword".

Parents' Perceptions of Negative Impacts

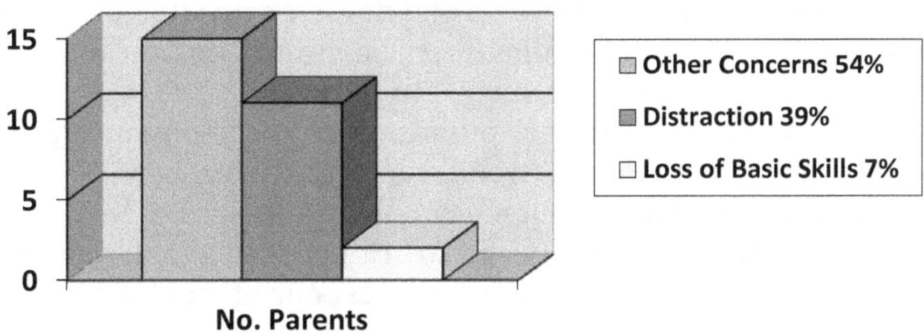

Figure 5: Parents' perceptions of the negative impact of technology on SRL

The following response captures the feelings of a number of parents who responded: "As much as I love technology, I also fear what technology could do to our children".

Parents definitely had a number of concerns around the use of technology as a tool to support students as self-regulated learners. The feeling that technology was making it difficult for students to be self-regulated learners as it was proving to be a distraction was an issue for over double the percentage of parents as compared to students (39% of negative parent responses compared to 15% of negative student responses). Parents had found that technology was a "hindrance to maintaining focus", students tended to stray off task with one parent explaining:

> Sometimes the student will be side-tracked whilst on technology and not much learning is achieved. I also find that it is taking a lot longer to complete tasks as friends are contacting without my knowledge while it is study time.

Parents seemed at a loss to know how to manage this situation: "Students are spending more time in Facebook and other social network sites. School/Parent need to have some guidelines on how to use these sites productively or limit their use".

While students focused on the loss of handwriting skills, this was just one of what parents referred to as "basic skills" that parents were concerned are being lost. A number of parents (7% of the negative responses) were concerned that technology use was impacting negatively on more traditional skills such as spelling while other parents were concerned about the impact on areas such as creativity: "I think technology could reduce a student's ability to create original thoughts and apply them in writing".

With the student responses there were a limited range of concerns emerging, however the parents raised a widespread set of issues. For example, the ease of access to information. As mentioned by students, parents were concerned this would make students lazy, that it "inhibits or stifles the get-up-and-go to meet and discover the practical reality of learning as an experience". Technology and in particular the internet was seen to be a band-aid solution by students with respect to their research needs: "Google makes finding information simple and "cut/paste" is just too easy to do and doesn't help students absorb information". The issue was raised that students sometimes just grab an answer off the web, without doing background readings to gain an insight into the topic.

Other areas of negative impact discussed were pitfalls regarding anonymity, privacy and discretion, the expense, reduced interaction between students and teachers, dependence on technology and lack of resilience when technology fails, lack of scaffolding for technology use, student perception of technology as a toy rather than a tool, constant changes and difficulty in keeping up, over-reliance on what is just one of many different tools – all of these concerns were raised.

Parents' Perceptions of Positive Impacts

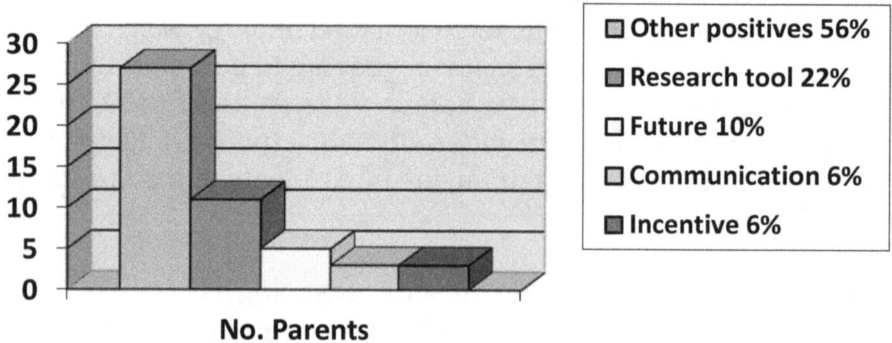

Figure 6: Parents' perceptions of the positive impact of technology on SRL

As with the students, the main advantage of technology for SRL was seen to be as a research tool (cited by 22% of positive parent responses and 32% of positive student responses). While students focused more on the ease of use and speed of accessing research materials, parents also pointed out the advantage of having current information, a contrast for some maybe to the days of printed encyclopedias, and perhaps something taken for granted by students. A number of parents also pointed out that the Internet allows students access to multiple sources of information, allowing them a wider scope to their research.

Like the students, parents (10% of the positive responses) also pointed out the importance of students being kept up-to-date with technological skills they may need in the future. There was also satisfaction in making communication easier (6% of the positive responses) and in particular the introduction of Engrade which allows parents to stay informed about their student's progress: "Engrade is our online service for parents and students to check their progress in class. Students can self-assess and ask for help from teachers if needed with the click of a button".

A few parents (6% of the positive responses) discussed how technology gave students a greater incentive to learn: "it is making the students a lot more independent...working with technology seems to make them want to learn...they enjoy using computers". One parent commented that "I love how technology is used, I love how the students can be creative with schoolwork".

Other positive impacts were giving students equal opportunity to learn, reducing the amount of textbooks they need to carry to school, making planning easier and allowing students to support each other through Facebook.

Discussion and Conclusions

The majority of students and parents at this school see technology as a tool to empower self-regulated learners, with the ease of access to information in a time and manner of their choosing. This in turn enhances student perceptions of self-control and efficacy, building positive self-perceptions that contribute to the motivational basis for self-regulation during learning.

The use of technology to assist in research was widely overshadowed by those who cited the principal benefit was that technology was purely for 'fun'. Students appreciated the opportunities for research and acknowledged that the speed and ease of use led to individual investigations beyond the limits of the curriculum. Anderson and Balsamo (2007) refer to the concept of 'just-in-time' learners. Past experiences have given these students the confidence that when they need to spontaneously locate information, they will find it. The findings demonstrate that technology has assisted these students to become more self-regulated in their learning, despite the challenges technology may also present.

While it is encouraging to see some students espousing many of the perceived benefits of technology that educators have long aimed for, such as the ability to work independently, it was surprising that a larger number of students did not articulate this in their responses.

Despite the overwhelmingly positive perception of the role of technology in SRL, there were a number of concerns raised in this study. The loss of handwriting skills will continue to be of concern while students need to take pen and paper examinations that determine their university entrance possibilities. Educators need plans in place to ensure handwriting issues are addressed and that these plans are communicated to the parent body to alleviate parental concerns. Equitable access to technology is also an issue that some schools may need to address.

It is clear that students need more assistance in developing strategies to manage the balance between technology used for school work, and technology used for social purposes. While the lines between these may be blurring (students using Facebook to ask friends a question about an assignment), the data reveals that many students are struggling to control their addiction to certain forms of technology: from Facebook, to gaming, to simple web surfing. Ebner, Nagler and Schön (2012) found that students of today are more addicted than ever to Web technologies. Parents are at a loss as to how to manage this issue. As this is something that is happening outside of school hours, it is an area that does not tend to be addressed by educators. In order to help students become more self-regulated in their learning, we need to provide our students with practical support in how to deal with technological distractions (Palfrey & Gasser, 2009).

The research also highlighted areas where the school has an opportunity to further develop students' use of technology in underutilized areas, for example, as a study tool and/or a communication tool. Charsky et.al (2009) explain that even millennials need training in how to use technology as a communication tool that can facilitate teamwork.

As reported elsewhere (Salter, 2012), Phase 1 of this study identified four common approaches across schools taken to developing SRL: explicit teaching in welfare programs, curriculum integration, use of mentors, and a technological approach. However the use of technology-mediated processes focused only on the school intranet, class portal, or Moodle as a tool for helping students become self-regulated. The findings emerging from analysis of the Phase 2 case study online survey data, outlined in this paper, demonstrate that schools need to educate students about ways to use technology (as a learning and communication tool), and manage technology (when it proves to be a distraction), to further foster SRL. Perhaps educators have not seen the need to provide this guidance due to now questionable assumptions of the net generation as technically savvy digital natives (Bennett, Maton & Kervin, 2008). However this research indicates that students are not necessarily using technology in such diverse and innovative ways as might be expected. Empowering students towards a broader engagement with technology will play an important role in a whole-school approach or framework to developing SRL.

References

Anderson, S., & Balsamo. A. (2007). A Pedagogy for Original Synners. In T. McPherson, (Ed.), *Digital Youth, Innovation, and the Unexpected,* The John D. and Catherine T. MacArthur Foundation Series on Digital Media and Learning (pp.241-259). Cambridge, MA: MIT Press.

Bandura, A. (1986). *Social foundations of thought and action: A social cognitive theory.* Englewood Cliffs, N.J.: Prentice-Hall.

Bennett, S., Maton, K., & Kervin, L. (2008). The 'digital natives' debate: A critical review of the evidence. *British Journal of Educational Technology, 39(5),* 775-786.

Charsky, D., Kish, M., Briskin, J., Hathaway, S., Walsh, K., & Barajas, N. (2009). Millennials Need Training Too: Using Communication Technology to Facilitate Teamwork. *TechTrends: Linking Research & Practice to Improve Learning, 53(6),* 42-48.

Commonwealth of Australia (2010). Department of Education, Employment and Workplace Relations. Retrieved July 16, 2010, from http://www.deewr.gov.au/Schooling/Pages/overview.aspx

Denzin, N.K., & Lincoln, Y.S. (2005). *The Sage handbook of qualitative research* (3rd ed.). Thousand Oaks, CA : Sage Publications.

Ebner, M., Nagler, W. & Schön, M. (2012). Have They Changed? Five Years of Survey on Academic Net-Generation. In T. Amiel & B. Wilson (Eds.), *Proceedings of World Conference on Educational Multimedia, Hypermedia and Telecommunications 2012* (pp. 343-353). Chesapeake, VA: AACE. Retrieved 15 October 2012 from http://www.editlib.org/p/40766.

Entwistle, N., & McCune, V. (2004). The Conceptual Bases of Study Strategy Inventories. *Educational Psychological Review, 16*(4), 325-345.

EU Council. (July 2002). Council resolution of 27 June 2002 on life-long learning. *Official Journal of the European Communities, 9.*

Fries, S. & Dietze, E. (2007). Learning with temptations present: The case of motivational Education. *Journal of Experimental Education, 76*(1), 93-112.

Merriam, S.B. (2009). *Qualitative Research: A Guide to Design and Implementation.* San Francisco : Jossey-Bass Publishers.

Palfrey, J. & Gasser, U. (2009). Mastering multitasking. *Educational Leadership, 66*(6), 14-19.

Patton, M.Q. (2002). *Qualitative research & evaluation methods* (3rd ed.). Thousand Oaks, CA: Sage Publications.

Salter, P. (2012). Developing Self-Regulated Learners in Secondary Schools. *Proceedings of Joint International Conference of the Australian Association for Research in Education (AARE)*

and the Asia Pacific Educational Research Association (APERA). Sydney, Australia: University of Sydney.

Sharples, M., Taylor, J., & Vavoula, G. (2007). A Theory of Learning for the Mobile Age. In R. Andrews and C. Haythornthwaite (Eds.), *The Sage Handbook of Elearning Research* (pp. 221-247). London: Sage.

Stake, R.E. (2005), Qualitative Case Studies. In Denzin, N.K. & Lincoln, Y.S., *Handbook of Qualitative Research*, (3rd ed). Thousand Oaks : Sage Publications.

Weinstein, C.E. (1996) Self-Regulation: A commentary on directions for future. *Learning and Individual Differences, 8*(3), 269--274.

Zimmerman, B. J. (2002) Becoming a self-regulated learner: An overview. *Theory into Practice, 41*(2), 64-72.

Zimmerman, B.J., & Martinez-Pons, M. (1986). Development of a Structured Interview for Assessing Students Use of Self-regulated Learning Strategies. *American Educational Research Journal, 23*, 614-628.

Zimmerman, B.J., & Martinez-Pons, M. (1988). Construct Validation of a strategy model of student self-regulated learner. *Journal of Educational Psychology, 80(3)*, 284-290.

PART 3 GAMIFICATION

14 Play As You Learn: Gamification as a Technique for Motivating Learners

Ian Glover, Sheffield Hallam University, United Kingdom.

Introduction

Learning is an active process and, as with all active processes, it requires motivation to both begin and continue the process. In young learners, motivation to learn is often readily available, but it can wane in older learners, and this is especially the case when an element of self-direction and autonomy is required (OECD, 2000). Rollings and Adams (2003, p.34) define a game as *"a form of participatory, or interactive, entertainment"* and contrast this with passive activities, such as watching television or reading. As learning is a participatory process, it follows that there could be greater benefits from incorporating games concepts with education than with these other, passive activities.

Games, especially computer games, often excel in creating an illusion of autonomy from a highly structured set of rules. Juul (2003) provides a more detailed definition of a game, which makes the correlation with a learning process even more explicit: *"A game is a rule-based formal system with a variable and quantifiable outcome, where different outcomes are assigned different values, the player exerts effort in order to influence the outcome, the player feels attached to the outcome, and the consequences of the activity are optional and negotiable."* Many of the elements listed in this definition are directly comparable to elements within formal learning, from '*variable and quantifiable outcomes*' (grades) to the effort required by the learner ('player') to affect the outcome (gain a particular grade). A significant difference, however, is in the final clause, as the consequences of learning are typically more concrete and long lasting, for example failing within a formal learning process can have detrimental effects on the learner's future.

The idea that effortful activity encourages motivation and engagement is fundamental to gamification, which has been defined as *"the use of video game elements (rather than full-fledged games) to improve user experience and user engagement in non-game services and applications"* (Deterding et al., 2011a). This is a reliable definition in many instances, such as those related to learning; however, the concept is broader in that it is not necessary for the elements to be derived solely from video games - the use of elements from playground or board games would be equally valid. Gamification typically makes use of the competition instinct possessed by most people to motivate and encourage 'productive' behaviours (and, as a result, discourage 'unproductive' ones). However, it would be a mistake to assume that it is solely an individualistic concept, as the same mechanisms can be used to encourage collaborative and cooperative behaviours. While gamification has been particularly embraced by organisations seeking to encourage the creation of online communities, it has also been applied to situations beyond the scope of this computing-focused definition, including encouraging people to perform administrative tasks, exercise, or visit retail outlets. Gamification has the potential to be a 'disruptive innovation' in education, that is, an emergent change that can alter practices in a positive way (Christensen & Raynor, 2003).

Deterding et al. (2011b) claim that the first documented use of the term 'Gamification' was in 2008 within the digital media sector, but it has since been used in many different domains as the concepts become more pervasive, and so, more familiar. Some of the core concepts have been used for much longer than the term has existed. It has long been used in early years teaching, with 'gold stars' next to a student's name on a poster being a familiar feature of many classrooms, yet this motivational technique has been little used beyond primary education. Educational gamification is a method that could encourage some of the same sense of pride and achievement in learners of all ages.

Educational Gamification is not to be confused with Game-based Learning, Simulation, or Serious Games. These focus on creating games (and game-like experiences) which impart an educational benefit, and includes software such as simulators. This is the direct opposite of educational gamification, which seeks to add game-like concepts to a learning process.

Core Game Concepts

To understand gamification it is necessary to understand the core concepts of games. There are three basic parts in most games: goal-focussed activity, reward mechanisms, and progress tracking (Dickey, 2005). Each of these is briefly described below; however, it is clear from the broad labels that there is a significant correlation between the design of games and of learning activities.

Goal-focused activity

Smith-Robbins (2011) points out that activities in games are typically goal-oriented with a clearly defined set of 'win' conditions and a number of obstacles to overcome in order to complete the activity (Figure 1). From this definition, it is clear to see the similarity between games and learning, with players/learners being directed to undertake tasks in order to achieve a desired outcome, moving to the next level/mission in the case of a game, or complete understanding a complex topic in the case of education (Ames, 1990; Pintrich, 2003). This shared focus on achieving specific goals is a major reason for the applicability of gamification to education. Goals that lead to mastery of a topic or skill (as opposed to ones that focus on performance targets) have been shown to increase the amount of time spent on learning tasks, especially when the difficulty level is high, and so lead to increased engagement and motivation (Ames, 1992). For performance-related goals, motivation is increased when there is public recognition of achievement (such as by the use of class rankings), though actual learning may be unaffected (Meece et al., 2006).

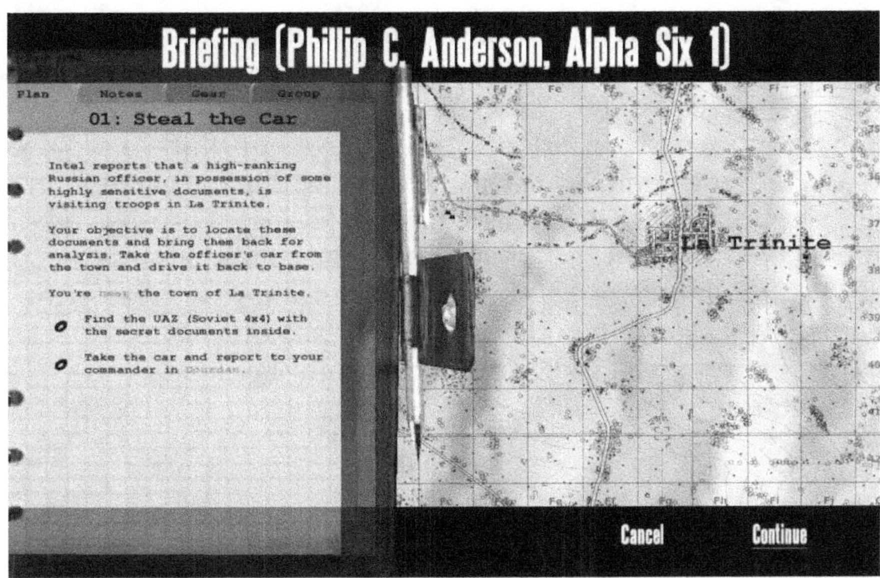

Figure 1: Mission Goals (on left) in Operation Flashpoint.

Reward Mechanisms

Games make use of many different reward mechanisms, depending on the context, but three main categories typically evident: Leaderboards, Prizes, and Achievements.

Leaderboards

As the name suggests, these are lists of players ranked according to their success within the game. The same concept is used within sport, but it is prominently used in multiplayer games, especially ones that use rounds of a fixed time or objective (Figure 2). A Leaderboard is a very coarse-grained technique as it lends itself to repetitive actions, but it can be a powerful motivator (though it provides little further motivation once the top of the leaderboard is reached). The leaderboard is typically used in competitive activities but can also be used to encourage teamwork.

Figure 2: Battlefield 3 End-of-Round Leaderboard.

Prizes

Computer games often feature customisation elements that allow players to adapt their character to their preferred playing style or personalise their character's appearance. This helps to make the player more engaged with the character and deliver a more tailored playing experience. In games that feature customisation options, the opportunity to acquire special items is typically linked to the completion of particular tasks within the game, and the desirability of the item motivates players to undertake these tasks. Prizes can also take the form of additional activities, which are unlocked after meeting the conditions of previous goals. Different players will be motivated by different prizes and so will perform activities accordingly, and learners will also vary in this way. Prizes should encourage further engagement, such as setting a research task for the cohort, and should not discourage it, such as being exempt from a test.

Achievements

Achievements are icons displayed publicly on online profiles that highlight activities completed by the person, and allow an individual to keep track of what they have done and to 'show off' to third parties. They can be seen as a combination of the two other mechanisms and have recently become popular in many domains due to their inclusion in popular recent games consoles. Beyond gaming, they have also been used to motivate people to do other activities, such as exercise (Figure 3), complete their share of household tasks (for example, Chore Wars [http://www.chorewars.com]) or maintain brand loyalty (such as FourSquare [http://www.foursquare.com]). A somewhat outdated example of this in education would be the top performing student being made 'head boy/girl' or 'class prefect'. The 'gold star' example would also fit into this reward category.

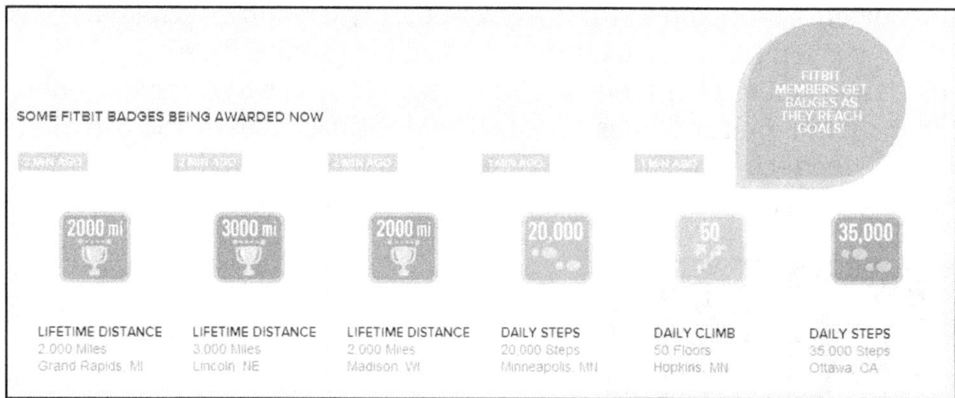

Figure 3: Achievement Badges Awarded to FitBit Users for Exercising (http://www.fitbit.com)

Progress Tracking

As with learning processes, tracking progress toward goals is important within games, because it would otherwise be impossible to identify the remaining tasks required to fulfil the victory conditions. Some of this tracking can be inferred from the reward mechanisms, but this is a very crude measure and many games have ways to quickly identify tasks have and have not been completed, and general play statistics. This method of progress tracking is somewhat analogous to the provision of feedback within education. Good feedback should outline what the learner has done and give guidance on how to improve or advance in the future, and progress tracking within games performs a similar duty by identifying the steps to take in order to make it to the next milestone.

Existing uses of Gamification

One of the most widely-known uses of Gamification is FourSquare, a mobile social networking application that encouraged users to 'check-in' to locations, with the person with most check-ins in the last 60 days being named 'Mayor' of that location. Other features include gaining points for check-ins and completed activities, and receiving 'badges', all of which can be displayed publicly. Many of these features make use of leaderboards to display people's activity, and the main reason for users is a sense of prestige. Some businesses provide additional incentives, such as discounts and gifts to people checking into their location, helping to further encourage consumer loyalty.

Red Critter Tracker (http://redcrittertracker.com) is an online project management system that rewards team members with points and badges for completing tasks and helping others. An organisation could provide further incentives by allowing staff to spend points on desirable items, such as days off or team 'away days'. This software is intended to ensure that people complete the required documentation about their work, particularly in industries such as Web and Software design where such administrative work is often seen as reducing the 'fun' of work.

Crowdrise (http://www.crowdrise.com) is a social fundraising system that also uses points and badges to motivate fundraisers to contribute to charity. Points and badges are displayed on a public profile along with information about the person and the charities they contributed to and support.

Figure 4: Web Development Badges Earned from Mozilla's Webmaker Site.

Most current examples of gamification make use of badges, images awarded when specific criteria have been met, and are based on the badge concept used, among others, by the Scout Association (http://scouts.org.uk/supportresources/search/?cat=56,135,156). Badges are a record of activity and competency that can be displayed in profiles on web pages to highlight a person's interests and work, though badges currently can usually only be displayed on the website where they were earned. Partly because of this limitation, since 2011 the Mozilla Foundation has been working with partners, such as the Peer2Peer University, to develop a standard method of awarding and displaying badges that would enable people to gather badges from multiple sources and create unique collections for display in different contexts. The Mozilla Foundation is using these 'OpenBadges' in its own educational projects, and Figure 4 shows badges earned for developing the skills to create websites via Mozilla's 'Webmaker' resource (https://badges.webmaker.org/). These would be added to a learner's 'badge backpack' for use as verifiable evidence of learning and self-promotion. They do not replace formal qualifications, but can help to expose acquired skills that may not be obvious from a grade transcript. This idea has influenced Purdue University, which has made badges a major part of a new initiative to provide students with a more comprehensive method of presenting their learning and achievements, and Figure 5 shows how badges are presented in a student's personal 'Passport' profile (Tally, 2012).

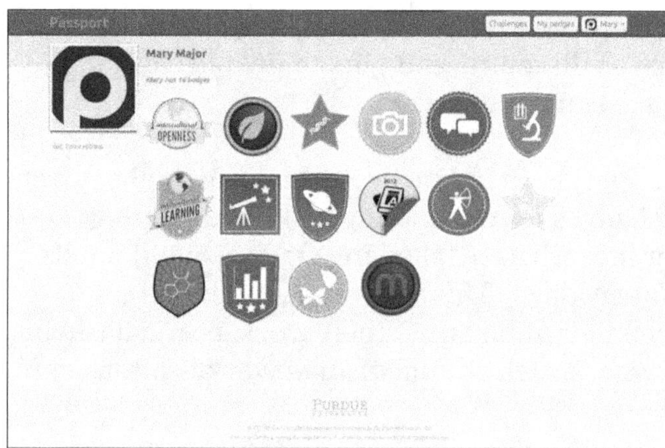

Figure 5: A Student's Badges Displayed in their Purdue University Passport Profile.

Criticism of Gamification

In a review, computer games journalist John Teti (2012) has stated that "[i]nstead of making work rewarding, gamification strives only to make work seem rewarding". Although this was a comment about gamification in the workplace, it has implications for educational uses. The act of gamifying an educational experience alone is not enough to make the experience rewarding, instead it should serve primarily to make something that is already rewarding *more* rewarding – perhaps by encouraging learners to invest more time than they otherwise would.

Gamification seeks to increase motivation by providing *extrinsic* recognition and reward for completing activities, however there is the possibility that such rewards can serve to de-motivate learners with an already high *intrinsic* motivation (Groh, 2012). This psychological concept, particularly evident in gifted children, is called the 'Overjustification effect'. In fact, a negative correlation between extrinsic motivation and academic achievement can sometimes be observed; that is, increased extrinsic motivation, such as rewards, reduces learning and achievement (Lepper, Corpus, & Iyengar, 2005). In order to mitigate the potential negative effects of Overjustification, it is therefore important to make the gamified elements of a learning process optional. This will allow those learners who are already motivated to remain so, and provide motivating elements to the remaining learners.

Another criticism of gamification is that it can encourage addicted or compulsive behaviour among people with relevant personality types (Zichermann, 2011). This could lead to a learner focusing on getting every point, reward, etc. from a past activity to the detriment of new activities and learning. The potential for these issues can be reduced by careful consideration of the design of the gamification elements in the learning activities, such as limiting the time in which awards can be earned.

In a panel discussion, Williams (2012) commented on the use of leaderboards at Microsoft, stating *"... leaderboards are great for people who are really aggressive, hardcore players and they want to get to the top. That can motivate them. At the same time, I'm not that person. I don't do leaderboards. The guy at the top has 500,000 points and I have eight. To me, that's a turnoff."* In learning situations, this highly public competitiveness could harm the learning and motivation of others by discouraging less competitive, status-seeking learners from engaging. This effect can be reduced by making competition internal rather than external, such as by having learners competing against their own personal best, and being rewarded for improvement rather than absolute achievement.

Thom, Millen and DiMicco (2012) investigated how removing gamification elements from a social networking system in a large organisation would affect levels of interaction and found that, without the extrinsic incentives, participation was dramatically reduced. However, analysis of the comments and posts on the system showed that the overall quality of the interactions was lower when the gamification elements were being used. This suggests that, without careful consideration of the rewards for interaction, gamification can be counter-productive and give tacit approval of distracting and time-wasting activities for some individuals.

Gamifying Education

This paper has outlined some of the key concepts and criticisms of gamification and shown how it is used in different domains. However, learning is something of a special case compared to many of the other examples listed. This is primarily because it is an activity with well-defined outcomes and requires more than token effort from the learner – whereas some of the other uses of gamification require little more than visiting a particular place regularly. Gamification, as a process which creates participatory learning experiences, is particularly suited to active learners and active learning. Yet, it can also provide a framework to encourage the use of different types of resources that target other learning styles, such as by incorporating audio, images and text into a single experience.

When deciding whether to gamify a learning activity/process it is necessary to consider some questions first:

Is motivation actually a problem?
This first, and most important, question needs to be answered before considering gamification. Learners could appear unmotivated when the actually issue is something else, such as the activity is too difficult/easy or they do not see the relevance of it. If these are the underlying cause of the problem then they should be addressed by learning design, rather than through gamification. Incorporating game-mechanics with an educational activity or process is non-trivial and cannot replace good learning design; therefore, it is essential that the pedagogy and level of the activity are appropriate before adding extra layers of complexity through gamification.

Are there behaviours to encourage/discourage?
Gamification is frequently used to provide incentives to modify specific behaviours, such as by encouraging group work or discouraging interruptions and distraction. This particular use can be effective, but it may not result in long-term changes without continued incentives.

Can a specific activity be Gamified?
One of the key concepts of gamification is 'Goal-focused activity' and this works best when there are clear 'checkpoints' in an activity that can be used by the learner to establish their progress and identify remaining tasks. This feature is often evident in good learning design, however there may be situations when this concept conflicts with the required learning outcome.

Am I creating a parallel assessment route?
It is important that gamification elements such as leaderboards and points are completely divorced from the formal assessment of learning, and that the learners understand this to be the case. Gamification should only be used to increase motivation and should not be another mechanism by which to grade learners. It is not a paradox that the person at the top of the leaderboard might also be the lowest achiever in formal assessments, but it would suggest that the gamification choices need to be refined.

Would it favour some learners over others?
While some learners would likely be motivated by having their activities gamified, others would be de-motivated by it. If this is likely to have an impact, it is necessary to ensure that those who would be adversely affected can ignore the gamification aspects – such as by making the rewards and tracking optional.

What rewards would provide the most motivation for learners?
Different rewards will provide different levels of motivation to different learners and therefore the reward(s) should be carefully planned in order to ensure that they would motivate everyone. For example, points could be earned and a 'price list' of different rewards could be used so that individuals can work towards something that interests them.

Will it encourage learners to spend disproportionate time on some activities?
Depending on the individual learners, it may be necessary to set limits on the gamified aspects of some activities, such as time or point limits, in order to discourage the learners from spending too long on particular tasks.

Are rewards too easy to obtain?
Rewards should be desirable by the learners and one of the ways to ensure desirability is through the creation of artificial scarcity (Glover et al., 2012). In order to encourage motivation, rewards should be achievable with a sufficient level of effort, but not so easily that all learners acquire it. This is particularly so when using online badges, because their zero-cost nature encourages them to be distributed too liberally.

Only after answering these questions should the implementation of gamification be considered.

Gamification in e-Learning

Gamification lends itself particularly well to e-learning because the necessary data for tracking progress is more easily collated, though it is important to remember that the process can be used on classroom teaching just as effectively. Engagement levels in e-learning activities are often lower and studies have shown that, while those with high intrinsic motivation are typically as engaged as they would be with face-to-face learning, the opposite is true for learners with low intrinsic motivation (Rovai, et al., 2007). Adding simple game features could encourage unmotivated learners to be more engaged in their own learning process and interactions with other learners. An advantage here is that existing associations between computers and games can be harnessed to encourage productive work; this may be more difficult in physical learning spaces, such as classrooms, because the idea of 'play' is the antithesis of the seriousness that is normally associated with these spaces. However, this latent association between computers and games has the potential of encouraging unwanted actions by the learners unless there is strong initial direction and the intentions of the game aspects have been clearly articulated.

Virtual Learning Environments (VLEs) and Learning Management Systems (LMSes) make an ideal location for the implementation of gamification. This is because they typically contain all of the functionality required to support activities, resource sharing, and collaboration, as well as providing methods to track a learner's progress and interactions. In some systems, manual analysis of this data might be necessary; however, the recent interest in personalised learning has resulted in most of the major platforms implementing features that can be harnessed to gamify learning. Sarah Thorneycroft (University of New England, Australia) has shown how the basic features of a Moodle VLE can be used to support gamification (http://www.youtube.com/watch?v=1rNfPyPCSi8). This could be further enhanced by making use of other features, such as using quizzes to assess the person's learning, or requiring a vote in a poll prior to moving to the next level (set of resources). When the learner has completed enough activities, or demonstrated a specific competency, a badge could be awarded automatically and displayed on their profile.

VLEs and LMSes sometimes also include peer rating mechanisms that can be used for gamification purposes. The Blackboard Learn VLE allows learners to rate each other's contributions to a discussion forum and these ratings could be collated and translated into points on a leaderboard, or learners with consistently high ratings could be given a prize or badge. This example serves two purposes, it encourages learners to contribute to online discussions and it also attempts to ensure that the discussion is focussed and of good quality. The long-running online discussion site, Slashdot (http://slashdot.org), uses a similar mechanism for rating contributions ,with posters earning 'Karma points' which help to increase the default visibility of their posts, and increase the overall quality of the debate.

The Peer2Peer University (P2PU), mentioned earlier in this paper, is a free online 'university' and provides a place for anyone to create or study on a Massive Open Online Course (MOOC). Unlike a traditional educational institution, there are no certificates or qualifications issued to learners who complete the course, and so there is no way of evidencing the learning that took place on the MOOC. P2PU is working with Mozilla to implement OpenBadges in order to verify learning and skills acquisition, for example, a 'Certified Networked Teacher' badge (https://p2pu.org/en/badges/certified-networked-teacher/) can be earned by completing the assessments in a specific MOOC and leads to eligibility for more advanced MOOCs and badges.

Gamification can also be easily adapted to use other learning technologies, such as Personal Response Systems (also known as Electronic Voting Systems, Classroom Clickers, Student Response Systems, etc.). In this case, it would be possible to track how many correct responses each learner makes and award points on a leaderboard. This would have the advantage that, if the leader's reward at the end of the course is something desirable to most of the learners, it will encourage learners to attend classes and vote on the questions. Gamification has been used with economics students at Pepperdine University and business school students are Pennsylvania State University to encourage students to engage with online quizzes (Educause, 2011)

The concepts can also expand to encompass complex tasks using multiple technologies in the same activity. For example, posts to a blog, edits to a wiki, contributions to a social bookmark list, assisting other learners in a chat session could all be worth points on the leaderboard. By varying the points gained for each task over the course of the activity it would be possible to guide learners through a set of tools, without limiting their freedom to be creative. This usage would cause the gamification elements to promote cooperativeness and sharing instead of competitiveness and 'selfishness', and encourage learners to be willingly involved in a wider range of tasks than they might otherwise.

These examples have outlined some ways in which gamification can be integrated with e-learning. The concepts are broad enough that most types of learning activity can be gamified, meaning it is possible to experiment on a small scale in order to identify what would and would not work in a given situation.

Conclusion

Gamification is a concept that can be used to make learning more engaging, but it should not be viewed in isolation to other tools and methods. There are many opportunities to implement the concepts of gamification within learning, both in traditional learning environments and, especially, in their electronic counterparts. However, to encourage meaningful learning experiences requires considerable thought about what is appropriate for the learners and the context. This is essentially the same as designing learning activities more generally, and gamification should be considered during this same design stage.

Yet, gamification is not a panacea, it can do little to make low quality materials, activities and experiences more engaging or meaningful. However, it can provide additional motivation to ensure that learners fully complete activities and, with careful consideration of the implementation, can encourage 'good' behaviour and discourage 'bad' behaviour. The principles of gamification are chiefly derived from computer games and therefore are a good fit for learning processes and activities that have some online element, such as being managed by a Virtual Learning Environment, but they can also be applied to non-electronic contexts.

There are many different game elements that can be used to gamify learning, and there is some skill in determining which are appropriate for a particular group of learners and activity and which are not. Many examples of gamification make use of easily quantifiable values, such as number of posts in a forum, but it is important to make use of qualitative measures too, such as ratings by other learners, in order to encourage high-quality interaction. The main consideration when assessing whether gamification could be of benefit for a group of learners is the level of intrinsic motivation. If this is high, then providing extrinsic motivation through rewards has the potential to *de*-motivate the learners, and gamification would not be appropriate in this case.

Finally, rewards need to be achievable and desirable in order to provide sufficient extrinsic motivation, but scarce enough that there is a sense of pride and accomplishment in receiving one; therefore, as a reward for reading this paper, you have earned the

'Gamification, Gamification, Gamification' badge (Figure 6). A digital version of the badge is available at http://badg.us/en-US/badges/claim/cfwcvk.

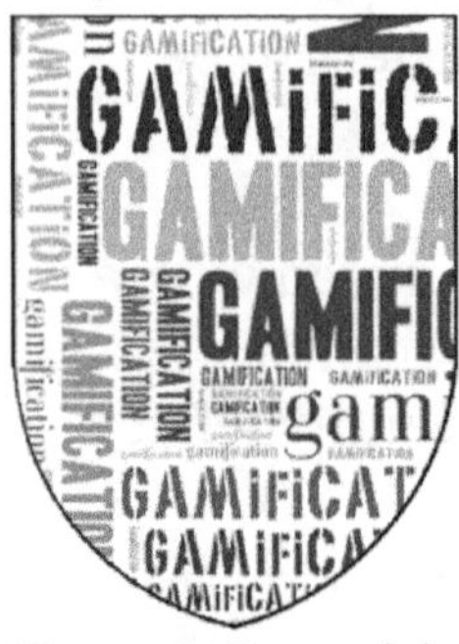

Figure 6: Reward for Reading this Paper – 'Gamification, Gamification, Gamification' Badge

References

Ames, C. (1990). Motivation: What Teachers Need to Know. *Teachers College Record,* 91 (3), 409-421. Accessed 29/11/2012 - http://www.tcrecord.org/Content.asp?ContentId=401.

Ames, C. (1992). Classrooms: Goals, structures, and student motivation. *Journal of Educational Psychology*, 84 (3), 261-271. Accesssed: 15/11/2012 - http://psycnet.apa.org/doi/10.1037/0022-0663.84.3.261

Christensen, C. M. & Raynor, M. E. (2003). The Innovator's Solution: Creating and Sustaining Successful Growth, Harvard University Press, Cambridge, MA. ISBN: 978-1578518524.

Deterding, S., Sicart, M., Nacke, L., O'Hara, K., & Dixon, D. (2011a). Gamification: Using Game-design Elements in Non-gaming Contexts. In *CHI '11 Extended Abstracts on Human Factors in Computing Systems* (CHI EA '11). ACM, New York, USA, 2425-2428. Accessed: 15/11/2012 - http://doi.acm.org/10.1145/1979742.1979575

Deterding, S., Dixon, D., Khaled, R., & Nacke, L. (2011b). From Game Design Elements to Gamefulness: Defining "Gamification". In *Proceedings of the 15th International Academic MindTrek Conference: Envisioning Future Media Environments* (MindTrek '11). ACM, New York, USA, 9-15. Accessed: 15/11/2012 - http://doi.acm.org/10.1145/2181037.2181040

Dickey, M. D. (2005). Engaging by design: how engagement strategies in popular computer and video games can inform instructional design. *Education Training Research and Development, 53 (2)*, 67-83. Accessed: 21/11/2012 - http://medicina.iztacala.unam.mx/medicina/Engaging%20by%20design.pdf

Educause. (2011). *7 Things You Should Know About ... Gamification.* Washington, DC, USA: Educause Learning Initiative. Accessed: 04/12/2012 [online] http://net.educause.edu/ir/library/pdf/ELI7075.pdf.

Glover, I., Campbell, A., Latif, F., Norris, L., Toner, J., & Tse, C. (2012). A Tale of One City: Intra-institutional Variations in Migrating VLE Platform. *Research In Learning Technology, 20.* Accessed: 27/11/2012 - http://dx.doi.org/10.3402/rlt.v20i0.19190

Groh, F. (2012). Gamification: State of the Art Definition and Utilization. In *Proceedings of the 4th seminar on Research Trends in Media Informatics*, 39-46. Accessed: 26/11/2012 - http://vts.uni-ulm.de/docs/2012/7866/vts_7866_11380.pdf#page=39

Juul, J. (2003). The Game, the Player, the World: Looking for a Heart of Gameness. In *Proceedings of Level Up: Digital Games Research Conference*, 30-45. Accessed: 22/11/2012 - http://www.jesperjuul.net/text/gameplayerworld/

Lepper, M. R., Corpus, J., & Iyengar, S. S. (2005). Intrinsic and Extrinsic Motivational Orientations in the Classroom: Age Differences and Academic Correlates. *Journal of Educational Psychology*, 97(2), 184-196. Accessed: 26/11/2012 - http://psycnet.apa.org/doi/10.1037/0022-0663.97.2.184.

Meece, J.L., Anderman, E.M., & Anderman, L.H. (2006). Classroom Goal Structure, Student Motivation, and Academic Achievement. Annual Review of Psychology, 57, 487-503. Accessed: 22/11/2012 - http://www.annualreviews.org/doi/abs/10.1146/annurev.psych.56.091103.070258

OECD (2000), *Motivating Students for Lifelong Learning*, OECD Publishing. Accessed: 29/11/2012 - http://dx.doi.org/10.1787/9789264181830-en

Pintrich, P.R. (2003). A Motivational Science Perspective on the Role of Student Motivation in Learning and Teaching Contexts. *Journal of Educational Psychology*, 95(4), 667-686. Accessed: 23/11/2012 - http://psycnet.apa.org/doi/10.1037/0022-0663.95.4.667

Rollings, A., & Adams, E. (2003) Andrew Rollings and Ernest Adams on Game Design. New Riders, Indianapolis. ISBN: 978-1592730018.

Rovai, A., Ponton, M., Wighting, M. & Baker, J. (2007). A Comparative Analysis of Student Motivation in Traditional Classroom and E-Learning Courses. *International Journal on E-Learning*, 6(3), 413-432. Accessed: 28/11/2012 - http://www.editlib.org/p/20022.

Smith-Robbins, S. (2011). "This Game Sucks": How to Improve the Gamification of Education. *Educause Review*, 46 (1), 58-59. Accessed: 16/11/2012 - http://net.educause.edu/ir/library/pdf/ERM1117.pdf

Tally, S. (2012, September 11). Digital badges show students' skills along with degree. Accessed: 27/11/2012 - http://www.purdue.edu/newsroom/releases/2012/Q3/digital-badges-show-students-skills-along-with-degree.html

Teti, J. (2012). Rev. of Assassin's Creed III. *The Gameological Society*. Accessed: 21/11/2012 - http://gameological.com/2012/11/review-assassins-creed-iii/

Thom, J., Millen, D., & DiMicco, J. (2012). Removing gamification from an enterprise SNS. In *Proceedings of the ACM 2012 conference on Computer Supported Cooperative Work (CSCW '12)*, 1067-1070. Accessed: 27/11/2012 - http://doi.acm.org/10.1145/2145204.2145362.

Williams, J. (2012). The Gamification Brain Trust: Intrinsically Motivating People to Change Behavior (part 2). *Gamesbeat*, Panel discussion, Wallace, M. [chair], Accessed: 26/11/2012 - http://venturebeat.com/2012/09/22/the-gamification-brain-trust-intrinsically-motivating-people-to-change-behavior-part-2/#h8geQcI5BUyR5Ihv.99

Zichermann, G. (2011). Gamification has issues, but they aren't the ones everyone focuses on. [Editorial] *O'Reilly Radar*. Accessed: 26/11/2012 - http://radar.oreilly.com/2011/06/gamification-criticism-overjustification-ownership-addiction.html

Acknowledgements

Thanks to Neal Sumner of City University London for his comments on the draft of this paper.

15 Attributes and Motivation in Game-Based Learning: A Review of the Literature.

Jina Kang & Min Liu, The University of Texas at Austin, United States

Introduction

Many scholars have asserted that games have several advantages for learning. Games are accessible, reasonably priced, and effective substitutes for traditional classroom activities (e.g., Belanich, Sibley, & Orvis, 2004; Driskell, & Dwyer, 1984; Rieber, 1996; Smith, Sciarini, & Nicholson, 2007). Despite attempts to prove the effectiveness of games, there are only a few studies regarding the relationship between specific attributes and specific effectiveness of the elements, for example whether the relationship is direct, or whether the specific impact of a combination of several game elements affects learning (Wilson et al., 2009). In addition, little research has investigated the relationship between learner motivation and attributes incorporated into the games. In this paper, attributes that Wilson et al. (2009) defined from studies prior to 2009 will be used to investigate current game-based learning environments, and this paper reviewed the literature from 2009 to present in an attempt to provide findings and insights for researchers and practitioners who are interested in using those game attributes to enhance motivation in game-based learning. The questions guiding this review are:

1. What attributes have been adopted by current game-based learning?
2. What is the relationship between the game attributes and learners' motivation?
3. Which game attributes have the bigger impact on learner motivation toward learning?

Defining Game Attributes

Several attempts have been made to define desirable game attributes for educational games, for example, Juul's six elements (2003): rules, variable quantifiable outcome, player effort, valorization of the outcome, attachment of the player to the outcome, and negotiable consequences. Garris, Ahlers, and Driskell (2002) suggested six features: "fantasy, rules/goals, sensory stimuli, challenge, mystery, and control. Thiagarajan (1999) asserted there are four components: conflict, control, closure, and contrivance. Walker and Johnson (1993) used four different features: dynamic visuals, interactivity, rules, and a goal whereas Malone and Lepper (1987) focused on these four elements: challenge, curiosity, control, and fantasy" (p. 228-229). Recently, Wilson et al. (2009) provided several key gaming attributes necessary for learning: (a) adaptation, (b) assessment, (c) challenge, (d) conflict, (d) control, (e) fantasy, (f) interaction, (g) language/communication, (h) location, (i) mystery, (j) pieces/players, (k) progress/surprise, (l) representation, (m) rules/goals, (n) safety, and (o) sensory stimuli. Brief definitions of each attribute can be found at http://exgalaxy.net/etc/Attributes.pdf.

As for the gradually growing research into learning and teaching with 3D games, 3D multiuser virtual environments have been considered as one of the trends in learning and teaching with technology (Omale, Hung, Luetkehans, & Cooke-Plagwitz, 2009). According to Alexander (2001), one of the most popular media will be a 3D online learning environment in which learners can feel "a sense of belonging" (p. 32). Since a 3D game attribute should be considered an important factor for learning, it is also included as one of the game attributes.

Method

This literature review covers research from 2009 to the present since other studies (e.g., Wilson et al., 2009) already conducted a review of literature related to game attributes and learner motivation before 2009. The review employed a two-phase search. The initial search surveyed the field using the following library databases: ERIC, Academic Search Complete, Communication & Mass Media Complete, Communication & Mass Media Complete, Computer Source, Library, Information Science, & Technology Abstracts, PsycARTICLES, PsycINFO, and Psychology and Behavioral Sciences Collection.

The second search relied on references from collected articles. To identify relevant articles, search terms included *game-based learning, game learning, game, simulation, motivation, engagement, attributes, 3D, three dimension, learning outcomes, effectiveness,* and *achievement*, using *and* and *or* operators. The search was also limited to peer-reviewed journal articles. To be included in the initial search, an article must reference games and assess learner motivation. These criteria focused on whether the study could provide enough information to answer the research questions stated above, as follows:

(1) focused on game attributes in game-based learning
(2) integrated game-based learning into the classroom
(3) focused on learner motivation or engagement in game-based learning.

Studies that did not satisfy at least one of the inclusion criteria were excluded. After examining each abstract, 20 articles were found to meet these criteria and were used for this literature review (See http://exgalaxy.net/etc/Review.pdf). In order to investigate games and attributes in the games, the relevant information was collected from the articles; Table 1 contains this specific information about the games reviewed in this paper is investigated. The different research issues of the studies reviewed are discussed and authors' findings and claims are evaluated in order to compare the impact of game-based learning on student motivation. Finally, based on the articles' findings, the specific game attributes that proved to affect student motivation are reviewed. The identified attributes are then discussed to better understand a trend of game-based learning that supports students.

Subject	Title	Description	Grade	Attributes
Computer Science	*TrainB&P*	3D Simulation game Study programming knowledge	Undergraduate	Piece, Representation, Location, Rule, Goal, Interaction, Conflict, 3D
Computer Science	*LearnMem1*	Study basic computer memory concepts	High school	Adaptation, Assessment, Rule, Goal, Fantasy, Interaction, Control, Mystery, Conflict
Economics	*Trade Ruler*	Online Flash game (http://nobelprize.org/educational_games/economics/trade/)	Undergraduate - Adults	Adaptation[1], Assessment, Interaction[1], Location, Control, Player, Piece[1], Sensory stimuli, Rule, Goal, Representation, Progress, Challenge[1], Conflict
Geography	Travel game	Role-playing game Study world geography	High School	Fantasy[1], Sensory stimuli[1], Challenge[1], Mystery, Control, Rule, Goal, Location, Representation, Adaptation, Interaction[1], Piece, Conflict
History	*Frequency 1550*	Location-based technology Study medieval Amsterdam	Middle School	Assessment, Challenge, Communication, Goal, Location, Piece, Player, Fantasy, Representation, Rule, Sensory stimuli, Conflict
Language	*It's a Deal!*	Serious game Study business English	Undergraduate	Challenge, Assessment, Interaction, Piece, Player, Control, Rule, Goal, Conflict
Language	*Nori School*	Study English Learning Management System including MMORPG game, community, and learning materials	Elementary School	Challenge, Adaptation, Assessment, Piece, Player, Interaction, Communication, Language, Assessment, Conflict
Language	*Hello You*	Study English	Elementary School	Assessment, Interaction[1], Rule, Goal, Piece, Communication[1], Sensory stimuli[1]

[1] Attributes to affect motivation

Subject	Title	Description	Grade	Attributes
Language	*HELLO*	Ubiquitous computing technology Study English	High School	Progress, Sensory stimuli, Interaction, Communication, Language, Representation, Control, Location
Pathology	*Path to Success*	Study Pathology courses	Undergraduate	Interaction, Rule, Goal, Progress, Assessment, Challenge, Sensory stimuli, Conflict
Science-Physics	*SURGE*	Unity 3D game engine Conceptually-integrated game Study Newtonian mechanics	7-9 grade	Adaptation, Challenge[1], Control, Goal, Piece, Player, Progress, Interaction[1], Representation, Safety, Sensory stimuli[1], 3D[1], Novelty[1]
Science-Biology	*CRYSTAL ISLAND*	Narrative-centered learning environment 3D game platform	Middle School	Adaptation, Assessment, Communication, Interaction, Language, Location, Mystery, Fantasy[1], Representation, Narrative[1], Sensory stimuli, Conflict, 3D
Science-Astronomy	*Alien Rescue*	Unity 3D game platform	Middle School	Representation[1], Challenge[1], Fantasy[1], Interaction[1], Sensory stimuli, Control[1], Rule, Goal, Piece, Mystery, Conflict, 3D
Science-Ecology	*Taiga, Quest Atlantis*	Multi-user virtual environment Study water quality concepts	Elementary – Middle School	Interaction[1], Location, Player[1], Rule, Goal, Communication[1], Representation[1], Piece, Sensory stimuli, Challenge, Assessment, Conflict, 3D[1]

Table 1: List of game-based learning environments and attributes in content areas.

Findings and Discussion

Game-based Learning Environments in the Content Areas and Game Attributes

This paper reviews the game-based learning environments in content areas of the current studies from 2009 to present, specifically examining the purpose of each game, target users' grades, and game attributes (See Table 1.). Fourteen games were included in these empirical studies. The target users ranged from elementary to graduate students. Various subject matters were developed to integrate game-based learning into the classroom, including computer science, economics, geography, history, language, pathology, physics, biology, astronomy, and ecology. Based on this review of the literatures, it seems that numerous educational games have been developed in many subject areas and that researchers and educators have been trying to incorporate such games into traditional classrooms.

Figure 1: Word cloud of the frequency of game attributes.

A word cloud that is a visual representation of the frequency of each game attribute in the games is provided in Figure 1. Interaction, which has the highest frequency among the attributes, is considered to be the most important and necessary attribute in the development of game-based learning (Prensky, 2001). On the other hand, the safety, fantasy, mystery, and language attributes are adopted less often than other attributes in the game-based learning environments. The representation attribute is incorporated in most games and is strongly asserted by researchers as a main feature. The role-playing feature, which is adopted in most of the games, especially allows learners to experience the cognitive process to solve given tasks like those in the real world and evoke learner motivation and curiosity. The 3D attribute is also adopted for the purpose of allowing learners to experience a simulation of the real world. The piece attribute is also considered as one of the main motivators; for example, extrinsic rewards or items are some necessary elements for motivation development in game-based learning. In general, although some attributes (e.g., fantasy, language, mystery, safety) are adopted in only a few games, regardless of the subject matter, most of the attributes are considered as important elements for learner motivation across all studies.

Research Issues in Game-based Learning

Game-based Learning vs. Non-Game-based Learning

Papastergiou (2009) compared an application with gaming aspects to an application with non-game aspects. The results revealed that learners using the gaming application were more engaged, effective, and active than learners using the non-gaming application. The author quoted a learner's saying; "You never get bored as in traditional teaching because you concentrate on a goal" (p. 10). Some learners also suggested the improvements of the game such as game graphics (e.g., 3D graphics), sounds, music, more adventurous plots, and a variety of activities. Papastergious (2009) argued that even though the improvements could encourage learners' motivation, they also might distract learners from concentrating on study.

In Barab et al. (2009), a mixed-method research was used to investigate learners assigned to four different groups: an expository textbook condition, a simplistic framing condition, an immersive world condition, and a single-user immersive world condition. The first group used an electronic textbook on a website in which there were four separate activities related to water quality problems. The second group used a website that contained the same content as the environment of the third and fourth group, which was an immersive world environment; however, the second group could get information in any order they selected, while the other groups could read information sequentially. The third and fourth groups used the immersive world, *Taiga*. As a result of the experiment, the third and fourth group showed that not only were the learners absorbed in the role of helping the world of *Taiga*, but also the learners performed significantly better on both standardized test items and performance-based tasks than other groups. Barab and his colleagues (2009) pointed out the situation of current science education, in which learners are passive and memorize scientific concepts and facts and suggested that an immersive virtual world could help learners' achieve deep and transferable learning.

Game-based Learning vs. Traditional Classroom

Suh, Kim, and Kim (2010) found learners in massive multi-player online role-playing game outperformed learners in a traditional classroom. In this study, motivation was one of the influential factors for effective learning; however, the researchers argued that a specific environment (e.g. network speed) was necessary for improving learners' motivation.

Huizenga, Admiraal, Akkerman and Dam (2009) conducted quasi-experimental design research in two groups: a group who played the mobile history game, *Frequency 1550*, and a group who attended regular lessons. They found that in terms of motivation for learning history, there was no significant difference between the two groups, whereas learners who played the game were more engaged and gained more content knowledge. They suggested that their definition of motivation could be the reason for the lack of significant difference, which was more focused on the motivation for learning history than on engagement or fun.

Tarng and Tsai (2010) also conducted a quasi-experiment using the counter-group pretest-postest design. Both the experimental group and the control group were taught by the same teacher with the same teaching material. However, the experimental group used a game to review what they learned after school while the control group used their own methods. The results showed that most learners who used the game were satisfied with the game-based learning as follows: learning motivation and interest (4.0) and reduction of learning pleasure (4.03) based on a five-point Likert scale.

Using the ubiquitous-learning environment, *HELLO*, Liu and Chu (2010) conducted a quasi-experimental study with two groups: a control group with a non-gaming environment and an experimental group with a gaming environment. They designed different curricula for the two groups; for example, the control group used printed materials and audio CDs, whereas the experimental group employed *HELLO* to play games embedded in the environment. They found that there were significant differences in learners' curiosity and interest toward learning between the two groups. The results revealed that learners who used the ubiquitous game demonstrated stronger motivation for attention, relevance, confidence and satisfaction and indicated a positive relationship between learning outcomes and motivation.

Liu, Cheng, and Huang (2011) conducted an empirical study to compare the learning experience of traditional lectures with the *TrainB&P* simulation game. They explored the learners' motivation as associated with the learning activities in the two different environments. As a result of the experiment, the learners' intrinsic motivation toward learning (mean = 3.95, S.D. = .6) was higher than the traditional environment (mean = 3.73, S.D. = .52). The result showed that the learners using the game tended to learn more and to be more intrinsically motivated when they actively solved the problems based on intrinsic motivation.

Pre- and Post-Experiment

Rowe, Shores, Mott, and Lester (2011) conducted pre-curriculum tests and post-experiments including questionnaires to measure learners' in-game action. This action included in-game quiz questions, character interactions, overall mystery solution, pathogen labeling activities, and a final game score calculated by the *CRYSTAL ISLAND* software to evaluate learners' progress and efficiency. Learners with more prior content knowledge seemed to be more engaged with the game; however, the researchers proposed that the results indicated different meanings for the different measures for engagement: presence, situational interest, and final game score. Regardless of the prior content knowledge, learners who were more engaged in the narrative environment gained more learning experience than other learners who were not engaged in the environment. Additionally, the researchers suggested that if learners experience greater presence in the game environment, they could be more motivated to complete their goals, pay attention to learning interactions, and engage deeply in the learning processing.

Using the *It's a Deal!* game, Guille'n-Nieto and Aleson-Carbonell (2012) conducted mixed-method research with 55 undergraduate learners. They collected qualitative and quantitative data from pre- and post-questionnaires and informal observations of the learners playing the game. Through informal observations, they found that learners were engaged and immersed in the game and also seemed to be very enthusiastic. It could be implied that the learners were motivated and fully involved in the game experiment.

Liu, Horton, Olmanson, and Toprac (2011) conducted mixed-method research in order to investigate the effects of a new media-enriched problem-based learning environment on science learning, motivation, and their relationship. They reported that most learners were motivated to use *Alien Rescue* and significantly increased their posttest scores as compared to pretest scores after using the game. In terms of the relationship between motivation and learning, the researchers found a significant relationship between learners' motivation scores and their science knowledge posttest scores.

Different Teaching Strategies

Different teaching strategies were applied to investigate their effects on learners' motivation. Chang, Peng, and Chao (2010) identified four specific principles to help teachers integrate games into the classroom and to strengthen their positive influence on learners' learning motivation: Challenge, competition, cooperation, and authentic tasks. In the study, different strategies that applied these four principles were used for three different courses in which learners played the same game. In two courses, teachers set the game to the single-player mode, while the other course was set to the multi-player mode. They reported that learners showed higher motivation in the course designed to encourage learners' competition in a cooperative learning environment than in the other two courses. On the other hand, they argued that different integration planning between courses led to different learner interests toward learning.

Different Levels of Free Choice

Barendregt and Bekker (2011) conducted mixed-method research on three different levels of free choice: free-choice learning activities, free-choice learning activities within boundaries, and no-choice learning activities. To determine choice, the first group of learners were asked whether they wanted to play the game and could decide to play the game by themselves. The second group of learners were asked if they were interested in the game and then scheduled to play the game. The third group of learners played the game in the classroom. Learners who were offered only limited-choice (Group 2) or no free-choice (Group 3) were more interested in playing the game than learners who were offered only free-choice learning activities (Group 1). The learners in Group 3 were the only ones who were eager to keep playing the game outside the classroom. Barendregt and Bekker (2011) pointed out that the explorative study had some limitations since they used one specific game with small samples of learners; for example, learners who are initially less interested in a specific game can become more interested when a large group plays.

Consequently, compared to learners involved in non-game-based learning, research suggests that game-based learners are engaged and motivated regardless of the use of computer applications. Even though all students were exposed to the computer-based learning environments, students who were placed in the game-based learning environments were shown to be more engaged and motivated in learning. Second, research suggests that learners in the game-based learning environments are more motivated and engaged in gaining knowledge than learners in the traditional classroom environments. Third, game-based learning designed to encourage competition and cooperation can highly motivate learners. Fourth, authentic narrative and presence embedded in game-based learning can spark learners' motivation and learning performance; motivation and learning are significantly related to each other. Finally, learners' autonomy or level of choice can affect learners' motivation. In order to encourage learners' motivation, it might be necessary to have proper restrictions or boundaries. Despite the range of topics across these studies, all of their results show that game-based learning can engender learner motivation and lead to better learning performance. Overall, this result can provide insights that educators and game developers can use to figure out what is a proper setting for specific target learners.

Relationship between Game Attributes and Motivation

Sweetser and Wyeth (2005) developed criteria to evaluate learner enjoyment of games, which included an evaluation checklist for influential factors such as goal, control, challenge, and feedback. Fu, Su, and Yu (2009) applied these concepts to develop more rigorous criteria and evaluated learners' enjoyment cognition with four different types of games that contained different levels of content. Eight factors were assigned to assess the enjoyment scale (Fu et al., 2009): Concentration, clear goal, feedback, challenge, autonomy, immersion, social interaction, and knowledge improvement. Fu et al. (2009) provided evidence that the enjoyment scale was both valid and reliable and each game had different enjoyment scales. The results show that no matter how technically advanced a game is, if the game had clearly stated goals, learners could attain a high score on the knowledge improvement scale. The researchers recommended that both competition and collaboration elements were necessary to complete students' learning experience.

Tarng and Tsai (2010) showed that game-based learning could reduce pressure on learning, which encourages learner interest and motivation. Specifically, in their travel game, they investigated several features that promote learners' positive attitudes such as the website design, billboard, problem report, and the challenge tasks. Additionally, they suggested that various situations, themes, or narratives in the game environment could be considered influential factors contributing to learners' attitudes. Huang, Huang, and Tschopp (2010) argued that the *Trader Ruler* game enables learners to be fully motivated and to have better learning outcomes because there are interaction components that arise between learners, the game itself, and multimedia components. They also pointed out that the novel content of the game motivates learners regardless of their prior knowledge. Some studies in game-based learning have suggested that the reward system enables learners to sustain their motivation; for example, in some studies, learners tended to choose a lower level of difficulty in order to acquire rewards or scores. As in the previously mentioned studies, learners who played the *Trader Ruler* game reacted to extrinsic motives if they saw the scores of other learners among peer players (Huang et al., 2010).

Rowe et al. (2011) stated that if a game integrates content, narrative, and gameplay, it could have an impact on the relationship between learning and engagement. Specifically, they demonstrated that narrative elements play an important role in the relationship between learning and engagement. In the game *CRYSTAL ISLAND*, the narrative motivated learners to solve their tasks, which were not only simple but also sufficient in not distracting learners from the learning goals. Finally, they suggested that a well-designed story and elements are necessary in order to lead learners to concentrate on games and tasks. Barab et al. (2009) investigated the level of learner engagement with the game-based, multi-user virtual environment, *Taiga*. In this game, learners used avatars to interact with other game players, which indicated that avatars led learners to engage with their experience in the virtual space. Some learners suggested that having more interactivity between a user and a game would have enhanced the learners' engagement with the game. Additionally, learners who played the game reacted to the representation attribute integrated into the game; for example, they felt real or authentic while they were in communication with other game players in the virtual environment. Liu, Toprac, and Yuen (2009) found that several attributes incorporated in *Alien Rescue* triggered learners' curiosity and notions of fantasy, specifically, the role-playing as a scientist, the challenge of solving problems, the goal of saving aliens, and the sensory environment. This finding is related to prior studies that showed that challenge, curiosity, control, fantasy, and relatedness can improve learners' intrinsic motivation. The researchers also suggested that the use of optimal just-in-time feedback in a problem-based learning environment can be helpful for learning.

Uncertainty is also considered as one of the effective attributes in game-based learning. Howard-Jones and Demetriou (2009) conducted research to determine whether uncertainty was an important motivational element in the game-based learning. Regardless of age, the results showed that when elements of gaming uncertainty were included, learners' affective response to game-based learning was higher, which could prove that engagement with the learning is enhanced. The researchers suggested that uncertainty attributes could transform the emotional experience of learning to improve engagement.

Feedback was also shown to improve learner motivation in the study conducted by Charles, Bustard and Black (2009). They first identified forty engaging and motivating aspects of game design in six core dimensions: structure, identity, challenge, feedback, social and fun. Charles, Charles, McNeil, Bustard, and Black (2010) mentioned that timely feedback was a fundamental component that learners need to get during the process of a game in order to improve learners' motivation and engagement. After conducting their research, they concluded that avatar attributes and virtual worlds could be used for enhancing educational feedback and learners' engagement.

Focusing on an entirely different aspect, Clark et al. (2011) stated that the design, which connects intuitive understanding and formal learning, is important. First, they integrated physics ideas and terminology into the pre-level and the post-level of *SURGE*. A non-player character played by a teacher and feedback screen were embedded into the levels in order to deliver instructions. However, through the research, they found learners could easily skip the levels. Therefore, they recommended making the elements in the levels more interactive to encourage learner engagement.

Accordingly, the attributes that affect learner motivation are provided in Table 1. Among the 14 game-based learning environments, researchers conducted experiments involving only seven games to prove the relationship between learner motivation and game attributes. Many researchers investigated motivation in game-based learning; however, demonstration of the specific impact of specific attributes on motivation is still limited. Through the review of the empirical studies, this paper found that certain attributes can improve learner motivation. Researchers suggested most frequently that interaction can be considered as an important component of game-based learning. Secondly, the results showed that the fantasy and challenge attributes tend to immerse learners in the learning process. Some studies also identified narrative and novelty attributes as some of the most effective components to increase learner motivation. The results also showed proper extrinsic rewards should be considered in order to motivate learning when designing game-based learning. Specifically, designers should include some form of diegetic extrinsic reward while also balancing extrinsic types of motivation with intrinsic motivation. In some of the studies, several attributes were mentioned as important elements in designing games; that is, challenge, feedback, goal, interaction, uncertainty, and 3D. In addition, many studies stated that considering the level of difficulty, which is defined as adaptation, is necessary to motivate students who have different levels of prior knowledge or ability. However, few game-based learning environments adopted the adaptation attribute to improve learner motivation.

Conclusions

This review found every attribute defined by Wilson et al. (2009) was included in the 16 game-based learning environments. The interaction attribute shows the highest frequency, and conflict, goal, assessment, rule, and piece attributes are also often used. The result shows that these attributes are considered critical elements for designing game-based learning. Language and safety attributes were rarely adopted. All of the science game-based learning environments utilized the 3D attribute, specifically, 3D space. Therefore, the rich 3D environment is an important attribute that can help students understand the complicated science concepts in an efficient way.

In terms of topics, many studies conducting comparisons between game-based learning and non-game-based learning to demonstrate the positive effects of games. Most research indicated that game-based learning encourages motivation and leads to better learning performance than traditional teaching methods. In order to design or teach game-based learning, consideration of various settings or environments of specific target learners should come first. The findings of this review can provide helpful insights for educators and developers in designing games for educational purposes and applying them to the classroom.

There is limited evidence to demonstrate the impact of specific attributes on learner motivation and learning. Although there is not sufficient empirical evidence to show the discussed game attributes can impact learner motivation definitely, the studies reviewed indicate that interaction is the most highly used attribute in game-based learning. Prior to designing games, which factors are effective to motivate learners should also be considered. This can also help researchers better understand how to improve learner motivation in game-based learning. In addition, as mentioned in many studies, it is crucial to evaluate how motivation and engagement can be sustained over time with game-learning environments and how long-term motivation and engagement are related to deep learning and transfer.

References

Alexander, S. (2001). Learning in 3-D. *OnlineLearning*, July/August, 30–32.

Barab, S. A., Scott, B., Siyahhan, S., Goldstone, R., Ingram-Goble, A., Zuiker, S. J., & Warren, S. (2009). Transformational Play as a Curricular Scaffold: Using Videogames to Support Science Education. *Journal of Science Education and Technology*, 18(4), 305-320.

Barendregt, W., & Bekker, T. M. (2011). The Influence of the Level of Free-Choice Learning Activities on the Use of an Educational Computer Game. *Computers & Education*, 56(1), 80-90.

Belanich, J., Sibley, D., & Orvis, K. L. (2004). *Instructional characteristics and motivational features of a PC-based game (ARI Research Report 1822)*. U.S. Army Research Institute for the Behavioral and Social Sciences: Alexandria, VA.

Chang, Y. C., Peng, H. Y., & Chao, H. C. (2010). Examining the effects of learning motivation and of course design in an instructional simulation game. *Interactive Learning Environments*, 18(4), 319-339.

Charles, D., Charles, T., McNeill, M., Bustard, D., & Black, M. (2010). Game-based feedback for educational multi-user virtual environments. *British Journal of Educational Technology*, 42(4), 638-654.

Charles, M.-T., Bustard, D., & Black, M. (2009). Game Inspired Tool Support for e-Learning Processes. *Electronic Journal of E-Learning*, 7(2), 101-110.

Clark, D. B., Nelson, B. C., Chang, H. Y., Martinez-Garza, M., Slack, K., & D'Angelo, C. M. (2011). Exploring Newtonian mechanics in a conceptually-integrated digital game: Comparison of learning and affective outcomes for students in Taiwan and the United States. *Computers & Education*, 57(3), 2178-2195.

Driskell, J. E., & Dwyer, D. J. (1984). Microcomputer Videogame Based Training. *Educational Technology*, 24(2), 11-17.

Fu, F. -L., Su, R. -C., & Yu, S. -C. (2009). EGameFlow: A Scale to Measure Learners' Enjoyment of E-Learning Games. *Computers & Education*, 52(1), 101-112.

Garris, R., Ahlers, R., & Driskell, J. E. (2002). Games, motivation, and learning: a research and practice model, *Simulation & Gaming*, 33, 441–467.

Guille'n-Nieto, V., & Aleson-Carbonell, M. (2012). Serious Games and Learning Effectiveness: The Case of "It's a Deal!". *Computers & Education,* 58(1), 435-448.

Howard-Jones, P. A., & Demetriou, S. (2009). Uncertainty and engagement with learning games. *Instructional Science*, 37(6), 519-536.

Huang, W. H., Huang, W. Y., & Tschopp, J. (2010). Sustaining iterative game playing processes in DGBL: The relationship between motivational processing and outcome processing. *Computers & Education*, 55(2), 789-797.

Huizenga, J., Admiraal, W., Akkerman, S., & Dam, G. (2009). Mobile game-based learning in secondary education: engagement, motivation and learning in a mobile city game. *Journal of Computer Assisted Learning*, 25(4), 332-344.

Juul, J. (2003). The Game, the Player, the World: Looking for a Heart of Gameness. In M. Copier & J. Raessens (Ed.), *Digital Games Research Conference Proceedings* (pp. 30-45). Utrecht: Utrecht University.

Liu, C.-C., Cheng, Y.-B., & Huang, C.-W. (2011). The Effect of Simulation Games on the Learning of Computational Problem Solving. *Computers & Education*, 57(3), 1907-1918.

Liu, M., Horton, L., Olmanson, J., & Toprac, P. (2011). A study of learning and motivation in a new media enriched environment for middle school science. *Educational Technology Research and Development*, 59(2), 249-265.

Liu, M., Toprac, P., & Yuen, T. (2009). What factors make a multimedia learning environment engaging: A case study. In R. Zheng, (Ed.), *Cognitive Effects of Multimedia Learning* (pp. 173-192). Hershey, PA: Idea Group Inc.

Liu, T.-Y., & Chu, Y.-L. (2010). Using Ubiquitous Games in an English Listening and Speaking Course: Impact on Learning Outcomes and Motivation. *Computers & Education*, 55(2), 630-643.

Malone, T. W., & Lepper, M. R. (1987). Making learning fun: A taxonomy of intrinsic motivations for learning. In R. E. Snow & M. J. Farr (Eds.), *Aptitude, learning, and instruction: Vol. 3. Conative and affective process analyses* (pp. 223-253). Hillsdale, NJ: Lawrence Erlbaum

Omale, N., Hung, W., Luetkehans, L., & Cooke-Plagwitz, J. (2009). Learning in 3-D multiuser virtual environments: Exploring the use of unique 3-D attributes for online problem-based learning. *British Journal of Educational Technology*, 40(3), 480-495.

Papastergiou, M. (2009). Digital Game-Based Learning in High School Computer Science Education: Impact on Educational Effectiveness and Student Motivation. *Computers & Education*, 52(1), 1-12.

Prensky, M. (2001). *Digital game-based learning*. New York, NY: McGraw-Hill.

Rieber, L. P. (1996). Seriously considering play: Designing interactive learning environments based on the blending of microworlds, simulations, and games. *Educational Technology Research & Development*, 44(2), 43-58.

Rowe, J. P., Shores, L. R., Mott, B. W., & Lester, J. C. (2011). Integrating Learning, Problem Solving, and Engagement in Narrative-Centered Learning Environments. *International Journal of Artificial Intelligence in Education*, 21(1-2), 115-133.

Smith, P., Sciarini, L., & Nicholson, D. (2007). The utilization of low cost gaming hardware in conventional simulation. *Interservice/Industry Training, Simulation, & Education Conference*. National Defense Industrial Association, Orlando, FL. 965-972

Suh, S., Kim, S. W., & Kim, N. J. (2010). Effectiveness of MMORPG-based instruction in elementary English education in Korea. *Journal of Computer Assisted Learning*, 26(5), 370-378.

Sweetser, P., & Wyeth, P. (2005). GameFlow: A model for evaluating player enjoyment in games. *ACM Computer in Entertainment*, 3(3), 1–24.

Tarng, W., & Tsai, W. (2010). The Design and Analysis of Learning Effects for a Game-based Learning System. *Engineering and Technology*, 61, 336-345.

Thiagarajan, S. (1999). *Teamwork and teamplay: Games and activities for building and training teams*. San Francisco, CA: Jossey-Bass.

Walker, F. J., & Johnson, R. T. (1993). Learning from Video Games. *Computers in the Schools*, 9(2-3), 119-134.

Wilson, K. A., Bedwell, W. L., Lazzara, E. H., Salas, E., Burke, C. S., Estock, J. L., . . . Conkey, C. (2009). Relationships between Game Attributes and Learning Outcomes: Review and Research Proposals. *Simulation & Gaming*, 40(2), 217-266.

16 Making Learning Fun Through a Ludic Simulation

Min Liu, Lucas Horton, Jina Kang, Royce Kimmons & Jaejin Lee, The University of Texas at Austin, United States

Introduction

The purpose of this paper is to describe a ludic simulation designed for middle school space science and examine students' experiences with it in an attempt to explore the value of ludic simulations in education and better understand how such environments can be designed to support learning.

Theoretical Framework

Play has received renewed attention in recent years as researchers have begun to consider the constructivist associations of this fundamental practice (cf. Singer, Golinkoff, & Hirsh-Pasek, 2006). At early stages of development, children engage with the world and people around them through playful interactions that allow them to learn by imitation, symbolic interaction, and cognitive representation, thereby constructing experiential knowledge about the world (Piaget, 1951). As a result, play for children is "an engaging and deliberate activity to which they devote great effort and commitment" (Rieber, 1996, p. 44), and out of such play, children can develop deep and important understandings. Current research in a variety of fields suggests that "play is an important mediator for learning and socialization throughout life" (Rieber, 1996, p. 44; see also Csikszentmihalyi & Bennett, 1971).

The introduction of digital technologies has empowered people to think about play in new and innovative ways. The rapid growth and the prevalence of digital games in our culture have led many to consider the questions we might answer and the problems we might solve through play. McGonigal (2011), for instance, argues that games in today's society "are fulfilling genuine human needs that the real world is currently unable to satisfy" and that games, if properly harnessed, have the potential to address real-world problems. Current gamification or ludification movements agree with this stance and hold that a "new ludic system" is arising in conjunction with a variety of ludic social phenomena (e.g., the video game industry, theme parks, etc.). Ortoleva (2012) explains that this "new ludic system would not exist without thinking machines, to which we owe a great variety of playful practices, from video games to casual games, to those peculiar games that are social networking websites," and in the words of Fuchs (2012), "we have a society with a 'high lusory attitude' ... in using these ludic interfaces [e.g., digital games], we increasingly turn work, war, sport and health into gamified processes." Focusing on specific problems in education, Squire (2003) has argued that digital games can "elicit powerful emotional reactions in their players, such as fear, power, aggression, wonder, or joy" (p. 2) and that designers of educational products have much to learn from game developers with regard to designing "interface, aesthetic, and interactivity" (p. 11) to support learning. Gee (2003) has further argued that good commercial games incorporate "learning principles that ... are all strongly supported by contemporary research in cognitive science" (p. 1) and even believes that "games may be better sites for preparing workers for modern workplaces than traditional schools" (p. 3).

From these perspectives, games and the play that people engage in through them have the potential for serving important and transformative roles in education and society; many have attempted to harness the power of games for educational pursuits (e.g., Barab, Pettyjohn, Gresalfi, Volk, & Solomou, 2012; Clark, Dede, Ketelhut, & Nelson, 2006). Throughout these endeavors, however, there has been a great deal of confusion and lack of clarity with regard to what types of games might have the most potential within education, what aspects of games are valuable, and what we even mean when we use the word "game." As a result, in modern vernacular, *computer, digital,* or *video game* is used inclusively to refer to a variety of types of programs that do a variety of things. Although a clear, universal definition of *games* has yet to emerge, researchers continue to consider the diverse range of games and game-like environments and their potential impact on teaching and learning. Lindley (2003), for example, attempts to capture some of the complexity of "what is a game" by offering a "high level framework for game analysis and design." According to Lindley's framework, games can be classified in accordance with how heavily they emphasize four factors: gambling (or chance), ludology (or playfulness), simulation (or representation of a system), and narratology (or story). Lindley places these four factors in a three-dimensional tetrahedron (see Figure 1) and explains that different genres of games may be effectively placed into different locations within the tetrahedron. Lindley's framework is important for game and educational researchers, because it empowers us to talk about games in ways that are more intentional, meaningful, and directed while simultaneously allowing us to escape the confines of restrictive game definitions.

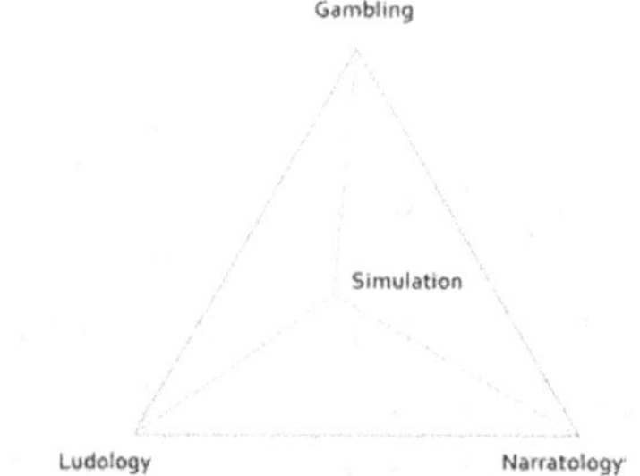

Figure 1. Lindley's (2003) three-dimensional classification space for game analysis and design (p. 2).

Within education in particular, Lindley's framework is valuable, because it allows us to focus upon certain aspects of games that are educationally valuable for a given context (e.g. play, real-world fidelity, etc.) without having to address other elements that may not be as relevant (e.g. chance, etc.). The framework also gives us flexibility to talk about a diversity of educational media that in cultural vernacular might be called "games" but may not fit a strict definition of the word. Within this tetrahedron, simulations are of particular interest to educators for their emphasis on skill development. In Lindley's words: "Simulations ... are not interesting as games or stories, but for understanding how a particular system functions in different circumstances" (p. 1). For this reason, simulations have been used in a variety of fields to support educational goals. Many of the popular commercial games could also be considered simulations, since they provide representations of systems that can be tweaked and manipulated by players. For example, games such as *Flight Sim X* (2006) simulates airplane flight, *Grand Theft Auto* (2008) simulates many aspects of city and criminal life, and *Civilization* titles (1991) simulate aspects of economics, warfare, and diplomacy.

Ludic simulations offer an interesting and engaging blend of skill development and playfulness that would be lost in a simulation that did not incorporate ludic elements or a game that did not simulate interactive systems. Unlike true simulations, which would replicate a system with absolute fidelity and realism, ludic simulations hold ludicity to be as important as fidelity or realism. Up to this point, the term *ludic simulation* has not been frequently used in educational game research, though many research projects have utilized games and virtual environments that might be meaningfully classified in this manner (DeNeve & Heppner, 1997; Ketelhut, Dede, Clarke, Nelson, & Bowman, 2007; Kimmons, Liu, Kang, & Santana, 2012). For example, much research involving the development and use of virtual worlds, multiuser virtual environments (MUVEs), and multimedia enhanced learning environments might be meaningfully discussed from the perspective of their ludicity and simulation properties. Current interest in ludic simulations reflects a larger ludification movement in society (Fuchs & Strouhal, 2008; Raessens, 2006), and current research into educational games should consider the ways in which ludic simulations can support learning by focusing on the value of ludus and simulation.

Research Context

This study focuses on a ludic simulation called *Alien Rescue. Alien Rescue* (AR) is a problem-based educational ludic simulation for sixth-grade space science (Liu, Horton, Olmanson, & Toprac, 2011; Liu, Williams, & Pedersen, 2002; see also http://alienrescue.edb.utexas.edu). The goal of AR is to engage students in solving a complex problem that requires them to use the tools, procedures, and knowledge of space science and apply processes of scientific inquiry while learning about our solar system.

Acting in the role of a space scientist, the learner's goal is to find suitable homes within the solar system for six different alien species, each with different habitat requirements, who have been displaced from their home planets. The experience challenges students to learn how scientists work, plan, and conduct scientific inquiry and to develop well-justified problem solutions. The inquiry process presents an authentic context in which students must exercise high level thinking skills, such as goal setting, hypothesis generation, problem solving, self-regulation, evaluation of various possible solutions, and the presentation of evidence. AR is designed as a sixth grade science curriculum unit to be completed over the course of approximately fifteen 50-minute class sessions and aligns with National Science Education Standards and Texas Essential Knowledge and Skills (TEKS). To support students in this endeavor, AR's design centers on a collection of tools, each of which is intended to support various aspects of the learner's thinking and problem solving process.

AR engages learners in roleplaying, as they take on the role of a space scientist aboard the fictional International Space Station Paloma. Roleplaying directly engages learners in the problem context of the simulation and allows learners to participate in its narrative structure. Students are first situated in the narrative through a video introduction that features a variety of audio and video elements. In this opening video, a series of breaking news segments, delivered by professional news anchors, relays the news that aliens have entered Earth's orbit and have broadcasted a plea for help. Subsequent reports depict Earth's response to the plea and shifting public consensus, which lead to the eventual formation of a special United Nations task force to address the crisis. Through the introductory video, students are introduced to the goals and context of the simulation and are oriented to their role as scientists tasked with saving the alien species.

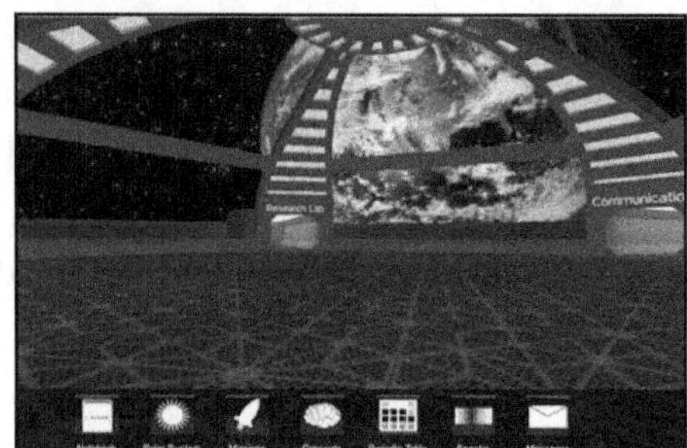

a. Students find themselves as scientists aboard an international space station.

b. The introductory video introduces students to the problem of relocating homeless aliens.

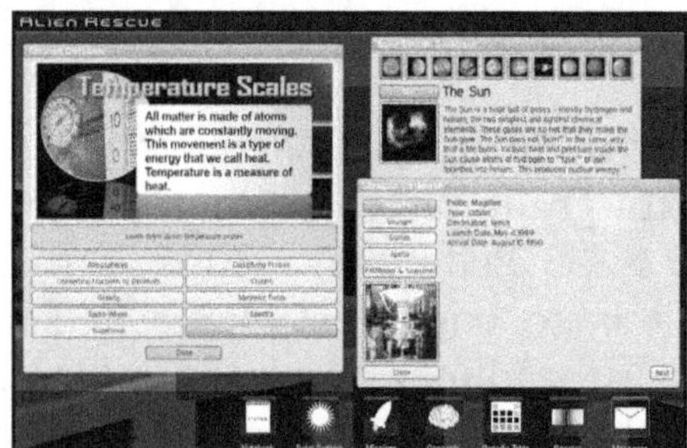

c. Students use tools such as the Concept Database, Solar System Database, and Mission Database.

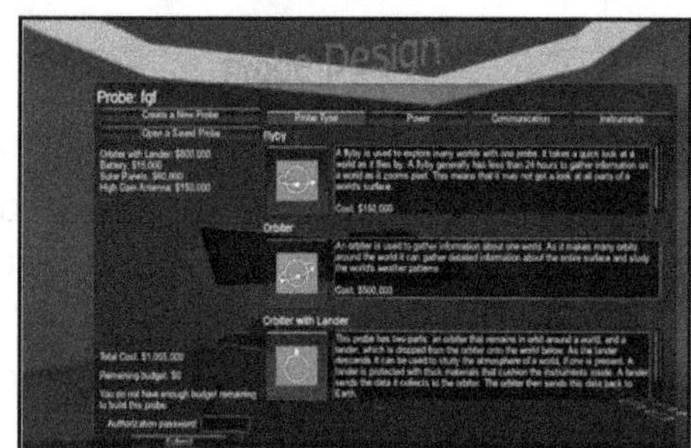

d. Students select probe design options based upon hypotheses.

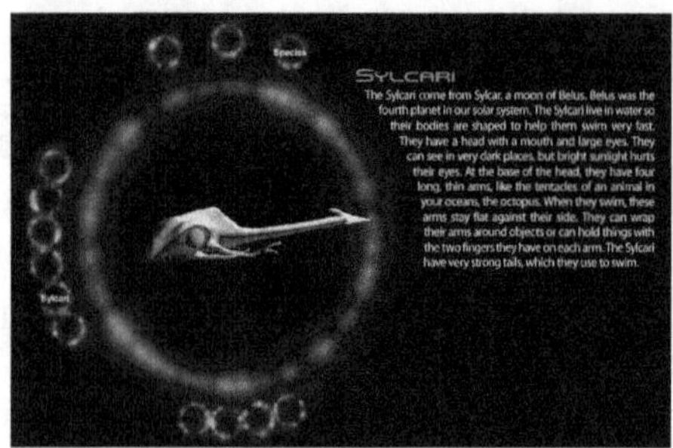

e. One of the alien species, called the Sylcari, is depicted in the Alien Database.

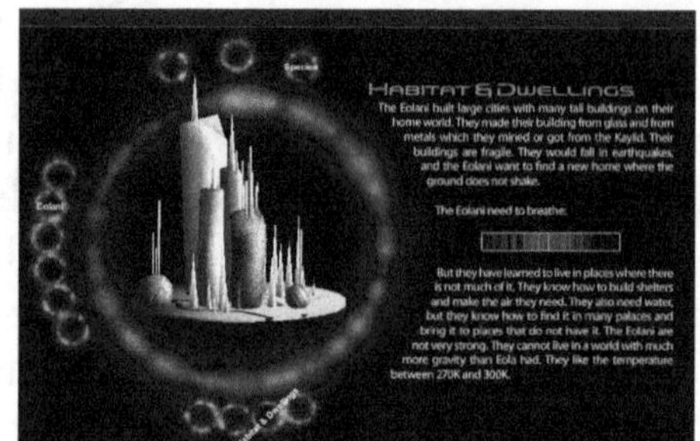

f. Information on alien habitats and dwellings are provided.

Figure 2: Screenshots of various tools provided in Alien Rescue to support the process of scientific inquiry.

After being situated in the problem context by the introductory video, students are free to roam the 3D environment of the Space Station Paloma, the primary setting of the simulation, through a first person perspective. Paloma includes five independent rooms that are connected to one another via a central area. These rooms include the Research Lab, Probe Design Center, Probe Launch Center, Mission Control Center, and Communication Center, and each room provides access to a specific scientific tool. Additionally, an augmented reality interface presents students with a toolbar that can be used to access persistent tools (e.g. Solar System Database, Concept Database, Notebook etc; see Figure 2).

In *Alien Rescue*, an array of tools is available for information gathering, data recording and analysis, experimentation, and reporting (see Figure 2 for examples). These tools are designed to support complex thinking and problem solving processes. The Probe Design Center is of special emphasis, because it allows students to design their own probes by selecting a probe type and equipping it with the scientific instrumentation required to test a given hypothesis. The process of designing and launching probes simulates the actual process of scientific investigation in space science, and a budget system simulates a real-world constraint that requires students to be strategic in the configuration of their probes. An incorrectly designed probe can malfunction, thus wasting crucial funds. As a gamification element, the Probe Design Center aims to help students identify efficient methods of scientific investigation and recognize realistic constraints that impact scientific inquiry. After designing a probe, students have the opportunity to launch it from within the Probe Launch Center, a process that includes a simulated rocket launch. Data from each probe are available from the Mission Control Center and are presented using a variety of images. Invalid probe configurations and randomization result in error messages, further supporting the authenticity of the simulation and encouraging students to refine their approach to designing probes.

Additionally, fantasy components are incorporated into the narrative of the simulation via the story of the distressed aliens, the shifts in public opinion, and the urgency of the situation, as depicted in the introductory video. The narrative of the video uses a familiar TV news format, while the incorporation of well-known international organizations, such as the UN, enhances the realism of the scenario. Beyond the introductory narrative, the playful science fiction inspired interface of the Alien Database provides background information on the alien species alongside interactive 3D models of the aliens, their home planets, and their food sources, each of which was designed according to the principles of educational fantasy (Kim, 2009; see Figure 2). Although the alien narratives are fictional, they are presented in a realistic way that promotes the fantasy of the simulation, thereby encouraging students to respond to the aliens with empathy and emotion.

Two recent research studies were conducted to investigate students' learning after using *Alien Rescue* (Kimmons, Liu, Kang, & Santana, 2012; Liu, Horton, Olmanson, & Toprac, 2011). It was found that sixth graders significantly increased their science knowledge following use of the simulation and there was a significant positive correlation between student knowledge scores and overall motivation. Of particular interest was when students were asked "How would you describe *Alien Rescue* to a friend?" or "What do you think of *Alien Rescue*?," their responses included ludic explanations like: "freaking awesome!!!" "soooooooooooooooooooooooooooo FUN!!!!!!!!!!!!!!!!!" Students often referred to this ludic simulation as a game and expressed that it was fun to use.

This leads us to consider What aspects of AR do students consider to be fun and why? This study continued this line of inquiry and built upon our previous research by further examining the ludic aspect of the simulation. We asked the following research questions:

1. What do middle school students think of *Alien Rescue* as a tool to learn science?
2. Is AR fun for them to use it? If so, in what way? If not, why not?
3. What features do middle school students consider fun?

Method

Participants, Setting, and Data Sources

Sixth graders (n = 383) from two public middle schools from different school districts in a mid-sized southwestern city in the United States participated in this study. The participants included sixth graders of all abilities groups, from talented and gifted (TAG) and regular education to students with limited English proficiency or learning disabilities. Demographic information of students at the first school indicates that approximately 4.3% are African American, 24.9% are Hispanic, 2% are Asian/Pacific Islander, 0.5% are Native American, 2.5% are multiracial, and 65.6% are White. Of these students, 22.6% are economically disadvantaged, 27.9% are identified as at-risk, and 2.1% are identified as Limited English Proficient. Demographic information of students at the second school indicates that approximately 10.3% are African American, 25.7% are Hispanic, 6.9% are Asian/Pacific Islander, 0.5% are Native American, 4.8% are multiracial, and 51.8% are White. Of these students, 21.1% are economically disadvantaged, 20.9% are identified as at-risk, and 2.1% are identified as Limited English Proficient. These sixth graders used AR as their curriculum for space science in place of regular textbooks for three weeks in their daily 50-minute science classes. Each student had his or her own computer for use but also worked in a small group, which is a recommended instructional strategy for implementing AR. After they completed AR, students were asked to respond to the following open-ended questions:

- How would you describe *Alien Rescue* to a friend? Or what do you think of *Alien Rescue*?
- What did you learn from *Alien Rescue*?
- What did you like about *Alien Rescue*? Or what is your favorite part of *Alien Rescue*? Why?
- What did you dislike about *Alien Rescue*? What is your least favorite part of *Alien Rescue*? Why?

Analysis

Students' responses were first cleaned, removing meaningless words or sentences and empty responses, leaving a total of 358 responses (female=46%; male =53%). Not all students responded to all questions and the *n* in each table below reflects the actual response rate for each question. To analyze the open-ended responses, we followed the constant comparative method of analysis practice (Lincoln & Guba, 1985; Strauss & Corbin, 1990). In examining sixth graders' responses to the first question, our intent was to find out how the students described their experience in using the simulation. Before creating a frequency count of the words the students used, we removed words such as "to," "the," "a," "an," "that," and "and" to increase the prominence of relevant adjectives, nouns, and verbs. The reference to the program name, "*Alien Rescue*" or "program" or "I think" as the start of the sentence were also removed. Typos were eliminated or replaced with correct spelling, and variations and misspelled words, such as alieb/alien/aliens, gets/got/get, and probes/probe, were combined. For example, in this statement "I think alien rescue was a lot of fun. I learned a lot. And I got to help aliens," "I think," "alien rescue," "was," and "a" were removed. After the data were cleaned, a word cloud was generated using wordle.net from students' responses to question one, which was produced by coupling word frequency with font size (the bigger the font size, the higher the frequency).

Sixth graders' responses for questions two to four were read and chunked from a line-by-line analysis of the data. Relevant information was extracted through a systematic and iterative examination of the raw data. These extracted units were coded to describe what the students said about their experience through "focused coding" (Charmaz, 2006). As the codes were compared with each other, similar codes were combined, different ones were separated, and various categories emerged at the next level (Creswell, 2005). Such analyses continued until an "emergence of regularities" (Lincoln & Guba, 1985) was reached. We then examined and re-examined the codes, categories, and emergent themes in light of our research goal. Two researchers were involved in the process of coding, checking, and verifying the codes, categories, and themes until 100% inter-rater reliability was reached on their interpretations.

Findings

For the question: "How would you describe *Alien Rescue* to a friend?" Or "What do you think of *Alien Rescue*?," a total of 1,072 words were extracted out of the 358 statements. Words used by the students to describe their experience included: fun, learn, solar-system, aliens, find, helpful, home, information, interesting, probe, game, computer, and so on (see Table 1). The word "fun" has the highest frequency.

Table 1

Word Cloud of students' responses to "How would you describe Alien Rescue to a friend?" Or "What do you think of Alien Rescue?"

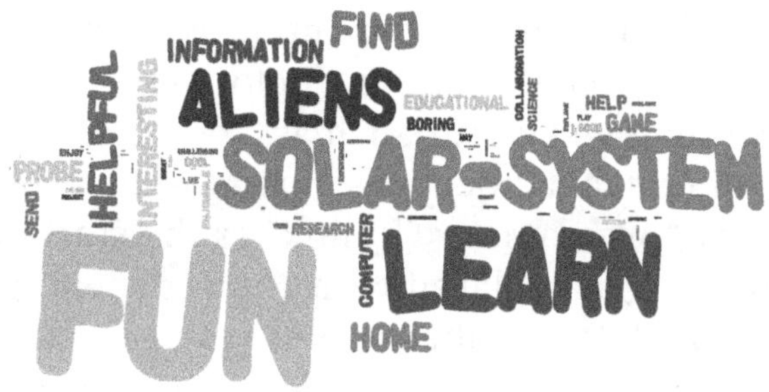

Word	Frequency (%)
fun	183 (17%)
learn	108 (10%)
solar-system	93 (8.7%)
aliens	74 (6.9%)
find	46 (4.3%)
helpful	41 (3.8%)
home	38 (2.7%)
information	30 (2.5%)
interesting	29 (2.7%)
probe	27 (2.5%)
game	24 (2.2%)
computer	20 (1.9%)

Note. Word count below 20 is not listed.

We then further examined 183 statements in which the word "fun" is positively used. Students' responses ranged from simple answers such as "fun" and "very fun" to more elaborate statements such as "it was really FUN and could help a lot of people! especially for the people who would like to go to space someday," "it is very FUN. it help[ed] you learn. i want to do it again," "i think was really FUN and enjoyable. i think was a good source to learn more about space." Reasons cited by the students ranged from more generic statements such as "a FUN way to learn," "it was very very FUN!!!!!!!!!!!," to more specific statements indicating the aspects of the program they considered fun. For example, students stated, "I think was very FUN and interesting. It was cool to see the alien and launch probe and get to learn about planet," "Its FUN. You can work with a group. Its a problem solving game," "It was FUN to do because you get to figure out what alien which to what planet and their needs," and "A FUN activity that get you to enjoy science and not just read out of the textbook. You get to help aliens find home in our solar system. But you also learn A LOT!!!" Table 2 provides the main reasons students considered AR to be a fun experience.

Table 2

Main Reasons Revealed in Student Statements in Which the Word 'Fun" Was used Positively

Why Students Considered Fun	Sample Quotes
a fun way to learn about solar system, space science, science	It is FUN an. It is a perfect way to learn. it is the best way to learn about the solar-system.
An educational or a learning experience	I would describe alien [rescue] to a friend to be really FUN. It is informational and valuable to a student's education. I would also say

	that it is creative.
a game	[It} was a FUN learn experience. The type of game like this should be more widely used among school districts. This was a healthy way for kids to learn about the planet.
Learn to collaborate, work in groups	I think that it was FUN because we had partners that we chose on our own and it was very delightful to be on the computers with a person we trust and know and we could communicate. Except i would like to do it more often.
Get to help aliens, learn about aliens, design/launch probes	i think [it] was FUN because we could buy things. because we could roam around the space station and see what the space station looks like. finally i think was FUN because we could send probe around the galaxy and see what the world look like.
Fun but challenging	its FUN learning about different planet and i love a challenge and this was a big one.
Problem solving, scientific process	it is a FUN activity that lets you interact and make your own probe. It is also educational because you can learn about different planet. You also have a budget, just like in real life.
Feel good, want to do again	I think that was a very FUN interesting thing to do. It was one of my favorite projects all year. I hope to do something like this again this year.

So what have students learned from using AR? Out of a total 515 coding units, approximately 51% of the responses were related to learning knowledge about our solar system (the planets, moons, and their characteristics) and about 16% were about learning the scientific instruments (creating and launching probes and various instruments needed for each type of probe). Other concepts or processes students stated they had learned include alien species (8%), scientific concepts such as magnetic fields, gravity and temperature scales (7%), problem solving (4%), conducting research (4%), managing a budget (2%), and working with others (2%). "Nothing" comprised about 4% of the responses. Below are a few sample statements:

> *I learned many different facts about the moons and planets in our solar system that I haven't known before, and some were quite interesting. I enjoy learning about outer space, therefore I thought that* Alien Rescue *was a neat game that could help us learn about the solar system.* (Student 1)
> *From alien Rescue how to really research and find information using tools and problem solving hard questions.* (Student 2)

Of various aspects the students liked the most, the top five were probe-related (33.84%), alien-related (22.28%), exploring the 3D environment (9.86%), learning about the solar system (9.52%), and problem solving or doing research (8.67%). Other aspects the students liked included: working with peers and managing the budget. 2% of the responses indicated that they did not like anything (see Table 3).

Table 3

Student Responses to " What did you like about Alien Rescue?" Or "What is your favorite part of Alien Rescue?"

Category	%	Sample Quotes
Probes related	33.84%	My favorite part was probe launching. I loved how the probes would send back info so quickly. It really boggles my mind how a probe could go off so quickly and give back so much information!!!!!!!!!!!!!!!!!
Aliens related	22.28%	My favorite parts were learning about the aliens. They have very different needs than humans. I also liked the time when you sent the aliens to the specific planet.
Exploring 3D environment	9.86%	Exploring Paloma. It was cool to see all the different rooms. Also looking at the aliens.... Great job an designer(s) part!! It was a cool 3D environment, and I enjoyed exploring it.
Learning about Solar system	9.52%	When we did research on the planets. Because we learned a lot of new things.
Problem solving/Research	8.67%	My favorite part was doing the research. I liked this best because it gave me an opportunity to learn about different worlds and moons.
Working in groups	3.06%	I love Alien Rescue because we got to work with friends and think on our own about how to get answers versus reading in a textbook to get answer.
Managing budget	2.04%	That there is a budget. Also that you get to send probes into space. I liked these because it gives people challenges.
Game	2.04%	It was a very kid-like gaming world, which made me feel free to do whatever I needed to win the game. This game is very fun and I liked being able to learn about the world we live in. It's very entertaining.
Other (including a sense of accomplishment, multimedia features, computer-based etc.)	6.63%	Getting to the end because I felt happy and confident. It gave me a reason to be happy with myself. The reason is because at first I did not understand what to do. The video the aliens sent. Because everybody thought it was real. I enjoyed how they added extra stuff like a note pad, the table of elements and other tools because it was very useful.
Nothing	2.04%	Nothing

Note. Total units= 588.

Students were also asked to tell us what they did not like. Out of a total 413 coding units, their top responses included: doing research (21.55%), limited budget (9.44%), not interactive enough (8.47%), too difficult (8.47%), note-taking (6.54%), and probe-related frustrations (6.54%). Other responses included that the simulation was boring, making mistakes, filling out worksheets (given by the teachers), and not having enough time to work out the problems. 12.11% responded that there was nothing that they disliked. Sample quotes are:

> *The researching was confusing because it didn't say what you were looking at.* (Research)
> *I didn't like losing money to send probes. I didn't like being denied when I asked for more money.* (Limited budget)
> *My least favorite part about Alien Rescue was placing the aliens because that took the longest and it took a lot of the work and time.* (Too difficult)
> *My least favorite part had to write down all the info that you had to gather. It took a long time to find and write the info down.* (Not-taking)

Discussion and Implications

The Role of Fun in Learning

It is clear that the sixth graders considered their use of AR to be a fun experience. The word "fun" has the highest frequency in their responses to an open-ended question as shown in the word cloud in Table 1. This finding is consistent with our previous studies (Kimmons et al; Liu et al, 2011) and supports the idea of gamified processes as described by Fuchs (2012) and the manner through which ludic simulations support a sense of playfulness, as suggested by Ortoleva (2012). Students indicated that they learned both the content (i.e. our solar system, various science concepts and scientific instruments) and thinking skills such as problem solving and researching. Students also learned about working in groups, managing a budget, and how to engage in problem solving. One student responded that AR "taught us useful skills such as time management, working in a group, computer skills, working independently too." Our qualitative data analysis supports previous quantitative findings on the positive relationship between use of the ludic simulation and student learning. The finding that students had fun while learning supports the literature emphasizing the value of play and playfulness (Barab, Thomas, Dodge, Carteaux, & Tuzun, 2005; Garris, Ahlers, & Driskell, 2002; Squire, 2003), and illustrates the possibility of creating playful and fun interactions for purposeful and intentional contexts such as school learning. That is, our findings support the idea that games can be contexts in which significant learning can occur, as suggested by Gee (2003).

Many students expressed their desire to use AR again: "It was FUN. You should do this every 6 weeks! Thanks!" and "It did teach me a lot of things I did not know! I would probably LOVE to do it again." Perhaps the most encouraging finding is that that some students expressed self-confidence and motivation toward learning science as shown in such statements as: "It was FUN. I learn a lot and now I am going to do this [be a scientist] when I get older," and "I did very well and I see that I am good at space science." Ample research has shown that motivation and self-efficacy play important roles in influencing learning and achievement (Bandura, 1997; Lane & Lane, 2001; Lepper, Iyengar, & Corpus, 2005). However, research has also shown a general reduction in students' interest in science beginning at the sixth grade level (Osborne, Simon, & Collins, 2003). Our finding that students' use of AR was shown to have a positive influence on attitude towards science should provide an additional impetus for educational designers and researchers to explore, design, and research technology enriched ludic simulations to support learning.

Attributes of a Fun Experience

Of particular interest to this study are those aspects of the ludic simulation that middle school students considered fun or enjoyable. The findings centered on two aspects (i.e. probe-related and alien-related) and features related to these two. In solving the central problem of finding relocation sites for the aliens, the students must engage in a series of problem-solving steps including gathering information from the databases (e.g. Solar System Database, Mission Database, Alien Database). However, the information in those databases is intentionally incomplete and therefore students must use the Probe Design Center, Probe Launch Center, and Mission Control Center to design and launch probes to gather more information and test their hypothesis. In designing each probe, students must select appropriate tools. These probe related tools simulate the tools scientists use and the inquiry process they typically apply in their work. Students are given opportunities to experiment and establish for themselves a suitable problem-solving path. The design intention of AR is to provide an authentic learning context where students can apply various thinking skills to find a solution. Students' responses related to the probe tools specifically demonstrated the importance of realism and the role of being a scientist:

> *Making probes were fun. I felt like an astronaut!* (Student 1)
> *Sending probes was cool, because you got to pick what probe you wanted to send and all the stuff for it. You kind got the feeling of being one of those people that work for NASA and other places.* (Student 2)

This sense of realism is a significant motivating factor for these young scientists. While the probe related tools were designed to provide a sense of fidelity and realism, the design of Alien Database is intended to create a sense of imagination and fantasy. The essential information about the aliens (i.e. their body, food, habitat, communication symbols, and their home planets) is presented through rich, colorful, and interactive 3D. Each species has its own distinct look and feel. The results suggest that this visual and playful interface elicits a strong sense of fantasy among these students aged 11-13; the aliens are one of the top features students liked about AR. In addition, the fantasy element is also embedded in the narrative of the simulation as presented by the introductory video. This approach of blending more realistic representation with fictional and imaginative elements apparently prompted strong empathy from this age group, a finding consistent with Squire's (2003) belief that games can evoke strong emotional responses in the player. Among those features that students indicated as their favorites (see Table 3), 22.28% are alien related, the second highest. Of this category, 42% are about helping or saving aliens, as shown in such sample quotes: "Finding homes for the aliens, because when you find one you just feel so excited" and "Sending an alien to their planet because it just makes you feel good to know that you worked hard for that moment."

In addition, the narrative of the young scientists tasked with saving the aliens is situated in an open-ended problem-based context where there are multiple built-in challenges. Once the students are presented with the central problem, there are no instructions within the simulation that direct their work. Students are encouraged to explore and discover in a self-directed way while negotiating one of many possible solution paths. There are also six different species, each of which can have more than one solution. Some habitats are more optimal than others, requiring students to weigh a diverse range of possibilities and develop well-articulated justifications. Additionally, the budgetary constrains present in designing and launching probes prompt students to make careful decisions so as not to be wasteful. While this problem-solving process is challenging, it represents an authentic level of real-world complexity and provides another motivational element that promotes joy and self-confidence in these students: "It was very FUN and help me learn more about science. Thank you for making this. I love it so much. :)"

The findings validate the design of the simulation and highlight several attributes that made AR a fun learning experience for these middle school students: exploratory, interactive, immersive, playful, media-rich, roleplay, engaging narrative, and a challenging problem scenario. Addressing the three factors in Lindley's tetrahedron (2003), AR places equal importance on simulation and ludology and delivers a playful experience in an intentional problem-based narrative. With these attributes, it is also necessary to point out designs of technology enhanced environments must be solidly grounded in learning principles and designed with social responsibilities.

Students' responses also indicated three aspects that they did not like: they perceived it as too difficult, were dissatisfied with the number of interactive features, and experienced some technical glitches. As discussed above, this problem-based ludic simulation presents a complex problem over a period of 15 days. For some sixth graders, this self-directed approach is difficult and time-consuming, highlighting the need to implement additional technology-based scaffolds to support students in acquiring the expertise necessary to fully engage with the problem.

Summary

In conclusion, the findings of this study confirmed our previous research and provided further evidence to show that sixth-graders perceived AR as having substantial ludic characteristics. The results indicated that having a playful experience is important for this age group and that a fun experience can help motivate the students to learn school subjects. Our research also highlighted several attributes of critical importance in designing learning environments for middle school students. We are very encouraged by the possibilities of creating sophisticated computer-mediated simulations that integrate both ludic and realistic elements to support learning.

References

Bandura, A. (1997). *Self-efficacy: The exercise of control.* New York: W.H. Freeman.

Barab, S. A., Pettyjohn, P., Gresalfi, M., Volk, C., & Solomou, M. (2012). Game-based curriculum and transformational play: Designing to meaningfully positioning person, content, and context. *Computers & Education, 58* (1), 518-533.

Barab, S., Thomas, M., Dodge, T., Carteaux, R., & Tuzun, H. (2005). Making learning fun: Quest Atlantis, a game without guns. *Educational Technology Research and Development, 53* (1), 86–107.

Charmaz, K. (2006). *Constructing Grounded Theory: A Practical Guide through Qualitative Analysis.* Thousand Oaks, NJ: Sage Publications Civilization [computer software]. (1991). Alameda, CA: MicroProse.

Clarke, J., Dede, C., Ketelhut, D. J., & Nelson, B. (2006). A design-based research strategy to promote scalability for educational innovations. *Educational Technology, 46* (3), 27–36.

Creswell, J. W. (2005). *Educational Research: planning, conducting, and evaluating quantitative and qualitative research* (2nd Ed.). New Jersey: Merrill.

Csikszentmihalyi, M., & Bennett, S. (1971). An exploratory model of play. *American Anthropologist, 73* (1), 45–58.

DeNeve, K. M., & Heppner, M. J. (1997). Role play simulations: The assessment of an active learning technique and comparisons with traditional lectures. *Innovative Higher Education, 21* (3), 231–246.

Grand Theft Auto IV [computer software]. (2008). New York City: Rockstar Games.

Flight Sim X [computer software]. (2006). Redmond, WA: Microsoft Corporation.

Fuchs, M. (2012). Ludic interfaces. Driver and product of gamification. *GAME.* Retrieved July 12, 2012, from http://www.gamejournal.it/ludic-interfaces-driver-and-product-of-gamification/

Garris, R., Ahlers, R., & Driskell, J. E. (2002). Games, motivation, and learning: A research and practice model. *Simulation & gaming, 33* (4), 441–467.
Gee, J. P. (2003). What video games have to teach us about learning and literacy. *Computers in Entertainment, 1* (1), 20-20.

Ketelhut, D. J., Dede, C., Clarke, J., Nelson, B., & Bowman, C. (2007). Studying situated learning in a multi-user virtual environment. In R. E. Mayer (Ed.), *Assessment of problem solving using simulations* (pp. 37–58). Mahwah, NJ: Lawrence Erlbaum Associates.

Kim, I. (2009). A Study on the Factors and the Principles of the Fantasy in the Educational Context (Doctoral Dissertation). Seoul National University.

Kimmons, R., Liu, M., Kang, J. & Santana, L. (2011-2012). Attitude, Achievement, and Gender in a Middle School Science-based Ludic Simulation for Learning. *Journal of Educational Technology Systems, 40*(4). 341-370.

Lane, J., & Lane, A. (2001). Self-efficacy and academic performance. *Social Behavior and Personality, 29*, 687-694.

Lepper, M. R., Iyengar, S. S., & Corpus, J. H. (2005). Intrinsic and extrinsic motivational orientations in the classroom: Age differences and academic correlates. *Journal of Educational Psychology, 97*(2), 184-196.

Lincoln, Y. S., & Guba, E. D. (1985). *Naturalistic Inquiry.* Thousand Oaks, CA Sage Publications, Inc.

Lindley (2003). Game taxonomies: A high level framework for game analysis and design. Retrieved June 18, 2012, from http://www.gamasutra.com/view/feature/2796/game_taxonomies_a_high_level_.php

Liu, M., Horton, L., Olmanson, J., & Toprac, P. (2011). A study of learning and motivation in a new media enriched environment for middle school science. *Educational Technology Research and Development, 59*(2), 249–265.

Liu, M., Williams, D., & Pedersen, S. (2002). Alien Rescue: A problem-based hypermedia learning environment for middle school science. *Journal of Educational Technology Systems, 30* (3), 255–270.

McGonigal, J. (2011). *Reality is broken: Why games make us better and how they can change the world.* Penguin Press HC.

Ortoleva, P. (2012). Homo ludicus. The ubiquity of play and its roles in present society. *GAME.* Retrieved from http://www.gamejournal.it/homo-ludicus-the-ubiquity-and-roles-of-play-in-present-society/

Osborne, J., Simon, S., & Collins, S. (2003). Attitudes towards science: A review of the literature and its implication. *International Journal of Science Education, 25*(9), 1049-1079.

Piaget, J. (1951). *Play, dreams, and imitation in childhood.* New York: W. W. Norton & Company.

Rieber, L. P. (1996). Seriously considering play: Designing interactive learning environments based on the blending of microworlds, simulations, and games. *Educational Technology Research and Development, 44*(2), 43–58.

Singer, D. G., Golinkoff, R.M., & Hirsh-Pasek, K. (2006). *Play = learning: How play motivates and enhances children's cognitive and social-emotional growth* (1st ed.). Oxford University Press, USA.

Squire, K. (2003). Video games in education. *International Journal of Intelligent Games & Simulation, 2* (1), 49–62.

Strauss, A., & Corbin, J. (1990). *Basics of qualitative research: Grounded theory procedures and techniques.* Thousand Oaks, CA: Sage Publications.

17 Assessments for Learning, of Learning, and as Learning in 3D Immersive Virtual Environments

Jillianne Code, University of Victoria & Nick Zap, Simon Fraser University, Canada

Introduction

The key to education reform lies in exploring alternative forms of assessment. The roles that assessments play in educational reform often coincide with the introduction of new philosophies of learning, driving major themes in policy change (Linn, 2000). Regardless of philosophical paradigms, advances in technology create new possibilities for learning and assessment (Behrens, 2009; Pellegrino et al., 2001). In September 2009, the US National Research Council held a workshop on games and simulations. The white papers from this research conference urge further research to determine the full potential of collaborative, immersive simulations to support assessment (Quellmalz & Pellegrino, 2009), as well as virtual worlds that integrate assessment while engaging learning (Clark et al., 2009). Current research aims to explore this potential through the use of immersive 3D technologies that aim to situate students in an environment that promotes inquiry and sets the context for assessment (i.e. Clarke-Midura, Code, Zap, et al., 2012; Ketelhut, 2010; Nelson & Eriandson, 2012). This research indicates that immersive environments can potentially support student experimentation and scientific reasoning in a virtual context by allowing students the ability to walk around an environment, giving students the opportunity to take on the identity of an avatar, a virtual personae, that can explore and interact the 3D environment by making observations, gathering data, and solving a scientific problem in context. As an extension to this work, current research is actively exploring whether immersive virtual environments can enable the automated, invisible, and non-intrusive collection of students' actions and behaviours during the act of learning so that the capture and assessment of learning is in situ (Clarke-Midura et al., 2011; Clarke-Midura & Dede, 2010; Quellmalz & Haertel, 2004; Shute et al., 2007). The purpose of this paper is to provide a case study of three innovative projects that are all actively utilizing immersive virtual environments as situated spaces for the assessments of learning, assessments as learning, and assessments for learning.

Assessment *of* Learning

Assessment of learning, or summative assessment, refers to those strategies designed to confirm what students know at a particular moment in time. These strategies usually come in the form of paper-and-pencil tests implemented by teachers as a snapshot of student achievement for grading and reporting purposes. Summative assessments also serve to demonstrate whether or not students have met curricular outcomes or the goals of individualized student programs to certify proficiency and make decisions about future programs or placements. In short, summative assessments take place at certain intervals when achievement has to be reported as it relates to the progression in learning against a defined criteria in the form or curricular standards often set by public bodies (Harvard

Graduate School of Education (HGSE), 2010c). As a further means of assessing program and curricular viability, summative assessments mandated by public bodies as high-stakes tests are designed to provide evidence of achievement to parents, other educators, the students themselves, and to outside groups (Ketelhut, 2010). Ongoing arguments in the literature suggest that most valid and reliable summative assessments are in the form of multiple-choice or numeric response questions that can be machine scored. Efforts by researchers over the past 20 years have led to significant gains in the use of performance based assessments along side the high-stakes paper-and-pencil tests (Linn, 1994).

Performance Assessment

Alternative performance measures provide a more valid measure than multiple choice tests of students' conceptual understanding and higher-level skills such as problem solving (Lane & Stone, 2006). Research findings indicate that these alternate assessments are more transparent to the content being measured (Lane & Stone, 2006) and valuable for providing formative, diagnostic feedback to teachers about ongoing student attainment. However, there are several limitations to their use as summative assessments in accountability settings: First, hands-on performance assessments (HoPAs) in accountability settings are cost-prohibitive when compared to multiple choice tests (Pellegrino, et al., 2001). Second, HoPAs often have issues around task sampling and occasion sampling variability (Cronbach et al., 1997; Shavelson et al., 1993). Finally, HoPAs suffer technical, resource, and reliability problems that undercut both their validity and their practicality (Cronbach, et al., 1997; Shavelson, et al., 1993; Webb et al., 2000). Current research explores the feasibility of using technologies, such as immersive virtual environments, as an answer to scalability, validity, and reliability issues. The Virtual Performance Assessment project is one such research project.

Virtual Performance Assessments (VPA)

The purpose of the Virtual Performance Assessment project (VPA; http://vpa.gse.harvard.edu) is to develop assessments that complement rather than replace existing standardized measures by assessing skills not possible via paper-pencil, multiple-choice or HoPAs (Clarke-Midura, Code, Mayrath, et al., 2012; Clarke-Midura, et al., 2012; Code et al., 2011a, 2011c). The VPA project identifies several potential benefits of using immersive virtual environments for performance assessment. First, using immersive environments alleviate the need for extensive training for teachers to administer performance tasks with students as research demonstrates that it is difficult to standardize the administration paper-based performance assessments as extensive training is often required to administer the tasks. Immersive virtual assessments can help ensure standardization of task and delivery. Second, immersive virtual assessments alleviate the need for providing materials and kits for hands-on tasks as everything student's need is inside the virtual environment. Third, scoring is all done automatically behind the scenes—

there is no need for raters or training of raters. Finally, immersive virtual assessments alleviate safety issues and inequity due to lack of resources.

For each of the three assessments developed in the VPA project, the main goal is to assess students problem solving capabilities by allowing students to make choices that advance the hypothesis and theory that they are attempting to build (Clarke-Midura, et al., 2012). The three assessments are built around two different paradigms of learning: instructivist and constructivist. The first assessment, *Save the Kelp!* (Harvard Graduate School of Education (HGSE), 2010b) uses an instructivist paradigm where students were guided through the science inquiry process. The second and third assessments, *There's a New Frog in Town* (HGSE, 2010d) and *Silence of the Bees* (HGSE, 2010c), whereas assessments two and three utilized more of a constructivist paradigm where students were able to freely explore the environment and practice inquiry though action and interaction. Regardless of philosophical paradigm in all three assessments the measure of a student's science inquiry performance is based on their in-world actions (see Figures 1 and 2; Code et al., in press). As students make choices, in-world actions and choices are captured and given a range of scores and weightings that contribute to an on-going student model of science inquiry. In this model, student's actions are temporally evaluated based on past, present, and future actions. In other words, a choice is evaluated in terms of the previous actions, their actual choice within the context of the available choices, and the outcome of their choice that sets the stage for the next set of actions. For example, if a character asks a student what they think the problem is and the student responds that they think the mutant frog is a result of pollution, the character will ask the student to provide evidence for their claim. The evidence that a student gives is weighted and evaluated based on their prior actions (data that they have previously collected) and by what they choose to present as evidence. Although both assessment paradigms evaluate the same learning outcomes and that are tracked, measured, and scored in the same way, the user experience in qualitatively and markedly different.

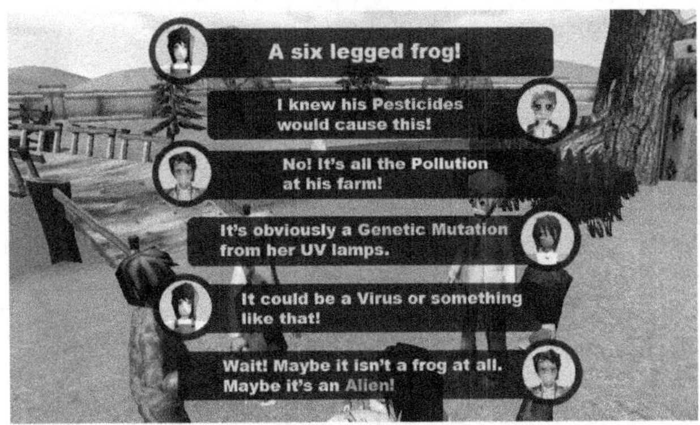

Figure 1. Presentation of competing hypotheses in a VPA environment.

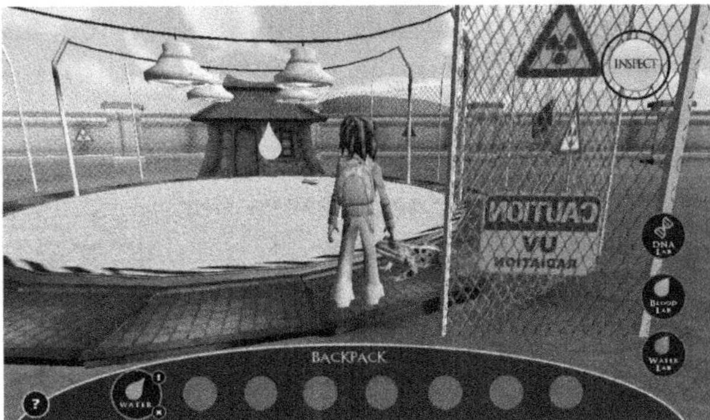

Figure 2. Collection of water samples in the VPA environment.

Results from the research published to date using the second and third VPA assessments (HGSE, 2010c, 2010d), reveal that the most successful students a) did a lot more external research in all areas and b) did a better job of supporting their claim with evidence (McCall & Clarke-Midura, 2011, 2013). Whereas unsuccessful students a) did not visit the Internet kiosk as much (external research), b) tend to engage in confirmatory activities, and c) were not skilled in reasoning from evidence (McCall & Clarke-Midura, 2011, 2013). Further, in relation to the engagement and in-world game behavior, results suggest that game behavior is not a good predictor of claim correctness as some students with high engagement and good reasoning chose the incorrect claim, and some people with low engagement and poor reasoning chose the correct claim. Although research is ongoing, one of the most salient features that is lacking in this approach is the one-way interaction between the student and the environment which is something that students expect more of this this kind of environment (Code, et al., 2011a, in press). In the next section, a case study of another project involves the students more intimately in their immersive assessment experience, engaging them in assessment as learning.

Assessment *as* Learning

The focus of self-assessment by students is not common practice, even amongst those teachers who take assessment seriously (Black & Wiliam, 1998). Despite significant evidence in the research that suggests that self-assessment improves persistence, self-efficacy, self-direction, achievement, and enhances metacognition it is an underutilized tool in the classroom (Black et al., 2006). Self assessment involves students in making judgments about their own achievement and learning processes and give them an active role in decisions about action for further progress in learning (Sebba et al., 2008). A recent systematic review of the research on student self and peer assessment reveals that there is evidence that self assessment improves: a) student attainment across a range of subject areas, b) student self-esteem, and c) students ability in learning to learn such as with goal setting, clarifying objectives, taking responsibility for learning, and increased confidence (Sebba, et al., 2008). Sebba et al. (2008) also found that self and peer assessment are more likely to impact on student outcomes when there is a move from a dependent to an interdependent relationship between teachers and students which enables teachers to adjust their teaching in response to student feedback. Thus "require[ing] learners to exercise a degree of autonomy from the teacher as the assessor and judge of quality" (Black, et al., 2006, p. 128). Ultimately, self-assessment means involving students in 'co-designing' the curricula for evaluation helping them to develop a better grasp of their own strengths and weaknesses. From the perspective of self-assessment, one such project putting students at the center of learning is the Transforming Engagement of Students in Learning Algebra project.

Transforming Engagement of Students in Learning Algebra (TESLA)

The purpose of the Transforming Engagement of Students in Learning Algebra project (TESLA; HGSE, 2010a; Figures 3 and 4; http://tesla-project.org) is to investigate the relationship between specific technology-based motivational activities and students' interests in Science, Technology, Engineering, and Mathematics (STEM) careers along a developmental span (Chen et al., 2012). Utilizing Expectancy-Value theory, TESLA explored how immersive virtual environments can be designed to promote students' interest and motivation. The TESLA environment accompanies a four-day blended experience that integrates technology-based activities with classroom-based instruction for 5th grade students in Mathematics. The immersive virtual activities the students are involved in (see Figures 1 and 2 as examples) enable the them to take on the identity of a STEM professional to solve a number of puzzles. Each of the puzzles must be solved correctly before the students can continue on in the environment.

Figure 3. First self-scoring puzzle in the TESLA environment.

Figure 4. Second self-scoring puzzle in the TESLA environment.

One of the critical features in the research design of TESLA project is that it is hypothesized that students attribute their successes and failures to factors that they could controllable thus highlighting that successful completion of the puzzles is not dependent on some innate mathematical intelligence that is completely out of their personal control (Chen, et al., 2012). Although the initial intention of the TESLA project was not necessarily aimed to serve specifically as a self-assessment, in effect it does just that, through the use of scaffolds assisting students in the solving of mathematical puzzles embedded within the curriculum. This highlights that the use of scaffolds as a means of formative feedback is a critical factor for student success enabling the use of assessment as an embedded learning experience.

Assessment *for* Learning

Current assessment approaches are inadequate at diagnosing how students develop critical thinking, problem solving, and sophisticated scientific reasoning which are all key 21st century skills (BC Premiers Technology Council (BCPTC), 2010; Partnership for 21st Century Skills (P21), 2009). Formative assessments carried out during instruction can be used to help teachers tailor instruction; aid in deepening students' understanding, and enable students to self-regulating their learning. Formative assessments however, are often too time consuming for teachers to do on a regular basis (Black & Wiliam, 1998). Teacher-made assessments tend to replicate multiple choice and open-response tests designed for benchmark or accountability settings and rarely tell teachers what they need to know about their students' thinking (Black & Wiliam, 2009). Such benchmark tests are also typically designed based on psychometric models that are better suited for assessing curricular program outcomes rather than based on a cognitive model of how students learn. This further contributes to the failure to formatively assess students' learning at the classroom level leading to a decrease in critical thinking and problem solving scores on a national scale. For example, on the 2010 Pan-Canadian Assessment Program (PCAP) of Mathematics, Science and Reading, middle school students from provinces and territories outside of Ontario and Quebec scored significantly below the national average on problem solving ability (Council of Ministers of Education Canada (CMEC), 2010). Similarly, on the 2009 Program for International Student Assessment (PISA), the average score of Canadian fifteen year olds on the use of elaboration and summarization strategies (critical skills for problem solving, science inquiry and the self-regulation of learning) is significantly below the international average of participating OECD nations (CMEC, 2011). In looking at the literature, there is a direct link between student use of self-regulated learning (SRL) strategies (such as elaboration and summarizing) and the development of complex cognitive reasoning and problem solving specifically in science (e.g. Winters & Azevedo, 2005). The fact that students in Canada are behind their international peers on the use of self-regulated learning strategies (i.e. elaboration and summarizing) is alarming and suggests that this will have a significant impact on their ability to conduct meaningful scientific inquiry.

Formative assessments have the potential to provide important feedback to both teachers and students. This feedback is critical in helping teachers adapt instruction so students can overcome any misconceptions they have in moving along a learning progression. Teachers need tools to adequately identify, measure, and evaluate what individual students know and do not know during learning. Without the aid of technology formative assessment is difficult to accomplish regularly during classroom instruction. Research findings suggest that formative assessments delivered using technology have the capability to record very detailed observations of students' actions not possible via paper-and-pencil tasks or through anecdotal teacher observations, as well as to adapt to students' responses in real time (Pellegrino, et al., 2001). "Practice in a classroom is formative to the extent that evidence about student achievement is elicited, interpreted, and used by teachers, learners, or their peers, to make decisions about the next steps in instruction that are likely to be better, or better founded, than the decisions they would have taken in the absence of the evidence that was elicited" (Black & Wiliam, 2009, p. 9). A limitation of current teacher developed assessments include an over-emphasis on rote learning and recall of facts which has led to a focus on grades and class level learning instead of individual learning that emphasize completing tasks as opposed to taking risks and engaging in cognitive activities. The quality of interactive feedback in formative assessment is a critical feature in determining the quality of overall teaching and learning activity, and is therefore a central feature of pedagogy (Black & Wiliam, 2006). Ironically, research on the success of feedback is mixed because it is often not used correctly (Shute, 2008). In her comprehensive literature review on feedback, Shute (2008) claims that formative feedback should address the accuracy of a learner's response to a problem or task and may touch on particular errors and misconceptions. Since research establishes that immersive environments have considerable potential to assess and scaffold science inquiry learning (Code et al., 2011b; Code, et al., 2011c, in press), the Assessment for Learning in Immersive Virtual Environment research project proposes to integrate these identified needs by focusing on the use of immersive virtual environment technologies to scaffold science inquiry and self-regulated learning strategies through the use of formative assessment and feedback.

Assessment for Learning in Immersive Virtual Environments (ALIVE)

The Assessment for Learning in Immersive Virtual Environments (ALIVE; http://alive.uvic.ca) project is a research program in the pilot stage that aims to examine how three-dimensional immersive virtual environments (3IVEs; \'thrīvz\) can enable student success by (a) providing formative feedback embedded during the process of learning; (b) visualizing students' cognitive models of problem solving *in situ*; and (c) scaffolding students' self-regulated learning. Self-regulated learning is an active, effortful process in which learners set goals for their learning and then attempt to monitor, regulate, and control their cognition, motivation, and behaviour (Pintrich, 2000). Specifically, this project aims to investigate ways that the 3IVE technology, designed around a model of science inquiry, enables individual students to (a) utilize formative feedback to adapt their learning behavior; (b) engage with log-file data-based visualizations; and (c) monitor their 3IVE activities to regulate their cognitive and behavioral processes to maximize learning success. The ALIVE project will integrate and build upon TESLA and VPA by utilizing 3IVE technology as a means to visualize and formatively assess science inquiry enabling a student to self-regulate their learning. The specific goals of the ALIVE project are to:

1. Focus on the use of 3IVE technologies to scaffold science inquiry and self-regulated learning strategies through the use of formative assessment and feedback.
2. Explore whether 3IVEs can enable the automated, invisible, and non-intrusive collection of students' actions and behaviors during the act of learning that will enable the capture and assessment of science inquiry in situ.
3. Use well established models of scientific inquiry to examine the use 3IVEs to assess learning processes as they happen and how students use this feedback to regulate their learning.
4. Design the 3IVE technology to non-intrusively collect log-file data of students' actions and behaviors during the act of learning and present this data as a means to provide feedback that helps students regulate their learning and teachers regulate their teaching.

It is the intention of the ALIVE project to design and develop 3IVEs to use as a formative assessments to research whether this feedback can help address students' misconceptions in science inquiry and help students regulate their learning and teachers adequately address what students know and do not know about science inquiry processes. The 3IVE will enable the capture of rich sets of student behavioural observations (log-file or trace data) in a database, which can then be analyzed with the intention of diagnosing student misconceptions in scientific inquiry.

Directions for Future Research

Authentic assessment requires students to apply knowledge and reasoning to situations similar to those they will encounter in the world outside the classroom (NRC, 1996). Since existing assessment frameworks do not provide information on how learning processes develop, a cognitive model is necessary to examine these processes in situ. Projects such as ALIVE aims to use established cognitive models to examine whether immersive virtual environments can assess learning as it happens and how students utilize feedback to regulate their learning goals.

Formative assessment provides feedback that can be used by teachers to regulate instruction, by students to regulate their learning, and by classroom peers to collaboratively regulate, monitor and overcome any misconceptions in complex reasoning. Research needs to specifically explore how teachers can use these measures to: 1) clarify and share learning intentions and criteria for success; 2) engineer effective classroom discussions and other learning tasks that elicit evidence of student understanding; 3) provide feedback that moves learners forward; 4) activate students as instructional resources for one another; and 5) empower students as the owners of their own learning (Black & Wiliam, 2009).

References

BC Premiers Technology Council (BCPTC). (2010). A vision for 21st century education (13th ed.). Victoria, BC.

Behrens, J. T. (2009). Response to Assessment of Student Learning in Science Simulations and Games: National Academy of Sciences.

Black, P., McCormick, R., James, M., & Pedder, D. (2006). Learning how to learn and assessment for learning: a theoretical inquiry. *Research Papers in Education, 21*(2), 119-132.

Black, P., & Wiliam, D. (1998). Assessment and classroom learning. *Assessment in Education, 5*(1), 7-74.

Black, P., & Wiliam, D. (2006). Developing a theory of formative assessment. In J. Gardner (Ed.), *Assessment and learning* (pp. 81-100). London: Sage.

Black, P., & Wiliam, D. (2009). Developing the theory of formative assessment. *Educational Assessment, Evaluation, and Accountability, 21*(1), 5-31.

Chen, J. A., Zap, N., & Dede, C. (2012). Using virtual environments to motivate students to pursue STEM careers: An expectancy-value model. In S. D'Augustino (Ed.), *Immersive environments, augmented realities, and virtual worlds: Assessing future trends in education* (pp. 42-56). Hershey, PA: IGI Global.

Clark, D. B., Nelson, B., Sengupta, P., & D'Angelo, C. M. (2009). *Rethinking Science Learning Through Digital Games and Simulations: Genres, Examples, and Evidence.* Paper presented at the National Academies Board on Science Education Workshop on Learning Science: Computer Games, Simulations, and Education, Washington, DC.

Clarke-Midura, J., Code, J., & Dede, C. (2011). *Assessment 2.0: Rethinking how we assess science inquiry with technology-based assessments.* Paper presented at the National Science Teachers Association 2011 Annual Conference, San Francisco, CA.

Clarke-Midura, J., Code, J., Mayrath, M., & Dede, C. (2012). Thinking outside the bubble: Virtual Performance Assessments for Measuring Inquiry Learning. In M. Mayrath, J. Clarke-Midura & D. Robinson (Eds.), *Technology Based Assessment for 21st Century Skills: Theoretical and Practical Implications from Modern Research* (pp. 125-147). New York, NY: Springer-Verlag.

Clarke-Midura, J., Code, J., Zap, N., & Dede, C. (2012). Assessing science inquiry in the classroom: A case study of the virtual assessment project. In L. Lennex & K. Nettleton (Eds.), *Cases on Inquiry Through Instructional Technology in Math and Science: Systemic Approaches* (pp. 138-164). New York, NY: IGI Publishing.

Clarke-Midura, J., & Dede, C. (2010). Assessment, technology, and change. *Journal of Research on Technology in Education, 42*(3), 309-328.

Code, J., Clarke-Midura, J., Zap, N., & Dede, C. (2011a). Student perceptions of immersive virtual environments for the meaningful assessment of learning. In T. Bastiaens & G. Marks (Eds.), *Education and Information Technology 2012: A Selection of AACE Award Papers* (pp. 185-194). Chesapeake, VA: AACE.

Code, J., Clarke-Midura, J., Zap, N., & Dede, C. (2011b). *Student perceptions of immersive virtual environments for the meaningful assessment of learning.* Paper presented at the World Conference on Educational Multimedia, Hypermedia and Telecommunications 2011, Lisbon, Portugal.

Code, J., Clarke-Midura, J., Zap, N., & Dede, C. (2011c). Virtual performance assessment in immersive virtual environments. In H. Wang (Ed.), *Interactivity in E-Learning: Cases and Frameworks. New York, NY: IGI Publishing* (pp. 230-252). New York, NY: IGI Publishing.

Code, J., Clarke-Midura, J., Zap, N., & Dede, C. (in press). The utility of using immersive virtual environments for the assessment of science inquiry learning. *Journal of Interactive Learning Research.*

Council of Ministers of Education Canada (CMEC). (2010). PCAP-2010 Report on the pan-Canadian assessment of mathematics, science, and reading. Toronto, ON: Council of Ministers of Education, Canada.

Council of Ministers of Education Canada (CMEC). (2011). Second report from the 2009 programme for international student assessment. Toronto, ON: Council of Ministers of Education, Canada.

Cronbach, L. J., Linn, R. L., Brennan, R. L., & Haertel, E. H. (1997). Generalizability analysis for performance assessments of student achievement or school effectiveness. *Educational and Psychological Measurement, 57*(3), 373-399.

Harvard Graduate School of Education (HGSE). (2010a). Transforming Engagement of Students in Learning Algebra Cambridge, MA.

Harvard Graduate School of Education (HGSE). (2010b). Virtual performance assessment: Save the kelp! Cambridge, MA.

Harvard Graduate School of Education (HGSE). (2010c). Virtual performance assessment: Silence of the bees. Cambridge, MA.

Harvard Graduate School of Education (HGSE). (2010d). Virtual performance assessment: There's a new frog in town. Cambridge, MA.

Ketelhut, D. (2010). Assessing gaming, computer and scientific inquiry self-efficacy in a virtual environment *Serious Educational Game Assessment: Practical Methods and Models for Educational Games, Simulations and Virtual Worlds* (pp. 1-18). Amsterdam, The Netherlands: Sense Publishers.

Lane, S., & Stone, C. A. (2006). Performance Assessments. In R. L. Brennan (Ed.), *Educational Meaurement.* Westport, CT: Praeger.

Linn, R. L. (1994). Performance assessment: Policy promises and technical measurement standards. *Educational Researcher, 23*(9), 4-14.

Linn, R. L. (2000). Assessments and accountability. *Educational Researcher, 29*(2), 4-16.

McCall, M., & Clarke-Midura, J. (2011). *Analysis of data from a game-based assessment from AHM and IRT perspectives.* Paper presented at the National Council on Measurement in Education, Vancouver, Canada.

McCall, M., & Clarke-Midura, J. (2013). *Analysis of gaming for assessment.* Paper presented at the Association of Test Publishers Annual Meeting, Orlando, Florida.

National Research Council (NRC). (1996). *National Science Education Standards.* Washington, DC: National Academie Press.

Nelson, B., & Eriandson, B. E. (2012). *Design for Learning in Virtual Worlds (Interdisciplinary Approaches to Educational Technology)* New York: Routledge.

Partnership for 21st Century Skills (P21). (2009). Framework for 21st Century Learning. Washington, DC.

Pellegrino, J. W., Chudowski, N., & Glaser, R. (2001). *Knowing what students know: The science and design of educational assessment.* Washington, DC: National Academies Press.

Pintrich, P. (2000). The role of goal orientation in self-regulated learning. In M. Boekaerts, P. Pintrich & M. Zeidner (Eds.), *Handbook of Self-Regulation* (pp. 451-502). San Diego, CA: Academic Press.

Quellmalz, E., & Haertel, G. (2004). Technology supports for state science assessment systems *Paper commissioned by the National Research Council Committee on Test Design for K–12 Science Achievement.* Washington, DC: National Research Council.

Quellmalz, E., & Pellegrino, J. W. (2009). Technology and testing. *Science, 323*(5910), 75-79.

Sebba, J., Deakin Crick, R., Yu, G., Lawson, H., Harlen, W., & Durant, K. (2008). Systematic review of research evidence of the impact on students in secondary schools of self and peer assessment: EPPI-Centre, Social Science Research Unit, Institute of Education, University of London.

Shavelson, R. J., Baxter, G. P., & Gao, X. (1993). Sampling variability of performance assessments. *Journal of Educational Measurement, 30*(3), 215-232.

Shute, V. J. (2008). Focus on formative feedback. *Review of Educational Research, 78*(4), 153-218.

Shute, V. J., Hansen, E. G., & Almond, R. G. (2007). *An assessment for learning system called ACED: Designing for learning effectiveness and accessibility.* (RR-07-26). Princeton, NJ: Educational Testing Service.

Webb, N. M., Schlackman, J., & Sugrue, B. (2000). The Dependability and Interchangeability of Assessment Methods in Science. *Applied Measurement in Education, 13*(3), 277-301.

Winters, F. I., & Azevedo, R. (2005). High-school students' regulation of learning during comuter-based science inquiry. *Journal of Educational Computing Research, 33*(2), 189-217.

18 The Academic Librarians: New Roles and Challenges: a Comparison to Kurt De Belder's "Partners in Knowledge"

Anne-Berit Gregersen, Learning Center & Library Oslo and Akershus University College of Applied Sciences, Norway

The Norwegian Academic Libraries

Today several of the university colleges are aiming to be fully acknowledged universities. This leads to a stronger emphasis on academic skills for both students and faculty. The students are required to improve their academic writing and information literacy skills. The faculty members are expected to publish in peer reviewed scientific journals, preferably with open access. They are also challenged by the new ways of publishing on the web, using e-books and printing on demand. The new paradigm with e-learning and MOOCs («Massive Open Online Courses») might lead to completely new ways of organizing higher education. This, and the technological change towards mobile technology and "bring your own device" ("BYOD") lead to a new ecology with easy and more frequent access to resources outside the institutions. These challenges must be met by university libraries offering highly specialized services in a rapidly changing environment.

Librarianship in Norway

The librarians' worktasks are changing with the technological development. ICT has long been a central part of the librarians field of activity and we are considered competent users. Many librarians work as Web-developers and we consider the web to be an important arena for organizing information. Now we have to face MOOCs and ask ourselves what impact this will have on the libraries.

The librarians are also faced with the "academization" of the university college. From building collections, giving access to information and providing reference services we are now giving support to learning and research. More effort is put in the task of making our students competent in information literacy – to make them able to update their professional knowledge throughout their working life. Norwegian nursing students should be able to evaluate research in order to decide upon best practices in nursing. The nursing teachers are cooperating with the librarians in the training of the students in evidence based nursing. The students meet the librarians in the classroom rather than behind the circulation desks. In my university college students also get counseling on their writing skills by trained language teachers.

The Norwegian research assessment system has created an arena for the librarians: The need for CRIS systems covering the entire scholarly publication production has made an opportunity for the librarians to work in closer connections with the researchers.

Support is given from choosing academic journals suitable for their publication to all the pitfalls of publishing Open Access and questions regarding publishing rights. My library is also in charge of managing the fees for open access publishing. The curation of research data is another task waiting to be taken care of.

Support to the learning environment by giving embedded courses in information literacy, curriculum support, EndNote, academic writing skills and general support to the students´ learning demands other competencies than the traditional library skills. The libraries are now shaped to provide the needs of the users, rather than the collections. "Customer relationship" and "the user in focus" calls for a new type of librarian, with new skills and new priorities. This provides a close collaboration with the teaching staff and research communities

The Need for change

These are some of the main challenges: (Langley, Gray, & Vaughan, 2003)

- Changes in the production and dissemination of scholarly communication
- Changes in higher education
- Growth of technology inside and outside of the library:
- New means of communicating with library patrons and collegues
- Materials in multiple formats, and read with varying systems, including mobile technology
- Competition from the "free web" and from commercial vendors and booksellers
- Technology in the workplace

"To meet the challenges of this electronic environment, you must be willing to aquire new skills and provide new services. You must become proficient in electronic collections management and further your commitment to public service. If you don't, your users will change without you." (Langley & al., 2003, p 86)

"The dynamic environment of the library and information sector dictates the need for library and information professionals to remain flexible and adaptable to change...Lifelong learning extends and develops the knowledge, skills and competencies of practitioners. It also enables them to prepare for their work more effectively, to broaden their careers and to undertake new tasks" (Fisher, Hallam, & Patridge, 2005, p. 49)

How do libraries deal with these challenges? According to Kurt De Belder (2013) libraries do change:

"Libraries have changed tremendously, have innovated, have added digital services, have generated more research/teaching time at the faculty level. But to a great extent have not ended services and have kept within the existing library paradigm Major drives for decisions about libraries within university administration is budgetary considerations. Change is outpacing us."

These are core areas of impact:

- Selection/Acquisition
- Cataloging
- Archiving
- Reference desk
- Outreach
- Making material available
- "Find it" business
- Special Collections
- Technology management

Local relevance

How does this apply for my library organization? To a great extent! We change all the time, but are still doing many of the traditional library tasks. I will answer the question by using De Belder's list of traditional functions:

Selection/acquisition is mostly done by librarians, but we are trying out Patron Driven Acquisition for e-books. Already 3 month into the fiscal year we have spent a substantial part of the budget and we were forced to cut down on the possibilities. We need more experience on the use of PDA in order to have control over limited resources, but we definitely think this is a road to follow.

Cataloging: The national academic library system, Bibsys, is both a joint catalog and a common ILL system for all the Norwegian academic libraries. This means saving time spent not only on cataloguing, but also in the acquisition process as well as for interlibrary loans. We reuse about 80% of the entries in the catalogue, but we still prepare the books for the shelves, with shelf tags and RFID etc.

Archiving: The OA and institutional repositories has created new field of work in libraries. This is a growth sector within Norwegian academic libraries and has taken over much of the work load previously spent on cataloguing and classification. Local archiving of materials in repositories also means a lot of work on management of copyrights towards both authors and publishers. In addition to the open archive we have established a closed archive for publications not permitted for OA. Data collections are in the early start in Norway but is a task that will need attention. If not the library is taking on the curation of research data, who will? This is parallel to the OA movement. The librarians are willing to engage in their institutions need for knowledge curation. We are hoping for a unified effort with Bibsys to build a national system for research data.

Reference desk: Staffed with highly qualified staff, this is one of our main priorities and an important meeting point with the users. We also have special "drop in" reference point for students needing a guidance in information seeking, and a "drop in" point for guidance in academic writing and Norwegian as a second language. Our "book a librarian" service is widely used by graduate students and researchers. This service requires booking in advance in order to match the needs of the users with our subject librarians. Virtual reference desk is in early beginning and the service must be further developed in order to meet the needs of education and research.

Outreach: There are faculty liasons with typical library services, but also partners in research and teaching. In 2012 we had 800 hours teaching in faculty with different levels of information literacy, reference management systems, tailored services to research and publishing support. The library is responsible for the quality control of students' reading lists with regard to new editions, reference styles etc. before they are published on the web. In addition to support in writing skill and study technique we have English for Academic Purposes, specially aimed at phd students and researchers. EAP is staffed with highly qualified staff fluently in English and holding a PhD degree. We have a staff of 6 persons within the library organization covering Research, 3 within e-learning and 3 within language and communication. In addition we handle Copyright questions related to OA, e-publishing (repositories and OJS) and Administration of a OA publishing fund were authors can apply for funding when publishing in OA journals with a publishing fee. Our University librarians are liasons to phd candidates. This is a librarian with minimum a master degree within the actual field of study and serves as a subject specialist. These positions are new in our learning center and library and a valuable addition to the traditional library staff.

Making available: We still have a growth in lending of printed materials, but a greater growth in use of e-publications. E-books needs to be retrieved the same way as printed books. We can make use of publisher's metadata, but need to add Norwegian terms as well. A lot of work goes into the institutional repositories. Has this work taken over for the traditional cataloguing and classification?

"**Find it" business**: A big part of our job! But increased use of e-resources turns us in to the "get it" business. This service in closely connected to teaching, making staff and students aware of the library's resources to become competent users of databases and library systems. "Googlification" of the library systems makes information retrieval easier for the end user, but the understanding of academic publications is scarce among fresh students. This support the importance of teaching information literacy in the library.

Special collections: This is not a big issue in my library organisation, but we do have a certain obligation to take care of the history of many small professions. Use of National Library is a possibility for deposit and digitalization of special collections.

Technology management: Bibsys, The National Library system means little local management. More systems must be shared in the future, like the accounting systems and acquisition systems used by the mother institution. We have a great advantage in a common library system within higher education in Norway. State institutions like most higher educational institutions, use the same administrative systems, the same purchasing systems etc which opens up for cooperation among institutions and between systems. Our new library system should make use of system integration on a wider scale. Other fields of technology management are institutional repositories. Bibsys have developed and is hosting the repositories for a group of minor educational institutions. The major institutions runs their own repositories – nearly all based on Dspace. In addition, NORA, the Norwegian Open Research Archive, is harvesting the local repositories. The library is responsible for Managing an Open Journal System to accommodate the institutions own scholarly open access journals. We also have the Management of library web-services within the institutional frames. The library´s web-pages is much about making available – collections and databases, but also user support. In the future we will have a stronger emphasis on the development of web-based services like Online tutorials – We have some very good Norwegian open source tutorials on information literacy and library support to phd candidates. In addition we are making short online tutorials locally available on YouTube, streaming of faculty lectures and management of e-learning content.

This overview clearly shows that there is a growth in the field of technology management, and the support and partnership in research and teaching. To become adequate partners in research and teaching within a university the librarians must also be skilled academics. They must be able to understand the needs of the researcher and the demands for academic information literacy faced by the students on different levels.

Lorcan Dempsey (2013) is speaking about three challenges for libraries: engagement, rightscaling infrastructure, and institutional innovation. The shift is in the engagement which is creating new services to research and education. Kurt de Belder is speaking about "Partners in research". Dempsey explains it as a shift in engagement. There is a clear shift in creating new services to research and education, but are we able to stop doing other tasks?

In an interview Carol Kuhlthau says: "So that´s where I see the librarianship as being in a time of change. The librarian is moving from something very structured to something that's much less structured, working with ideas and concepts, pulling in resources and working with the person who is going through various different stages of a problem. But I don´t think we´re quite there yet. It is a hugely changing profession." (Tonning, 2009, p. 52)

Future thinking

An abundance of online learning resources, coupled with the rise of Open Access also stand to affect the nature and services provided by libraries. We know very little of the impact of MOOCs in Norwegian academic libraries. If these courses continue to be massive and open online the whole way of dealing with access to journals and databases will have to change. Today the Open Access movement cannot meet the competition of the commercial information vendors – will the MOOCs change that and make the education sector a learning space for all? Or will the institutions limit their best courses to those who can pay? The International Federation of Library Associations (2013) trend report claims that online education will democratise and disrupt global learning. This trend report point to five trends, which all will have impact on library services. Trend 1 is "New technologies will both expand and limit who has access to information". This emphasis the importance of information literacy skills as tools for distinguishing authorative information and the question of ownership of information and content. Learning will focus more on how to authenticate and exploit information rather than memorise knowledge.

Libraries do change. Our skills and services are being used in new ways and on other work tasks. Instead of meeting the users behind the circulation desk, we meet the students and researchers in their classrooms or offices, teaching information literacy or giving support to reference management. We still perform cataloguing, but towards institutional repositories rather than the traditional library catalogue. The libraries are the working space and meeting place for students rather than a quiet area and a depository for printed books.

References

De Belder, Kurt (2013*). Transformation of the Academic Library.* Paper presented at the Bibsys brukermøte, Trondheim http://www.bibsys.no/norsk/bibliotekar/brukermoter/brukermote_2013/Presentasjoner/index.php

Dempsey, Lorcan (2013). Three challenges: engaging, rightscaling and innovating. Retrieved from http://orweblog.oclc.org/index.html

Fisher, Biddy, Hallam, Gillian, & Partridge, Helen. (2005). Different approaches - common conclusions: the skills debate of the 21st century. In P. Genoni & G. Walton (Eds.), *Continuing professional development: preparing for new roles in libraries : a voyage of discovery : Sixth World Conference on Continuing Professional Development and Workplace Learning for the Library and InformationProfessions* (Vol. 116, pp. 41-52). München: Saur.

Langley, Anne, Gray, Edward, & Vaughan, K. T. L. (2003). *The role of the academic librarian.* Oxford: Chandos.

The International Federation of Library Associations and Institutions IFLA. (2013). *Riding the Waves or Caught in the Tide? Insights from the IFLA Trend Report*: IFLA.

Tonning, Anne Sissel Vedvik. (2009). Carol C. Kuhlthau - interviews at the Conference Learning, Innovation and the Use of Information in Aalborg, Denmark, April 2008. *Nordic Journal of Information Literacy in Higher Education, 1*(1), 52-53.

19 New Library Tasks: A Dialog-based Approach to Guidance on Academic Writing.

Ingunn Nilsen, The Culture, Language and Learning Unit, Learning Center & Library
Oslo and Akershus University College of Applied Sciences, Norway

Introduction

The Study Skills Center; from project to a permanent unit at Oslo and Akershus University College for Applied Sciences. A description of choice of methodology, the focusing on dialog based guidance, student to student, on academic writing. A look into the future, with hopes and immediate plans for a dynamic Study skills Center.

A project was initiated in 2008, than a trial period followed, and 16 months ago The Study Skills Center became part of a regular activity at HiOA, Oslo and Akershus University College of Applied Sciences, with two centers, one in Oslo and one in Akershus. We started this year, 2013, with one senior advisor in an 80% post and six to eight (6-8) writing mentors working part time. We are planning to end this year with 1,5 (150%) posts and 8-10 writing mentors.

In the beginning, the project paid special attention to giving students with special needs; international students and students with Norwegian as a second language an extra service. It was thought of as a project in the work of creating an intercultural and international environment at the school. It also was looked at as interesting for students with special needs like for example dyslexia or mental challenges. The Learning Center and Library was from the beginning thought of as a natural environment when setting up the center. Both the Study Skills Center and the Learning Center and Library are directed towards all students, all departments and all faculties at the University College, and both are supporting the sections in academic work. The aim of the project was to implement the activity into the regular and permanent activities presented for the students. (Greek& Jonsmoen: 2010)

The reasons for success, for not becoming a project developed, implemented, and then disappearing when the funding was spent, were first of all, the thorough work done in the period of developing the project. The aim of implementing the Study Skills Center into the existing organization was part of the strategy from the start, the project leaders secured a group of inter faculty professionals in the reference group, and also had project partners from a range of departments. The project started with thorough research, what was needed and wanted amongst students and academic staff, and what did the research with observation, tell them. The research was followed by a trial period with trying out different locations for the Center, a variety of courses and guidance lessons were arranged, before it was decided on one location, and one model for mentoring, with students being writing mentors. (Greek & Jonsmoen; 2010).

The project was, from the beginning, aimed at and worked directly towards establishing the Center as a part of the existing organization, immediately following the project funding running out. It was thought of as important that there should be no time-lapse between the project funding ending, and the ordinary activity starting up. It is at this crossroad that many a good project strand.

In other neighboring European countries, for example Denmark, Sweden and Great Britain there had been similar activities and centers for years. Their experiences and how they were organized, was used as examples of what our organization was missing. Some of these Centers were visited, and success criteria were sought out and used in modeling the first Study Skills Center in Oslo.

Norwegian researchers with focus on writing for a university level have been emphasizing the necessity of opening similar writing centers at the universities and university colleges of Norway. In 2005 Torlaug Løkensgard Hoel wrote that Writing centers and writing courses that can give the students help to self-help, should be established as permanent activities at institutions for higher education (Hoel;2005, p114) (my translation from Norwegian)

Since the beginning of the project, the Center has been open for all students, even though some groups of students were specially invited to join,. We see that students with Norwegian as a second language keep visiting us, but we also see that students with Norwegian as their first language find your services valuable. In fact about 50% of our visiting students have been from each of the two groups. From the logs we see that students both with Norwegian as a first and a second language, find it useful to have a dialog about the constructing of their academic texts. Some of the students with Norwegian as a first language also want to speak about their uncertainties about their language, and many of them are interested in discussing the formal criteria an academic text requires. The students with Norwegian as a second language wanted and needed, in addition, more certification on their language skills. Some students learning the Norwegian language at a grown age have larger issues with language and also with understanding the learning culture and writing culture of Scandinavia.

A dialog based approach to guidance on academic writing has proved its success at HiOA. The project was duly documented and the students, the academic staff and the writing mentors involved were interviewed. The results were published and the heads of the project, the writing mentors and the students commented on the process. (Greek & Jonsmoen 2010)

On Asking the « Obvious »

The dialog between teacher and student tend to become more of a teaching/learning experience, one is the experienced, and one is the inexperienced. This has been taken into account when planning the Student Skills Center. The experience from neighboring countries, the recommendations from Norwegian professors with writing as their major focus, and the popular demand from teachers as well as student organizations from the inside of the institution, all pointed in the direction of starting something that could be a supplement not a competition to the already established system of teacher-student guidance (Greek & Jonsmoen; 2010).

When it comes to dialog concerning an academic text, the result of the learning experience for the student becomes different and more open when the dialog is between two students. It is crucial that both the student and the student working as a writing mentor knows, and at all times have in mind that the guidance is on the text as a an academic text and the guidance is not on the content of the subject the student is studying. At first, many students find it confusing and sometimes not satisfying, because they do not get what they expected to get. Many come to be assured that their text is "good enough", that they will pass and get a satisfactory grade. At first, many want straight answers, what is wright and what is wrong.

The students working as writing mentors at The Study Skills Centre have had a three day writing mentor course. The subjects emphasized during this course are: 1. How to practice guidance, student to student. 2. Developing awareness on writing process and text development. 3. Building a critical approach to your own work of writing, and to the work of writing of other students.

The job description for the writing mentors specifically describes what the writing mentors at our Student Skills Center are going to work with, with the visiting students. The focus is on these three topics; 1) Supporting the student in clarifying and organizing own thought, and developing writing strategies. 2) Developing a critical approach to own work, improve structure and understanding the academic genre. 3) Developing strategies for improving their own academic writing.

There has also been produced a mentor guide, used at other units at our University College as well, for student guides and study buddies (HiOA; 2010). This guide focuses on the win win situation, that the student mentoring and guiding other students will benefit and learn new skills themselves. The guide focuses on the increased competence in mentoring skills, the experience they are gaining in communicating with new people and the increase in their intercultural competence.

The guide states about the writing mentor that their work should focus on the writing process. Themes can be on how to get started with an assignment, how to make a register, how to structure the text, how to debate or make plausible arguments, conclude, or how to use references. The role of the writing mentor is described as working towards the aim of being a supportive listener, a critical reader and a partner in discussion (HiOA; 2010).

The writing mentors have a monthly follow up meeting with useful subjects on the agenda, as well as an exchange of good practices. We talk about what works well, what kind of questions do you ask to make the students learn from the experience, and what kind of questions do you not ask. The work on building the students' consciousness of their role as skilled writing mentors is an ongoing and crucial process for success (Johansen; 2013).

We have a log from every guidance session, and the findings from these gives us more than an indication; to have a dialog with an able student; a writing mentor, about the visiting student`s academic text versus the written comments from a teacher on text, gives the student an immediate possibility to respond and get a response.

The threshold for asking "the obvious" is reduced, and the session seems to give the student an opportunity to practice and improve meta language on own text. Since the talk is between two students, the possibility to have an open and actual dialog increases. Some of the students with Norwegian as a second language are not used to talking about their own unfinished texts, and therefore they find it difficult in the beginning, but also rewarding in the end. (Johansen; 2013)

The logs are semi structured with a form and it is obligatory for the writing mentors to fill in the forms and comment and reflect on every guidance session they have completed. We emphasize on the reflections the writing mentors do, and the reflections are partly about the students response to the guidance session, but also on the writing mentors own experience of how they succeeded in their professional role. They also come with ongoing suggestions on how the Study Skills Center can improve their service to meet the students' actual needs.

A new Dimension of "Librarianship";
Long-term Perspectives – A Blueprint for Further Development

As of this year, 2013, the Study Skills Center has become part of a new unit; The Culture, Language and Learning Unit at the Learning Center & Library at HiOA. The others in the unit are EAP; English for Academic Purposes and MIPP; Diversity in Pedagogical Practices. Both EAP and MIPP work mainly towards the academic staff, and we, the Study Skills Center work today mainly towards the students. Together we are building a robust, professional team working to enhance the quality of education through the work with professional communication amongst the academic staff and the students.

We are unconventional as a unit at libraries in Norway today, but does that need to be the case? We think not. The work with enhancing quality of education is also the work of building a library for the future.

A Norwegian network for Student Skills Centers is establishing. So far five institutions of higher education have participated. The network became a reality after numerous enquiries and inquiries to our Study Skills Center during 2012. The first network meeting was held in Oslo in the spring of 2012, and the second in Stavanger in May 2013. This time we had the overall theme of how to meet the student with Norwegian as a second language as well as general. Next year the network meeting will be held in Haugesund, and a permanent network is emerging.

We see that the thought of starting a student Skills Center no longer is a singular though amongst some idealists at one University College, in one city in Norway. The center in Oslo has proved its right to existence, and other cities and other institutions of higher education are finding their way of providing similar services for their students. The network may work as a platform for sharing practice and experience, both of organizing questions, but foremost on the content, the professional skills.

The basis of the work in the Student Skills Center will, at least for some years yet, be the dialog based guidance given of and to students. We have already other activities like courses in academic writing. Some courses are elementary; what is academic writing, how to discuss in an academic text, but we also arrange courses in writing a bachelor or master paper. The courses are held both of academic staff and of writing mentors that have undergone training. Courses in study technique are arranged annually as well.

We have a good working relationship with the Learning Center and Library, our courses and services are linked on our different web pages. Our web page and our Facebook account are main arenas for contact with students. You are welcome to visit our cites here;
http://www.hioa.no/LSB/Studieverkstedet
www.facebook.com/Studieverkstedet

The web page is updated with information on opening hours, new courses, and a short introduction to our services. On our Facebook account we also announce activities at our Center, but we keep a more informal tone, giving advice and recommendation on articles, apps or other useful sites focusing on study skills or academic writing. This work is time-consuming with updates two times per week, but the response is that many find our post interesting and inspiring, and therefore worth our while.

With the new unit, Culture, Language and Learning, we see and hope for a more extensive corporation on new projects. All departments in the new unit are working inter departmentally, all with an aim of strengthening the quality of the studies, and enhancing an intercultural environment for both academic staff and students. All three units have a main focus on the academic writing skills of students and staff.

This year, in September, Studieverkstedet have taken small role in the organizing of the annual Writing Week, arranged by MIPP since 2010. The Writing Week is open for all students and staff at HiOA. The lecturers invited are experts in their field, and come from different institutions of higher education in Norway .We were also represented on the program of the Writing Week this year with a two hour crash course in Norwegian grammar for students with Norwegian as a second language. The course was a an opportunity to focus on that even though you were accepted into higher education, developing a language as a second language speaker will always be an ongoing task.

The intention was also to launch the idea of a work shop for the same student group, arranged by our Center. The work shop will be a pilot project to explore the needs and the requests amongst students with Norwegian as a second language. We will explore the cooperation between the head of the unit and the writing mentors. The initiating idea is to have a topic of the day, followed by independent work by the students on their actual student texts, with the possibility of discussing language and assignment questions with us and each other. If there is enough interest, we hope to arrange a series of workshops during the fall of 2013 and spring 2014. From experience, we need to allow a modest number of visitors over some time. Most new project need time to settle.

For 2014 we are looking at increasing staff with one 50% position. With this we hope to make the Student Skills Centers second unit, at Akershus, a more rugged center. We also plan a project of on-line guidance at the Akershus campus. This because a number of students here take part time studies, a group are older students with other commitments, family, work etc. There are therefore fewer students here than in Oslo, that can make use of our on campus guidance.

The centers are situated at different campuses, 30 minutes apart. With one head of the unit, the work of implementing and keeping in contact with the faculties and academic staff is complicated. We hope that with the increase in personnel, the personal and frequent contact with students, staff and community will become an easier task than today. We see the daily the personal and frequent contact with students, staff and community as crucial in the establishment of a new center, but just as crucial in the continuous work of being a dynamic center meeting the needs of the students, the academic staff and the ever changing needs of society.

References

Dysthe, Olga, Frøydis Hertzberg & Torlaug Løkensgard Hoel. (2010). *Skrive for å lære.* Oslo: Abstrakt forlag

Greek, Marit &Jonsmoen, Kari Mari (2010*) Studieverkstedet ved Høgskolen i Oslo, PLUSS-rapport.* HiO-rapport 2010 nr 16. Oslo : Høgskolen i Oslo

HiOA, læringssenter og bibliotek; http://www.hioa.no/LSB/Mangfold-i-pedagogisk-praksis/Mentorarbeid/Mentorguide-hva-vil-det-si-aa-vaere-mentor

Hoel, Torlaug Løkensgard Hoel. (2008). *Skriving ved universitet og høgskolar – for lærarar og studentar*. Oslo: Universitetsforlaget

Johansen, Grethe Moen (2013) *Jeg vil gjøre, ikke bare snakke om.* In; *Gode pedagogiske praksiser.* HiOA Tema utgivelser 2013 nr 1. Oslo: Høgskolen i Oslo og Akershus

20 From Flash to HTML5: making a mobile web application for library with jQuery Mobile

Jingru Hoivik, The National Library of Norway, Norway

Background

"Flash was created during the PC era – for PCs and mice. ... But the mobile era is about low power devices, touch interfaces and open web standards – all areas where Flash falls short. New open standards created in the mobile era, such as HTML5, will win on mobile devices (and PCs too)." [Jobs 2010]

Adobe Flash is a multimedia and software platform used for vector graphics, animation and games on web pages. It has been widely used to create interactive library webpage as well, such as simulation of page turning, zooming and interactive touch screen for digital library exhibition, etc.

Adobe Flash was one of the most useful elements on the web. The following data are gathered in 2011:

- 98% of enterprises rely on Flash Player.
- 85% of the most used sites use Flash.
- 75% of web video is viewed using Flash Player.
- 70% of web games are made in Flash.

But now the trend has been reversed. HTML5 is quickly **becoming one of** the **most sought-after** web tools. In the past, Apple refused to enable support for Flash on the iPhone or iPad and the Flash Player was not going to be available on Apple's iOS. Google launched Chrome Web Store to focus on HTML5 in December 2010, followed by Facebook launched the HTML5 mobile site in 2011, and Amazon, LinkedIn also unveiled HTML5 products.
On mobile devices, HTML5 provides a similar level of ubiquity that the Flash Player provides on the desktop [*Mike Chambers*]. With its unique technological advantage in the mobile area, HTML5 has been steady taking over the market. HTML5 is the future. It is also a new challenge for librarians. There are quite a number of web presentations in the National library of Norway have been made based on Flash these recent years. However, the mobile era is the low-power devices, touch interfaces and open web standards-screens, Flash has been left behind. With the growth of the user market for mobile devices, the ability to create applications that run across platforms is very important for developers. The current situation marks a crucial acknowledgement by libraries that we need to change our strategy to remain relevant in a world that is increasingly turning to mobile.

Mobile Applications& jQuery Mobile

There are two types of mobile applications in the mobile market so far:

- Native mobile application, such as those sold in Apple's App Store or Google Play

- Mobile web application

Instead of running on a stand along desktop application, a web app is an application that runs on a web server through a web browser. Mobile web applications are an increasingly way to deliver web content to mobile devices, such as smart phones and tablets. Delivering through web, mobile web applications do not need to be downloaded and installed via an apps store. Native mobile apps request developers to create different types of applications for each type of device, i.e. Apple apps for iPhone/iPad and Android apps for Android phones and galaxy tabs, etc. In the past, developers need to program in Android, iOS, WindowsPhone and other types of operating system development corresponding to applications. The HTML5 opportunities, enabling developers to achieve a "write once, available everywhere" purposes. The ideal situation for developers is a cross-platform mobile web app, an application that reaches users through whatever devices, Android phone/tabs or Apple's iPhone/iPad, wherever they are. The ideal tools so far for us to build mobile web apps are HTML5/jQuery Mobile, which make it even quicker and easier to develop mobile web apps.

jQuery Mobile provides a set of touch-friendly UI widgets and an AJAX-powered navigation system to support animated page transitions. It provides cross-browser support for developers to build applications that can run across the various mobile Web browsers and provide the same or very similar user interface. It is a relatively new mobile web framework that helps us build mobile web apps that look and feel like native apps crossing a variety of mobile platforms.

The basics of a jQuery Mobile/html5 page may include the following:

- The doctype is the standard doctype for an HTML5 Web page.
- The page normally contains header, content and footer sections.
- The viewport is set in a metatag, normally is set to the screen width of the device
- The jQuery core JavaScript file;
- The jQuery Mobile core JavaScript file;
- The jQuery Mobile core CSS file;
- The jQuery Mobile CSS theme file

The Mobile web app solution for library

Users do not exactly browse the content on mobile in the same way they do on desktop. The main difference between desktop and mobile web application is the design for user interface.

There are three features for mobile devices we should take in consideration when we design:

- Portable sound and video system
- Sensitive touchable screen display
- Limited memory storage space
- Slow reaction and long processing time

A mobile web application should meet the following:

- Bigger and easy to control buttons
- Simple interface for information content
- Display limited information within one small "screen page"
- Take advantage of portable sound / video system

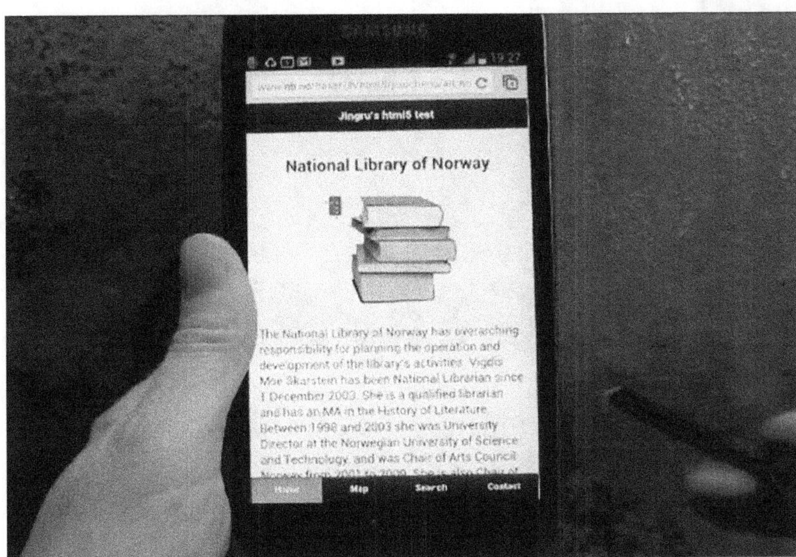

Figur 1

Fig.1 shows our web app interface showing on a galaxy note screen. Mobile web application's interface needs mainly to be optimized for the devices: limited memory and screen size, finger sweeping display. A clean interface with easy control buttons is suitable here. Four fitting buttons on the bottom will bring users to our library's information and collection.

Fig.2b is a screen shots from the free text search result. The search function is carried out by JavaScripts in our jQuery/html5 solution and search data were fetched from our library server. In Fig.2a, the Map button will bring users to an interactive map where the library's location and the user's current position will show on a Google map. The road from the user's current location to the library will be showed on the map. The Geo-location API provides a method to locate the user's current position. Several different sources could be used to obtain a user's location. Mobile devices tend to use triangulation techniques such as GPS, WiFi, etc.

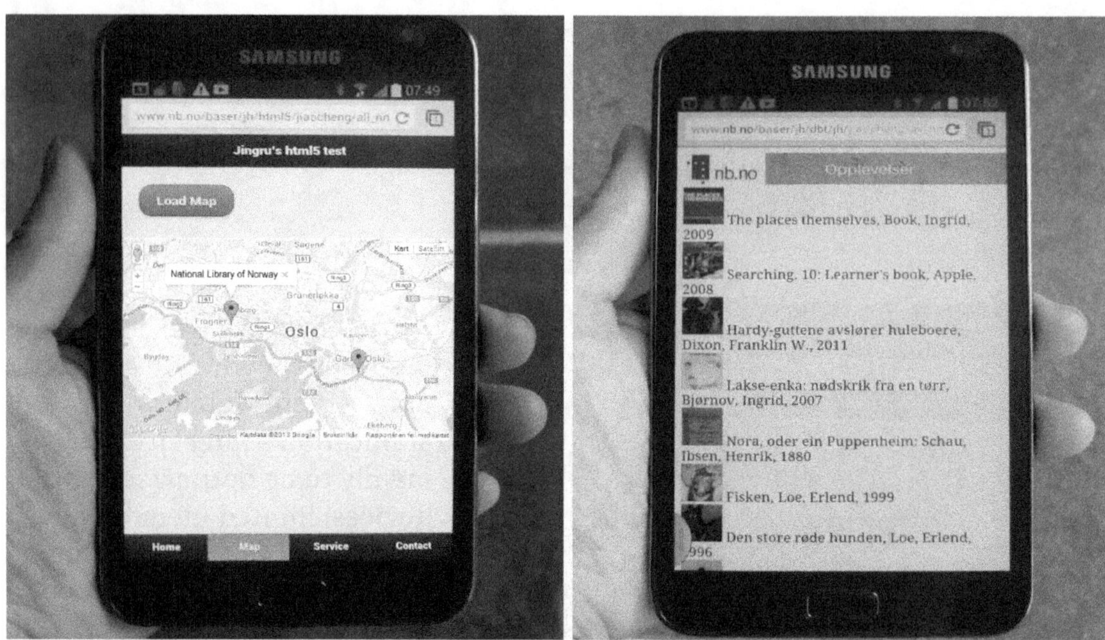

Figure 2a & 2b

In our case finding a user's position is realized with a function:
navigator.geolocation.getCurrentPosition();
The getCurrentPosition method retrieves the current geographic location of the user's mobile device and returns the location information in a position object.

Interactive presentation for the collection

There are many ways to make a mobile web application for the library's collections. Interactive presentation is one of the best ways to display library's resources online, especially suitable for mobile users with finger touch.

Figure 3a & 3b

In our solution, zooming function has been realized by jQuery/html5 for picture presentation (Fig.3a). Instead of click on a small picture and link to a large picture, zooming has been used here for mobile users. Since the limitation of a mobile device screen size, a large picture may only be showed part of the picture at a time. Fig.3a shows our web app in a mobile screen: a fit size picture is in the middle of the screen, mobile users may use their fingers or an active pen on the pen-enabled devices to drag and move the "magnifier" to any where inside the picture. In our jQuery mobile solution, zooming simulation was implemented by several JavaScripts and CSS files with function such as obj.hover( ) and obj.offset().

Under the Journal display, a page turning imitation has been used for turning the journal back and forth. Mobile users may experience with finger touch for an interactive view of the front and back covers of a journal (Fig.3b).

Selected references:

- Firtma, Maximiliano: Programming the Mobile Web, 2nd Edition -- Reaching Users on iPhone, Android, BlackBerry, Windows Phone, and more. O'Reilly Media, 2013
- **Firtman, Maximiliano**: jQuery Mobile: Up and Running, O'Reilly Media, 2012
- Chetan, K Jain: jQuery Mobile Cookbook, 2012
- Ben, ParrNov : Flash For Mobile is Done, HTML5 is the Future, 2011
- Campesato, Oswald: jQuery, CSS3, and HTML5 for Mobile and Desktop Devices, 2013

21 Applying the Model of Digital Literacy Assessment in English Reading and Writing

Feng Yang & Lihua Li, Beijing University of Technology, China

1. Background

Along with the wide use of computer and the rapid development of the Internet, literacy in language education has been expanding its original notion. English learners should have knowledge and skills not only in English but also in digital technology. Therefore, College English education should help college English learners to develop a whole new range of English-based skills under the circumstances of Web multimedia. The urgent need to prepare students for these future challenges has made it a priority to incorporate digital literacy development into university English teaching programs (Gu 2002). *The College English Curriculum Requirements* (2007) in China suggests that the extensive use of advanced information technology should be encouraged, and computer- and Web-based courses should be developed in designing College English courses. However, in China the new literacy skills are not reflected in the traditional standardized multiple-choice testing currently used to test. In this case, a new approach to curriculum and assessment based on digital literacy is required.

This study explores the use of an assessment model adapted for *Academic English* teaching at Beijing University of Technology (BJUT). The assessment model in the study is adapted from the model used in the framework of *Academic Writing* at Peking University (PKU) by Prof. Zhang Wei, as well as on the basis of the actual setting at BJUT. The original model was successful at PKU, a first-class national key university in China, so the study explores whether the adapted model of digital literacy assessment can be applied in College English education in ordinary colleges and universities and whether the adapted model can help to improve students' English and their English-based digital literacy skills.

2. Theoretical framework

2.1 Digital literacy

From a traditional perspective, being literate is perceived as being able to read and write. But in this information age, the need for the specific learned ability to use a computer and the Internet has generated terms such as digital literacy, information literacy and e-literacy.

Gilster (1997) uses the term "digital literacy" to describe the skills required in the Internet age. According to Gilster (1997), digital literacy is the ability to understand and use information in multiple formats from a wide range of sources when it is presented via network computers. Acquiring digital literacy for Internet use involves mastering a set of core competencies, including "knowledge assembly, Internet searching, hypertextual navigation, and content evaluation" (p.230). The most essential of these is the ability to search, assess and select online information. Thus, being digitally literate means more than mastering key-strokes or other low-level technical skills relevant to the use of basic computer hardware/software. It is about mastering and constructing knowledge based on the vast amount of information available on the Internet (Zhang 2003).

Hill (1998, 2000) developed the term computer literacy into English-based Digital Literacy, and claims that the new literacy consists of four skills: (1) use of resources such as search engines for locating and scanning relevant information on the Web and electronic databases; (2) use of critical thinking skills for evaluating the reliability of the information from various web sites; (3) use of organizational skills for integrating various bodies of information into a coherent framework; and (4) use of presentation skills for effectively communicating in both oral and written English in a technological environment.

It seems Hill laid an emphasis on the acquisition and practice of the new language skills for completing academic learning tasks in schools (Lu 2004). Actually, this framework specifies practical goals in developing curriculum and assessment for Chinese college students.

2.2 Assessment in the digital age

Assessment is a complex topic, the technical and sometimes political dimensions of which can often put teachers off. But here we are only concerned with language assessment.

Brindley (2004) defines assessment as "the act of collecting information and making judgment on a language learner's knowledge of a language and ability to use it" (p.310). Assessment is thus concerned with individual student learning. Bailey (2004) believes that "assessment is an integral part of teaching and learning, but should be subordinate to both" (p.24). She brings assessment into the heart of language teaching, and teachers can make sense of it and therefore direct it to support effective teaching and worthwhile learning in their classroom.

The best explanation comes from Angelo (1995):

> Assessment is an ongoing process aimed at understanding and improving student learning. It involves making our expectations explicit and public; setting appropriate criteria and high standards for learning quality; systematically gathering, analyzing, and interpreting evidence to determine how well performance matches those expectations and standards; and using the resulting information to document, explain, and improve performance. (p. 7)

Thus, we know assessment is important to educational process because it provides feedback on whether the course and learning objectives have been achieved to a satisfactory level. Appropriate assessment instruments can offer valuable information to teachers, students and administrators. On the one hand, it gives teachers a better idea of what students understand as well as what still needs to be clarified, and then enables teachers or other decision makers to make appropriate decisions (Wang 2005). On the other hand, students may take active part in the process of the assessment, and get some valuable feedback from teachers so that students may gain insights into the educational process and become more interested in the assessment

3. Research questions

What is mentioned above becomes the theoretical foundation for the present study. Considering the major difference between students at PKU and BJUT, the researcher used assessment as a way to help students at BJUT find their place in school and in the world community of language users. The present study targets English-based digital literacy skills such as searching on the Internet, gathering information from the Internet, and synthesizing the evaluated information into a coherent framework as curricular and assessment goals.

Research questions are addressed here:

(1) Can the adapted model of digital literacy assessment be effectively applied in Academic English for Science and Engineering teaching at BJUT?

(2) In what way can the adapted model of digital literacy assessment improve students' English and digital literacy?

(3) What are the students' attitudes toward this new adapted model?

4. Methodology

4.1 Participants

Thirty second-year non-English majors of 2011 from BJUT participated in this project by taking the 16-week course *Academic English for Science and Engineering* in Fall, 2012. They major in Electronics, Civil Engineering, Chemistry, Mathematics, and Physics, etc. and most of them have learnt English for over 7 years. These students entered into the College English program as Band-3 students. After one year of study in the College English program, they passed the BJUT Band-4 test and the nationwide Band-4 test in China. Then they participated in the project.

They had never attended a writing course before, and none were familiar with English research paper technique or even Chinese research paper. In the use of the Internet and the skills of using computer, most of them just used the Internet to send email, chat or play online games, and a few of them even had no experience of using the Internet before they entered BJUT. No one had had the experience of using the Internet and digital databases for research purposes.

4.2 Collection of Data

The assessment design consists of five parts, which were adapted from the assessment model for *Academic Writing* by Professor Zhang Wei at PKU (2003, 2006).

4.2.1 The achievement target

Based upon the infrastructure and digital database at BJUT as well as the quality of students at BJUT, the learning objectives of this study include:

- Use of search skills for locating and scanning relevant information from the Internet and digital databases;
- Use of organizational skills for integrating various bodies of information into a coherent framework;
- Use of presentation skills for effectively communicating such information in written English in a technological environment.

The learning objectives were set not only to encourage students to cultivate their sense of culture and society after reading more English after class, but also help students to develop knowledge and skills in utilizing digital resources online and in communicating what they learned from these resources. This is also the basic step for students to learn to write a research paper in their major field of study when they are juniors or seniors or even after graduation. Here the researcher did not include the critical thinking skills in the learning objectives as Professor Zhang did, just because of the lower English level of these BJUT students.

4.2.2 The assessment task

In the 16-week course, each student was required to select a topic relevant to their major field of study or an issue relevant to culture or social problems, develop an exposition or an argument supported by sources from the digital databases and the Internet, and then present the project to a general audience in written English. The length of the written presentation was expected to be no less than 800 words, but no more than 1,500 words. Students are required to learn how to use library sources, take notes effectively and master the conventions of documentation, i.e., proper use of quotations, footnotes or endnotes, and bibliographies.

All the students of 2011 were divided into three levels based on the scores of National College Entrance Examination. The students in the top of the score list were A and B-level students. Among 2,500 students, 350 students are A-level, 1000 are B-level and 1,150 students C-level. The participants in the study were all A-level students. Teacher selecting five interesting units with topics concerning such controversial issues as the vulnerability of a computer, nanotechnology, global warming, nuclear radiation, and genetically modified foods will make students more serious with their study and more responsible for their study. Students also had freedom to choose a topic relevant to the field of their study or topics concern other social problems, allowing them to develop a strong personal commitment to their projects.

4.2.3 The scoring rubrics

Heidi Goodrich, a rubrics expert, defines a rubric as "a scoring tool that lists the criteria for a piece of work or 'what counts' " (*Just what is a rubric* 1997). A rubric for an essay might tell students that their work will be judged on purpose, organization, details, voice, and mechanics. A good rubric also describes levels of quality for each of the criteria, usually on a point scale.

The scoring rubrics evolved from the use in studies in PKU made by Zhang Wei and their use in pilot studies, as well as the evaluators and the students who participated in this study.

The adapted written rubrics consist of three major criteria: content, clarity, and creativity. Content consists of the central idea, the relevance of the supporting evidence and the reliability of the sources for the supporting evidence. Clarity includes the coherence in organization (informative introduction, logical body paragraphs and consistent conclusion), sentence grammar and word choice. Creativity includes originality of personal thought which goes beyond the original material cited and the consistent control of materials used by the students.

Here the researcher changed 'the criteria of critical thinking' in Zhang's rubric into 'creativity' just because she knew that even students at PKU found it most challenging, so she lowered the requirement for BJUT students in this respect. Table 1 presents the scoring rubric used for this study.

Categories	Accomplished	Promising	Developing	Beginning
Content	*Defined central claim *Highly sufficient support *Varied sources	*Central claim *Moderately sufficient support *Some sources	*Unclear central claim *Slightly sufficient support *Few sources	*Unclear central claim *No sufficient support *No sources
Clarity	*Overly organized *Varied and appropriate choice of words; highly effective cohesive devices	*Organized *Appropriate choice of words; effective cohesive devices	*Organization mixed up *Frequently inappropriate choice of words; limited cohesive devices	*Organization mixed up *Inappropriate choice of words; no cohesive devices
Creativity	*Fresh personal thought *Highly consistent control of material	*Personal thought *Moderately consistent control of material	*No personal thought *Slightly consistent control of material	*No personal thought *No consistent control of material

Table 1 Scoring Rubric

4.2.4 Instructional design

In the mid-1980s, educators were introduced to a new approach to writing instruction that focused on writing as a process, as opposed to writing as a product. Since then, writing teachers have learned to guide students through a process for writing that encouraged a repeated set of activities focused on planning, drafting, revising, editing and publishing (Roblyer 2005).

This course, in which writing is as a process, uses both face-to-face and online modes of instruction. Students worked both in and out of class, with the support of face-to-face instruction and an online learning environment.

In face-to-face instruction, the teacher introduces the five topics in the textbook (the vulnerability of a computer, nanotechnology, global warming, nuclear radiation, genetically modified foods). These topics are currently controversial issues people are interested in nowadays. Students can read these passages and refer to the courseware and reference materials either using textbook or school intranet.

In online instruction, after registering the course named *Academic English for Science and Engineering* in Education Online on BJUT website, the researcher posted the references in Education Online on campus network of BJUT as well as sent the instructions (search online, hypertext reading, criticizing and analyzing information and reorganizing information, checklist, etc.) into public mailbox, so students can generate a range of ideas and solutions relevant to their self-selected research report using the resources and tools provided.

4.2.5 Application of the rubrics

At the beginning of the semester, the students and the teacher used the rubrics to evaluate previous student presentations so as to become familiar with the rubrics and offer suggestions for the revision of the rubrics. Then students use the revised rubrics for self-evaluation and peer-evaluation when they were writing their research report. At the end of the semester, the two evaluators used the rubrics to evaluate the students' final drafts.

The two evaluators are female English teachers from BJUT. Both of them are associate professors of English and have years of marking students' writings in the nation-wide CET-4 and CET-6. One of them graduated from Beijing Normal University in 1985. The other evaluator started teaching College English after she received her Master's Degree in English literature from Jilin University in 1997. Both of them have been teaching *Reading and Writing* for many years.

As for the score, equal weight was given to each of the three criteria --- content, clarity and creativity, because it is hard to determine in what way each criterion contributes to the quality of the whole writing. High performance in each of the three criteria is equally graded as 5 points, Mid performance 3 points, and Low performance 1 point. Between High and Mid performance is 4 points and between Mid and Low performance is 2 points. Therefore, the average total score of High-level papers is within the range of 12-15 points; the Mid-level papers within the range of 9-11 points; the Low-level papers below 9 points. The thirty writings were evaluated by the two evaluators independently.

4.3 Data Analysis

4.3.1 Quantitative Methods of Data Analysis

The purpose of quantitative data analysis is to examine whether the adapted model of digital literacy assessment can be effectively applied in *Academic English* teaching at BJUT.

To address this research question, the researcher estimated inter-evaluator agreement between the two written evaluators at two levels: composite evaluation results and results under each individual criterion so as to know the stability of the evaluation results by the two evaluators based on an evaluation rubric built around content, clarity and creativity. Composite results were measured by Pearson's Product Correlation Coefficients to test the correlation between the two evaluators because the nature of the data is continuous. The results under each individual criterion including content, clarity and creativity were measured by Spearman's Rank Correlation Coefficients because the nature of the data based on a scale of 1 to 5 is ordinal. Besides, quantitative data were analyzed with SPSS 17.0.

4.3.2 Qualitative Methods of Data Analysis

Qualitative data were collected from the students' written presentations, evaluation results by the two evaluators and students' reflections upon the writing as well as the informal interviews of the evaluators upon the completion of their evaluation.

To illustrate how the scoring rubrics operate for evaluating student performance at different levels, text analysis methods are used to analyze six written presentations: two High-level papers within the range of 12-15 points, two Mid-level papers within the range of 9-11 points and two Low-level papers within the range of 0-8 points.

Three levels of evaluation are used to analyze the representative papers: the first is the evaluation by the students themselves; the second is the evaluation by the two evaluators; the third is the evaluation by the researcher. Here the focus is on the evaluation by the two evaluators.

5. Results and Discussion

5.1 Effective application of the adapted model at BJUT

Inter-evaluator agreement is estimated between the written evaluators at two levels: 1) composite evaluation results and 2) results under each individual criterion. Correlation coefficients at both levels are shown in Table 2:

Evaluators	Content	Clarity	Creativity	Composite
Written evaluators	rs =.657**	rs =.466**	rs =.403*	r =.709**

(*p<.05; **p<.01)

Table 2 Correlation Coefficients between Two Written Evaluators

For composite results, Pearson's Product Correlation coefficients indicate a strong correlation between the two evaluators ($r = .709$, $p < .01$). The strength of this correlation indicates that the application of the written rubrics has produced highly consistent results by the two evaluators. This positive result is due to their substantial practice in using the rubrics before the actual work of evaluation.

Spearman's Rank Correlation coefficients are significant for all the individual criteria between the two evaluators. There is a high correlation in content (.657) and clarity (.466) and a moderate correlation in creativity (.403). The correlation coefficient for content (.657) is higher than that for clarity (.466) and the coefficient for creativity is lower (.403). Actually, from the scores the evaluators assigned to these 30 presentations, there is highly consistent agreement in content and clarity and there is moderately consistent agreement in creativity.

In the following talks with these two evaluators, both of them appreciated the topics the students chose and the content in their compositions. Both said that it was a good attempt for these college non-English majors to write an article concerning social problems as well as topics in their field of study. Both of them appreciated the way that these students searched online for useful information and read it before they wrote. Both are tolerant of the incorrect way the students document their reference materials and quotations, and they think as long as these non-English majors document these information, it is OK. Therefore, their high appreciation of student writings might explain the high correlation between the two evaluators for the criteria of content.

As far as the criterion of creativity is concerned, the two evaluators seem to have different ways in which they apply the criterion of creativity. Evaluator A seems to have a relatively tight schema in this respect. She pays more attention to the consistent control of materials by the students.

However, these differences are not sufficient to affect the overall consistency in applying the rubrics built around content, clarity and creativity, as evidenced in the significant coefficients in the composite results and in the results under almost all individual criteria. With the high inter-evaluator agreement for the composite results and for the individual criteria, we can conclude that the application of the written rubrics has produced consistent results between the two evaluators in the study, which proves that other English teachers are also able to evaluate the writings which involve the use of new literacy skills with the rubric designed, if properly trained. The results of the study show that this adapted assessment model is effective in assessing English-based digital literacy for Academic English studies at BJUT. This proves that the model of digital literacy assessment used at PKU can be successfully repeated at such second-class universities in China as BJUT. The project can be promoted elsewhere and can benefit teachers and students in other schools.

5.2 The adapted model improving students' English and digital literacy

Most students are quite satisfied with this course as stated in students' reflections. In this project, students saw themselves as developing important new life skills that integrated technology and language. They are happy that they are getting familiar with the process of writing an English research report, and they have learned the advanced skills required in digital age.

Many students stated that their reading comprehension has been greatly improved through reading various materials in English to select suitable articles as references and their vocabulary has been enlarged in the process of sifting information. It indicates that reading skills are intimately bound up with research skills in the online language learning environment, because with so many resources online, people often have to read with some purpose in mind and with a critical eye, in order to find something useful. Students also acquired some good usage of the language and useful supporting evidence in the reading process, which "heightened the awareness of the new language, identified macro-structures in text, and helped them formulate rules for themselves in their research paper writing" (Yan 2006).

Students seemed to have gained more valuable research and writing skills. Most of them know how to choose a topic, search for information, organize their materials and draw conclusions. But the high-level achievers do well under the three criteria (content, clarity, and creativity), while the mid-level achievers do well only under one or two of the three criteria. The low-level achievers do poorly in almost all the three criteria. This indicates that the participants' different language proficiency, basic computer skills, past writing experience and commitment to their project work may affect their digital literacy development and application. Students with more computer skills seemed to be more comfortable in this new learning environment. Those with higher language competence benefited more from the process of writing a research report. This result is the same as what Professor Zhang (2003) found in her study.

This study also shows that students generally lack awareness of documentation and citation. Thus teachers need help to cultivate and improve their awareness of the copyright or the intellectual property right of other people to document.

5.3 Students' active attitudes toward this adapted model

There are several factors that seem to have positive influence on the student attitudes and learning performances. Firstly, students appreciated the new Web-based project environment that was not available in their normal classrooms. It was the first time for students to write a research paper by using some advanced computer technology to complete the task. Second, they perceived English and information technology as inseparable means to achieve success in their future career and personal development. Third, many students made good use of the computer tools (email, blog, forum) to directly exchange their opinions with the teacher and their partners, which improved the efficiency of their writing and helped them maintain the positive attitude to the task all the while. That's why most students in this study overcame the difficulties, maintained their positive feelings and kept active involvement in the writing tasks throughout the project. At the end of the project, many students conveyed their intention that they wanted to take part in this kind of project if they had the chance in the future.

But there are still a few students who changed their initial positive attitudes toward the writing task in the process of the project just because of their low English proficiency and poor computer skills. They felt that too much time and effort was put into technology and it was difficult for them to understand English papers on the Internet. It was especially a headache for them to go beyond the sources to express their own viewpoint.

This indicates that the participants' different language proficiency, basic computer skills, past writing experience and commitment to their project work may affect their digital literacy development and application. Therefore, it is preferable to ensure that students have mastered basic computer skills before the project begins and the project is implemented among students at a higher level of language competence so that the students might not be frustrated by these technical problems and they may gain more confidence and acquire a sense of accomplishment.

6. Conclusion

The study shows that the assessment model developed gives full play to the advantages of traditional classroom teaching while fully employing modern digital technology. This adapted assessment model can potentially improve both students' English proficiency and their digital literacy. Students generally hold positive attitudes towards this kind of projects and kept the active involvement in the projects. The success of the study at BJUT proves that the model of digital literacy assessment used at PKU can be successfully repeated at such second-class universities in China as BJUT. The adapted model can be promoted and repeated among other college students with different levels of English proficiency at different universities, and it can be adapted to English majors and students of humanities in college and it can also be conducted in middle schools or primary schools.

As an important part in current curricular reforms at BJUT, the adapted model in turn promotes the reform of College English teaching at BJUT. Therefore, this study provides an alternative assessment model for other Chinese universities to complement national standardized College English testing. This study can also provide some valuable references for the reform of College English teaching in China. However, such a Web-based project requires not only the efforts of individual instructors but also collaboration between College English instructors and experts in other fields as well as administrative support from school leaders.

References

Angelo, T. A. (1995), Reassessing (and defining) assessment, in AAHE Bulletin, 48(3), 7. <www.tss.uoguelph.ca/id/newfac/assessment.pdf>

Bailey, K. M. (2004). *Language About Language Assessment; Dilemmas, Decisions and Directions.* Beijing: Foreign Language Teaching and Research Press.

Brindley, G. (2004). Classroom-based assessment. In Nunan, D. (Eds.) *Practical English Language Teaching* (pp.309-328). Beijing: Higher Education Press.

Gilster, P. (1997). *Digital literacy.* New York: Wiley Computer Publishing.

Gu, P. Y. (2002). Effects of project-based CALL on Chinese EFL learners. *Asian Journal of English Language Teaching*, 12, 52-66.

Higher Education Department of the Ministry of Education. (2007). *College English Curriculum Requirements.* Beijing: Foreign Language Teaching and Research Press.

Hill, C. (1998). *English in China: Educating for a global future.* <http://www.columbia.edu/~cah34/EIC/EnglishInChina.html>

Just what is a rubric. (1997). <http://www.middleweb.com/CSLB2rubric.html>

Lu, Q. (2004). *Electronic literacy development from school to workplace: A process evaluation.* Unpublished master dissertation. Suzhou: School of Foreign Languages, Suzhou University.

Roblyer, M.D. (2005). Learning theories and integration models. In Roblyer, M. D. (Ed.), *Integrating Educational Technology into Teaching.* (pp.51-82). Xi'an: Shan Xi Normal University Press.

Wang, Y. P. (2005). *Assessment in the Computer-and-classroom-based Multimedia College English Teaching Model.* Unpublished master dissertation. Fuzhou: Fujian Normal University.

Yan, L. H. (2006). *Effects of needs-based CALL tasks on EFL writing.* Unpublished master dissertation. Suzhou: School of Foreign Languages, Suzhou University.

Zhang, W. (2003). *Doing English digital: An assessment model for a new College English curriculum in China.* Unpublished doctoral dissertation. NY: Teachers College, Columbia University.

Zhang, W. (2006). Digital literacy assessment: A model for a new College English curriculum. *Foreign Language Teaching and Research*, 38(2), 115-121.

22 Results from implementation of the Trans-Media book iMAGiNETICspace

David Slykhuis, James Madison University & Troy Cline, NASA, United States

Introduction

The improvement of P-20 science, technology, engineering, and mathematics (STEM) education is a central part of American educational priorities. Indeed, President Obama has made the improvement of STEM education a focus of the initiative "Educate to Innovate," declaring that

Reaffirming and strengthening America's role as the world's engine of scientific discovery and technological innovation is essential to meeting the challenges of this century. That's why I am committed to making the improvement of STEM education over the next decade a national priority. (The White House, Office of the Press Secretary, 2009)

Efforts like "Educate to Innovate" as well as other initiatives are careful to recognize that developing the STEM workforce is a process that needs to begin early in the education pipeline.

Emergent disruptive technologies are subject to restrictions designed to control and limit their use. Invention of the printing press gave rise to licensing laws designed to constrain the dissemination of information. In the twentieth century the president of the Motion Picture Association of America (MPAA) famously called for restrictions on home recording, stating in congressional testimony that "the VCR is to the American film producer and the American public as the Boston strangler is to the woman home alone" (United States Congress, 1982). The following year the Supreme Court ruled that home use of videocassette recorders was legal, but only by the narrowest margin in a five-to-four decision. The irony, of course, is that ultimately recording technologies generated profits for the motion picture industry that equaled or exceeded revenues from screenings in theaters. However, this was far from evident at the time that the MPAA attempted to ban use of these technologies.

A white paper issued by the non-profit policy group Public Knowledge identifies digital fabrication as the next disruptive technology and notes that, "Policymakers and judges will be asked to weigh concrete losses today against future benefits that will be hard to quantify and imagine" (Weinberg, 2010). Currently we are in a transitional window during which regulatory restrictions have not yet been established.

During this transitional period it will be important to pilot as many potential uses of digital replication in educational settings as possible in order to establish conditions under which this use is beneficial. These groundbreaking uses will help establish boundaries within which future educational uses may be permitted as well as guide educationally sound practice.

The Study

A group of science educators met to develop a T-book around the upcoming NASA Magnetoshperic Multiscale Mission launching in 2014.

The Storyline: Our earth is under attack from outer space! Earth is being bombarded by cosmic radiation, a complex solar magnetic field, and high-energy particles from solar storms. The Earth is largely protected from this attack by the magnetosphere surrounding out planet. Most of the energy is directed around the planet by this magnetic field. The detailed nature of this magnetic field is still not completely understood. For that reason, NASA is undertaking the MMS mission.

Big Questions/Concepts covered in the T-book: The focus of this book explores magnetic fields and interactions between magnetic and other forces. Additional STEM topics include science concepts relating to angular velocity and momentum, centrifugal force, and space weather; math concepts relating to geometric shapes; and engineering concepts relating to design under constraint.

Activities related to background concepts:

- The first activity in the book is the construction of a soda bottle magnetometer. This is set up for the duration of the unit to detect changes to the magnetic field in the classroom. Despite the simplicity of the instrument, it is surprisingly sensitive and yields interesting results.
- The interaction of forces from charged particles is explored through a simple experiment using scotch tape.
- Bringing a magnet near, but not touching, another magnet to effect its movement and using magnetic film explore the interaction of forces between magnets.
- Simulations at the PhET site are explored.

Activities related to the MMS mission:

- An experiment is designed and conducted by the students to determine the most feasible shape for the MMS satellites. This involves placing solar panels around a perimeter in a variety of shapes and rotating the shapes. A fixed light source is placed at a distance and the configuration must be adjusted to maintain a specified minimum current output to be satisfactory.
- The size of the model satellites is explored, as this mission will involve a set of four identical satellites launched in a single rocket. They must be compact enough to fit in the payload area of the rocket.
- Once deployed, the satellites will need to extend antennae to collect data. As the satellites will be spinning, the students will design and build an apparatus to spin the model satellite at a range of revolutions per minute. They will then insert a wire in the model satellite to simulate its antenna and explore the spin rate necessary to extend the antenna.
- The culminating activity will be to build four model satellites with their antennae for a scaled tetrahedral mobile.

The T-book was implemented with all the eight grade students in school district with a more typically urban student population in a rural setting. The school district has two middle schools and the T-book was tested first in one building, some minor changes were made, and then tested in the second building.

Findings

Two instruments were used to study the implementation of a FabLab classroom curriculum activity. One was related to the content while the other instrument measures attitudes toward STEM areas as well as interest in STEM careers.

Twenty content items were developed to assess student learning during this two-week curriculum project. Five items were written by the science content specialist and the remaining 15 items were taken from released state tests in Virginia.

The STEM Semantics Survey is a new instrument created to assess general perceptions of STEM disciplines and careers using Semantic Differential adjective pairs from Osgood's (1962; Osgood, Tannenbaum, & Suci, 1957) evaluation dimension. This survey was created by adapting Knezek and Christensen's (1998) Teacher's Attitudes Toward Information Technology Questionnaire (TAT), which was itself derived from earlier Semantic Differential research by Zaichkowsky (1985).

The five most consistent adjective pairs of the ten used on the TAT were incorporated as descriptors for target statements reflecting perceptions of STEM subjects. A fifth scale representing interest in a career in STEM was also created. Each of five scales consisted of a target statement such as "To me, science is:" followed by five polar adjective pairs spanning by a range of seven choices. For example, "To me, science is: exciting _ _ _ _ _ _ _ unexciting."

Previous internal consistency reliabilities for middle school student perceptions of science, math, engineering, technology, and STEM as a career have typically ranged from alpha = .84 to alpha = .93 (Tyler-Wood, Knezek, & Christensen, 2010). These numbers are in the range of "very good" to "excellent" according to guidelines provided by DeVellis (1991). As shown in Table 1, internal consistency reliabilities for this set of data were also considered to be in the range of "very good" to "excellent". An additional six items were added to the Career scale to enhance measurement accuracy, including a test-retest reliability of .60 for the pre-test and .71 for the post test.

Table 1.

Internal Consistency Reliabilities for STEM Semantic for 8th grade FabLab Data

	Pretest	Post test
Science	.89	.94
Mathematics	.91	.95
Engineering	.95	.96
Technology	.88	.92
Career with 5	.91	.94
Career with 11	.92	.95

Examination of correlations among the STEM disposition measures at pretest and again at post test times indicated that the students changed their cognitive structure as a result of participating in the digital fabrication activities. In particular, as shown in Table 13, only dispositions toward science and engineering were correlated at the r = .4 level or higher with STEM Career Interest at the time of the pretest. By the time of the post test, technology and math as well as science and engineering were all correlated at the r = .4 level or higher, and in fact technology and math were both correlated r > .5 with STEM Career Interest. Math and technology become much more closely aligned with STEM Career Interest.

Table 13.
Pretest correlations

		SciTot	EngTot	TechTot	CarTot5	CarTot11	MathTot
SciTot	Pearson Correlation	1	.395**	.304**	.476**	.466**	.149*
	Sig. (2-tailed)		.000	.000	.000	.000	.015
	N	268	268	266	267	267	268
EngTot	Pearson Correlation	.395**	1	.435**	.481**	.451**	.263**
	Sig. (2-tailed)	.000		.000	.000	.000	.000
	N	268	268	266	267	267	268
TechTot	Pearson Correlation	.304**	.435**	1	.395**	.378**	.146*
	Sig. (2-tailed)	.000	.000		.000	.000	.017
	N	266	266	266	266	266	266
CarTot5	Pearson Correlation	.476**	.481**	.395**	1	.903**	.367**
	Sig. (2-tailed)	.000	.000	.000		.000	.000
	N	267	267	266	267	267	267
CarTot11	Pearson Correlation	.466**	.451**	.378**	.903**	1	.334**
	Sig. (2-tailed)	.000	.000	.000	.000		.000
	N	267	267	266	267	267	267
MathTot	Pearson Correlation	.149*	.263**	.146*	.367**	.334**	1

	Sig. (2-tailed)	.015	.000	.017	.000	.000	
	N	268	268	266	267	267	268
**. Correlation is significant at the 0.01 level (2-tailed).							
*. Correlation is significant at the 0.05 level (2-tailed).							
a. prePost = 1							

Table 14.
Posttest correlation

		SciTot	EngTot	TechTot	CarTot5	CarTot11	MathTot
SciTot	Pearson Correlation	1	.522**	.499**	.594**	.547**	.445**
	Sig. (2-tailed)		.000	.000	.000	.000	.000
	N	260	260	258	259	259	260
EngTot	Pearson Correlation	.522**	1	.620**	.436**	.437**	.303**
	Sig. (2-tailed)	.000		.000	.000	.000	.000
	N	260	260	258	259	259	260
TechTot	Pearson Correlation	.499**	.620**	1	.518**	.486**	.316**
	Sig. (2-tailed)	.000	.000		.000	.000	.000
	N	258	258	258	258	258	258
CarTot5	Pearson Correlation	.594**	.436**	.518**	1	.928**	.530**
	Sig. (2-tailed)	.000	.000	.000		.000	.000
	N	259	259	258	259	259	259
CarTot11	Pearson Correlation	.547**	.437**	.486**	.928**	1	.525**
	Sig. (2-tailed)	.000	.000	.000	.000		.000
	N	259	259	258	259	259	259
MathTot	Pearson Correlation	.445**	.303**	.316**	.530**	.525**	1
	Sig. (2-tailed)	.000	.000	.000	.000	.000	

	N	260	260	258	259	259	260
**. Correlation is significant at the 0.01 level (2-tailed).							
a. prePost = 2							

Table 2 shows the pre-post means for the combined two middle schools for the content portion of the surveys. There were significant differences ($p<.008$) for the content as a whole. The pre-post effect size is .23. There were significant differences between the gains in the two middle schools. As shown in Tables 3 and 4, only Harrison MS showed significant ($p<.002$) gains pre-post. The effect size in those changes is .34, which can be considered educationally meaningful.

Table 2.
Pre-post Content Gains for Skyline and Harrison Middle Schools Combined

	N	Mean	Std. Deviation	Sig	ES
Pre	270	14.87	3.480		
Post	254	15.70	3.600		
Total	524	15.27	3.560	.008	.23

Table 3.
Content Gain By School - Skyline MS

	N	Mean	Std. Deviation	Sig.	ES
Pre	108	15.47	3.161		
Post	105	15.67	3.712		
Total	213	15.57	3.437	.681	.06

Table 4.
Content Gain by School - Harrison MS

	N	Mean	Std. Deviation	Sig	ES
Pre	162	14.47	3.632		
Post	149	15.72	3.532		
Total	311	15.07	3.633	.002	.34

Conclusions

This presentation is a follow-up to a presentation from SITE 2012. In Austin we presented the parameters of the project and shared the experience of the implementation of the book with the 8th grade students. We did not, however, at that time have available the results of the assessments instruments that were given. We now can present this research project in much greater detail. Participants will learn how the T-book came to be developed and written. The procedure and test results will be explained in much greater detail. Participants will understand that projects that are focused on real world problems and incorporate all areas of STEM can both stimulate students interest in STEM and school as well as prepare students to perform more proficiently on State mandated tests.

This presentation should have wide interest to SITE membership. Researchers will be interested in how the study took place in the 8th grade and the results that are presented. Curriculum developers will be interested in how this was written and how the T-Book went through the NASA review process for distribution to teachers. Methods instructors will also be interested as undergraduate pre-service teachers were involved in the research and implementation process and how a T-Book could be used in methods classes.

References

DeVellis, R.F. (1991). Scale development. Newbury Park, NJ: Sage Publications.

Knezek, G., & Christensen, R. (1998, March). Internal consistency reliability for the teachers' attitudes toward information technology (TAT) questionnaire. In *Proceedings of the Society for Information Technology in Teacher Education Annual Conference (Eds.)* S. McNeil, J. Price, S. Boger-Mehall, B. Robin, & J. Willis, pp. 831-836. Bethesda, MD: Society for Information Technology in Teacher Education.

Knezek, G., Christensen, R., & Tyler-Wood, T. (2011). Contrasting perceptions of STEM content and careers. *Contemporary Issues in Technology and Teacher Education, 11*(1). Retrieved from http://www.citejournal.org/vol11/iss1/general/article1.cfm

Osgood, C.E., Suci, G., & Tannenbaum, P. (1957) *The measurement of meaning.* Urbana, IL: University of Illinois Press

Tyler-Wood, T., Knezek, G., & Christensen, R. (2010). Instruments for assessing interest in STEM content and careers. *Journal of Technology and Teacher Education, 18(*2), 341-363.

Zaichkowsky, J. L. (1985). Measuring the involvement construct. *Journal of Consumer Research, 12*(3), 341-352.

www.ingramcontent.com/pod-product-compliance
Lightning Source LLC
Chambersburg PA
CBHW081841230426
43669CB00018B/2772